I0762906

COLE NICOLE LEFAVOUR

IN THE ARMS OF MOUNTAINS

A MEMOIR OF LAND, LOVE, AND QUEER RESISTANCE IN RED AMERICA

BEACON PRESS, BOSTON

BEACON PRESS
24 Farnsworth Street
Boston, Massachusetts
www.beacon.org

Beacon Press books
are published under the auspices of
the Unitarian Universalist Association of Congregations.

Printed in the United States of America

29 28 27 26 8 7 6 5 4 3 2 1

This book is printed on acid-free paper that meets the uncoated paper ANSI/NISO specifications for permanence as revised in 1992.

Text design and composition by Kim Arney

Library of Congress Cataloguing-in-Publication Data is available for this title.
Hardcover ISBN: 978-0-8070-2418-8
E-book ISBN: 978-0-8070-2419-5
Audiobook: 978-0-8070-2451-5

The authorized representative in the EU for product safety and compliance is Easy Access System Europe 16879218, Mustamäe tee 50, 10621 Tallinn, Estonia: https://beacon.org/eu-contact.

CONTENTS

PART 3: FORGIVENESS

AUTHOR'S NOTE

This story is my recollection of events in my life told with a great deal of love. While some dialogue is reconstructed and approximate, I've made every effort to reflect my understanding of the intent and nature of what was said. In some dialogue, people use gender pronouns for me that I used at the time but no longer use. A few names have been changed and identities obscured. Otherwise, this is the story, accurate to the best of my abilities.

PROLOGUE

GOAT PASTURE

FEBRUARY 2014

Boise, Idaho

For four years in the middle of my already wild life, I lived as that slam dancer who has strayed from the mosh pit at a Joan Jett concert. I wandered out into the alley with an empty flask, dancing with a wall until my bones ached. Occasionally, I drew a crowd to dance there with me in the street light and snow, but mostly in those years I spun alone between the trash cans, music distant but ever in my head—"Bad Reputation" at high volume.

On this night, I am living alone in a goat pasture, a literal goat pasture with two ponies, two large goats, and a barn. On tall posts, yard lights shine, reflecting off snow. I squint, frost on my lashes. Goat bodies blur in the ice fog. Their hooves scrape gravel and straw. I am returning from a night downtown and they follow me.

The city around me is a hiss of quiet. Hills in darkness hang and the sage desert stretches west to the Cascades and Oregon, a state away. I can make out my motor home parked under a willow tree on the back side of a subdivision. I've taken up residence here, unpermitted, uninvited, uncomfortably close to comfortable homes. Sometimes my food and toothpaste freeze in the night. Sometimes my lack of a bathroom and water plagues me and I improvise in uncomfortable ways.

Trailed by two pairs of horns and yellow eyes, I move toward the trees, toward the fence of wire panels that protects my lawn chairs and flowers from the barnyard animals. Inside my kitchen, I switch on the lamp beside my disco ball. Tiny squares of light pierce the ceiling and cabinets. I smile, a small smile. I've upended a life lived in houses, bringing paintings and books, folders of paper for teaching and for making and breaking laws.

From that room set inside a goat pasture, I remember Carol's voice, "Lawmaker, lawbreaker," eyebrows raised, a tight curve at the corner of that genderless mouth. Carol. I cannot help but think of Carol, the one still dancing in the pit, the one waiting when the hall empties and the music dies.

In the bits of light there in the goat pasture, it's long past midnight. The clock ticks. I've used up another day waiting for a hearing on our bill. But again we made trouble. We blocked doors and the Senate sent seventy of us to jail rather than let us testify.

I'm a former lawmaker with a growing arrest record. Miles away, they still call me "Senator" when I walk in the door. But I'm living in a goat pasture and strategically I'm back where I started a month earlier, or worse, because I have no exit plan for this civil disobedience, this slam dance in the alley. My exit plan requires several simultaneous miracles: a public hearing and passage of our law in a Capitol miles from the goats and my disco ball.

Though I do not have a real exit plan, I do have a ransom note scrawled on a cocktail napkin.

I settle at my kitchen table. From earlier in the day, I can still feel the cold steel, heavy, the scratch-echo of voices outside the jail cell. The arrests in the Capitol got theatrical. Someone in the Senate decided the police needed long jangling belly shackles and handcuffs to arrest us. They skipped the easier plastic zip ties, for dramatic effect, I suppose, to send a message of some kind, a deterrent. As if we cared. We are slam dancing in the alley, not literally but figuratively. We hope our trash cans make some noise.

PART 1

LAND

1
WOODY CREEK

1964

Woody Creek, Colorado

I was born in 1964, in the West, in a town with dirt streets set in pine and sagebrush, five years before the queer uprising at the Stonewall Inn in New York.

My parents left the East Coast when they were young, went West separately for the counterculture.

Woody Creek, Colorado, was nothing then but a single gas station, a trailer park, and a country store off the river bank. An unstriped paved road ran from the store upstream toward Lenado and the borrowed cabin with wood heat and an outhouse where my dad carried me, bundled against the February cold on the day I slipped into this world.

My dad was a walking man with thin, strong legs, calloused hands, kind blue eyes, and a stovepipe beard. When he met my mom, he worked as a janitor and maintenance worker on the ski hill in Aspen. Their first date was a day of duck hunting together. Mom was good with a gun. Dad, too, but he didn't like to shoot, didn't care for killing. A lover of food, nature, and physics, he had left college in his twenties and buried a mentor and friend in the Canadian Arctic after three boats capsized on a canoeing expedition, dumping six men into freezing waters. For eighty days, they paddled as winter came on, killing caribou and ptarmigan, catching fish, and struggling to stay dry so they didn't freeze.

The first ten years of my life, my family lived with other young families in remote cabins and wooden houses. My parents bought land for

$160 an acre and settled at the end of a wild side canyon off Woody Creek, thirteen miles outside Aspen. Aspen was already a ski town but still felt a little like a mining town. The valleys off Woody Creek hung with hay fields and homesteads populated by counterculture intellectuals, physicists, carpenters, East Coast pot smokers, writers, musicians, and artists. Hunter S. Thompson lived there with his wife, Sandy, and son, Juan.

The year my parents met, my mom, Pat, was cook and kitchen manager for a lunch spot on Aspen Mountain. She was taller than most men, wore her hair back in a long braid, her pale skin often tan, nails short, Irish nose sharp.

Her mom was Irish and Catholic. Her dad, though, was a tall, big-jawed son of a Swedish immigrant. Mom grew up ever braced to run from home to escape being beaten by him. She hid under bridges or ran, carrying her dog into the cemetery. Conscience wasn't in my grandfather's wheelhouse. He claimed to work as a door-to-door salesman. With this excuse, he left my grandma to do the work of wrenching herself from life as an immigrant's daughter to middle class on her own. At the same time, she cared for her mother-in-law and raised her two kids, Mike and Pat, both of whom, it would turn out, were gay.

My dad, Bruce, was raised by his father, a widowed newspaper publisher with a mountain of privilege. Dad was humble, thoughtful, and embarrassed by wealth, even when, for a time, he had it himself.

In nearly every photo that my grandmother took of my parents before their lives were consumed with their restaurant, my dad is the one holding me. He looks down into my face or holds my chunky, overall-clad body in his lap while my mom smiles. He is tipping a glass of beer up to give me a sip or holding my hand as my feet wheel out to take first awkward steps.

My mom was a wild thing. Unlike my dad, the empathetic staring into an infant's eyes that's said to create attachment wasn't something she took to. It wasn't in her nature. Inside her brain, her machinery of imagination was taken up with ink drawings and sculptures, with imagining monsters with her father's face, or often with conjuring the perfection of her evening cocktail. Every day was marked by the crack of ice in our aluminum ice tray, the clink of a cube in the glass, the gentle sound of the tonic, the sting and zest of lime, gin slipping from the bottle, its gurgle and sigh.

In my first eighteen months of life, I went everywhere with my parents. At three months old, I traveled with them in a VW Bug through France and Germany. I slept quietly under dinner tables as they researched local dishes and restaurants, planning to open one of their own. Bundled in a basket at their feet, I was whisked off into kitchens by waitstaff, my parents' ticket to meeting the chef.

Cheerful and tiny, all the change and closeness of that first year and a half knit itself into my being, fed my little brain, made me trustful. I grew confident and secure, wild like my mom, with my dad's gentle sense of justice. For me, those two humans made the universe in all its chaos make sense.

My brown-eyed sister, Cree, was born after the calm I thrived on. She was dropped into the bustle and intensity of my parents' long workdays of turning an aging building in downtown Aspen into a restaurant that critics from New York and Los Angeles came to write about. Dad stood at the helm of his kitchen, while my mom was the bread baker, sauce maker, and prep cook. Dad had spent his early twenties on leave from college roaming the Adirondacks and Canadian wilds and then was stationed in France, becoming fluent in French as he enlisted in the army and was assigned counterintelligence work. He never finished college. After all he saw, he chose a life that let him live in the mountains and cook for others.

Cooking became his love, his gift, his art form. He labored at it, invented, gave everything to a set of tiny rooms where, every day, the menu was different, built with ingredients he would shop for and combine in unheard of ways. As the years passed, he grew more certain, even wild in how he made a meal of meats, tubers, vegetables, flour, butter, and cream.

Once the restaurant opened, a series of live-in babysitters came to stay in the basement of our house. Each one cooked, corralled, changed diapers, and fed us.

In Woody Creek, the tangle of oak trees and sage on the south slope beside our house became Cree's and my playhouse. There, the ridge at the top of the hill wound round the valley, climbing thousands of feet to mushroom-filled meadows, hung high above the houses scattered below. We feasted after family hikes on wild morels, chanterelles, Suillus, boletes, and puffballs.

In the scrub oak, I'd play house with Cree and my best friend, Juan. We'd sketch out bedrooms, kitchens, and living rooms in the dried leaves and act out scenes from double-feature Saturday matinees we watched in town, films like *The Poseidon Adventure*, *The Sound of Music*, and *Swiss Family Robinson*. Juan and I married each other dozens of times, cooked dinner, and put my stuffed animals or Cree to bed. We fit ourselves into roles for men and women like those in his house where his mom, Sandy, cooked and cared for him while his dad wrote, traveled, and questioned all things establishment.

For nine years, we had no television. Books filled our shelves. Outside, in the rectangle of my dad's carefully plotted garden, I'd sit on the soil as he worked his shovel or hoe. I'd pick up earthworms to hold, listen to him talk as he pulled weeds, explaining how a person made seeds grow, offering water, sunlight, and soil. Clouds traipsed the strip of sky above us. Birds argued and conspired. Leaves and pine branches hissed in the wind.

I picked up a dried-out creature with wings and a half inch-long needle at the end of it.

"It looks mean," I whispered.

"That's an ovipositor there, not a stinger," Dad said, lifting the black beetle with its orange stripes and turning it over.

I carried the motionless creature upstairs to join the tidy rows of found carcasses of moths, dragonflies, yellow jackets, mountain cicadas, and road-kill snakes. All sat on the orange folding table below the window in my bedroom. These were my marvels. I'd stare at them, learning about scales, exoskeletons, wings, odors, armor, and biological self-defense. In my head, a web of relationships between living things took shape. I developed theories about how one creature relied on another and studied how ants worked more as one being than as many.

Outside our house at the end of the road, a dense pine forest lay on the north slope, which climbed steeply—up to where I wasn't sure. My dad would stand in an upstairs window looking out into the twilight, listening for owls, coyotes, and one night called us from our bedrooms to glimpse a bobcat staring back at us from the edge of the trees.

When he was home, Dad was usually our cook. Mom rode her horses and shot her guns. They mixed around the notion of gender roles.

"Your dad wanted kids," Mom said years later, no shyness in her voice. "I got pregnant and had you two because it was expected."

For four years, while she worked the restaurant with Dad and they could afford sitters, she escaped having to be our stay-at-home mom. Dad seemed happy at the center of our family, being the level, the force for gentleness. Mom was glad to wield the wild part, be the one who pushed outward at the calm, upending norms, dragging things to extremes to keep our life from feeling staid.

As for me, I owned a cap gun, microscope, and stuffed animals I worried would feel neglected if put away in a box.

"Oh, Neee-cole, you're such a priss," Mom would say.

Compared to her, I was soft. Yet, in photos of me at the time I wear my favorite red felt Western hat, sometimes a plaid skirt, tights, and my brown leather cow boots. I looked out through my hazel-blue eyes and saw a world in three dimensions, seasons turning, insects hatching, snow falling, drifts melting, grass poking through the soil. To me, time was never a calendar, a clock, or a straight line. It revolved around cycles, causality, seasons, which colored the stations of the big oval ribbon that was the calendar of time in my head.

On the wall in the bathroom of the house that my dad designed and helped build was a poster that read, "Stop the Rising Tide of Conformity." On it, a row of identical White men marched in line, one behind the other. If I didn't know the word "conformity," I sensed what it meant. It meant following orders, bowing down to do what you're expected to do.

Political posters and paintings of naked men and women hung on the walls of our living room and my parents' bedroom. In my bedroom, a large print hung beside my bed. In it a row of Black women in brightly colored head scarves and skirts stood outdoors surrounded by trees. One played a xylophone that filled the width of the painting. She beat on wooden keys set on a frame, attached to gourds so massive they hung from waist-height almost to the ground.

A window at the foot of my bed looked down the canyon to a meadow and three snow-covered peaks set against a blue-black sky. Not a house lay within sight of us. My parents walked nude onto the deck or swam naked in the pond near my mom's horse corral.

My world was as small as a ten-year-old's might be. My sense of the land then was that every part of it had a human purpose. Beyond the lumber mill was forest where trees grew and were cut for the mill. Cow Camp on the high ridge above Lenado set sage slopes and forest apart for grazing. In the meadows in the valley below us, horses lived in fenced pastures, and neighbors grew wheat or hay. The three hulking peaks in the distance hung almost like pyramids, crusted with snow, even in early summer. They felt distant and ornamental. Estes Park was there and images of the mountains rose up out of postcards, murals, paintings, and plastic tourist souvenirs. On our one and only family camping trip into the park, Cree and I woke in the morning and left our tent to wander the wide meadow at the base of the peaks, picking tiny wild strawberries and plunking them into tin cups. Dad, who gathered wild mushrooms, currants, and raspberries when he hiked, had shown us how the tiny plants that greened the hillside below our tent also had fruit to offer.

Every part of the land seemed similarly arranged, divided up according to human expectation, molded by our hands, or just ready to meet our needs.

As far as I knew, every person in the houses and ranches around us owned a gun and could sink a bullet into a target with one pull of the trigger. Before my parents stopped hunting, Cree and I stood in the kitchen as Mom and Dad brought home limp pheasants, rabbit skins, and deer my dad skinned and cleaned to eat. The killing was remote, abstract, even though the guns were present and real.

One day, when I was tall as my mom's elbow, I stood on the deck in front of our house. Little Woody Creek flowed below us in thaw. In bare feet and a nightgown, I looked up at Mom, tall, her black hair pulled back, feet spread wide.

In the chill air, her voice rose. "Can't—you—read?" she shouted in the direction of the driveway, her voice flat, humorless. The metallic click of her shotgun cocking silenced the roar of the creek. Aspen leaves clattered in the wind.

Even then I knew this amused her. She stepped forward on the footbridge between our house and the road, barrel low, walking purposefully toward the men ahead of us, climbing out of their bland white car.

Mom had carved and hand-painted no trespassing signs. She'd nailed them to the gate, which the two men in white shirts and ties had driven past, a quarter mile back. The most obvious sign just said "NO" in curly red letters.

NO trespassing. NO, don't keep driving. NO, you are not the exception.

This was pretty much all I knew of religion in my early years: Mom meeting missionaries on the bridge with her shotgun. She'd cock it with a loud "chukkkk-chuuuk" and then smile.

I didn't quite grasp the way the world might be hostile. However, in the years ahead when we traveled and she and Dad set us free to wander in towns and cities, she taught Cree and me about self-defense. Plucking her knife from the sheath on her belt where she always kept it, she held it out in front of her.

"Keep the blade up," she said, "so you can slash their wrists if they try to grab you."

Mom claimed people knew the sound of a shotgun being cocked. She and Dad occasionally left us alone at night, paid us to babysit each other when I was just eight. Instructing us in how to scare off intruders, she'd remove the shells and hold her shotgun out in front of her, lifting the long muzzle. The gun's black double barrels would rise, gleam briefly, then fall as she pulled the hammer back and snapped the stock closed with a reverberating metal-on-metal click.

"Hear that sound?" she asked. "That sound is all you'll ever need."

Out in the world, where Cree and I had to ride the bus into town to go to school, I wore a sort of impervious shield, knowing my life was full of love and kindness, even when my classmates were cruel. Things kids disliked about me were not things I did by choice. By extension, I understood that when others were taunted for their clothes, way of speaking, skin color, or gentleness, the taunting wasn't a remark on their goodness, only on features they simply might not be able to walk away from.

On a spring day in my second-grade classroom at the big public school in town, little faces stared up at me. I'd climbed on a table in the middle of Mr. Fuji's class. In my hand, a wad of dollar bills gave off a metallic smell I knew was getting on my skin. I raised the bills above my head. The money was fresh from Mom's dresser. As that kid in special ed, still sucking my middle two fingers, it was safest if I stayed inside at recess. There, I could pretend to read. If I went out, I might again be sat on, buried in a snow pile, then taunted for wetting my pants.

High on the tabletop, I looked down at the faces of the children below me and let a dollar bill fly. It fluttered past my waist into the shrieks and scrambling. I let another flutter down.

Juan, with his big brown eyes and long black lashes, was kind, but other kids seemed to see something in me, some weakness, some failing. It gave them license to be cruel. I don't recall that anyone could name what was different in the jumble that was me—that thing that sketched out the target on my chest.

On our first day of second grade, I sulked when Juan got to stand in the boys' line for the bathrooms and I couldn't. With his round face and shiny black hair, Juan could already read. I couldn't. Like my little sister, Cree, Juan had a finely tuned sense of what was appropriate. I didn't. I tilted toward disturbing the peace, dragging Juan in while he scrambled to smooth the chaos and apologize.

From the age of three, Juan's life was intertwined with mine as our parents hosted and went to parties. Juan and I floated in irrigation ditches on rough-cut boards. We wandered sage-covered mesas while his dad, Hunter, and my dad played two-on-two volleyball or while Hunter and my mom shouted, whistled, and gestured in a sort of competition of drinking, being outrageous, and talking about guns.

In 1972, as Juan's dad ran for county sheriff, my dad posed in his chef's hat for one of Hunter's wild photo shoots where friends in bandoliers, big hats, and costumes sat at tables in the Jerome Bar. In the photo, Hunter sat in the center, sedate, staring at the camera, the skin of his clean-shaven head covered by a white bucket hat—just like the one Mom wore.

Juan skirted a world that spun around his father's unpredictability. He lived with a sort of fear of breaking rules I never had. My mom threatened punishments like the dreaded lifting in the air that was part of an "undershirt trick." Often she grabbed our shirt fronts leering, "I'll knock your little heads together!" But never once did she actually do it.

I crept around Juan's house, allowed to eat Space Food Sticks and powdered Tang. I was hushed or hauled out, cautioned never to wake Hunter as he slept through the day in the big bed set on shag carpet in the basement, resting so he could write all night.

The Thompson house was filled with electronic gadgets and rubber pranks. Rubber dog shit piles lay at the edges of the back hall. Record covers, masks, hats, and a painted human skull decorated the living room. A bird cage with a live talking mynah bird hung in the open kitchen among the potted plants.

The house had two separate land lines. I was intent on trying out the contraptions that let Hunter record phone interviews. At least once, I had to beg an operator not to disconnect Hunter's phone because I'd dialed numbers at random, pretending to be a reporter from *Playboy* magazine, doing a survey on American sexual habits.

While rules functioned more as an enticement than a deterrent for me, by third grade, most days, Cree and I dressed ourselves for school, made our breakfast and lunch, and followed the path along an abandoned irrigation ditch to the mesa and hay field where our new elementary school sat. One morning, coats zipped, backpacks on our backs, breakfast in our bellies, we crossed the meadow out the back door. In the early light, snow-covered peaks rose in the distance. A quarter mile down the trail, we arrived in a stand of aspens with tall white trunks, all of them dormant then, waiting quiet until spring.

Chickadees called. Long shadows stretched across the path. Looking down, we found the ground littered with white branches. Small trees had been clipped to clear the trail, limbs cut clean with shears or a blade. It was carnage. Maybe Dad had told me or maybe one of my science teachers had explained that aspens are not separate trees, but like bees, they're clones, interconnected underground to form a single being.

I fell to my knees, scrambling to gather up lost parts, matching little trunks to tiny stumps.

"We'll get tape," I said dropping my pack and running back up the trail, through our field, to the quiet house where Mom and Dad still slept after a long night of work in their restaurant.

I am a little of each of my parents. With pale, freckled skin, I have my dad's small blue eyes and firm nose, his curiosity, compassion, and moral compass but my mom's lack of self-consciousness and need to mix it up.

My sister and I were freer than most children. We had wilds to roam, parents who worked long hours and trusted us to climb ridges or slip out in winter darkness, into fields, running in our socks across a crust of snow under the full moon. I learned to fear little, to love the dark, and to know the sounds of the night.

What I loved most was time with my dad.

At dinner on a good night when Dad wasn't working, we all sat together to eat. Until I was eleven, he might stay after at the table and talk with me. He'd answer my questions, explain biology, evolution, or physics from books he was reading.

"Imagine you're this saltshaker. Your life exists only on one thin, straight line." Above his brown beard with its streak of blond, Dad's blue eyes drew lines, planes, cubes in the air as he moved the saltshaker back and forth in two directions along an imaginary tangent. "Here in the first dimension on this line," he tapped the saltshaker on the table, "a person living there can't imagine a world where people live in the next dimension. They can't imagine living a life able to move in many directions, at different angles, not just back and forth along a line."

Dad's hands now moved the salt in a circle across the wooden top. "Even for the person who lives on a flat plane in the second dimension, they can't imagine the person whose life is lived in the third dimension, in a universe where they move not just forward and back, or side to side, but up and down as well. For someone in the second dimension, climbing a hill, flying, or going underground feels impossible. The rules of our dimension are just too different. They're beyond experience, beyond imagination."

"What's the fourth dimension?" I asked. We'd talked already about the first, second, and our own, the third.

"We can't imagine it," Dad said.

2

DELICATE THINGS

1976

Stanley, Idaho

My early memories of moving to Idaho are of the cold, the White, and the blue. The sounds were those of Dad's new kitchen in motion, outside every window a depth of wild I did not fully comprehend.

During our final years in Colorado, our neighbors planted a TV antenna on the ridge above our houses. Hundreds of yards of black cable connected it to our living rooms. At last, briefly, our family had television.

I'd passed through tribal lands to the desert on school camping trips, had traveled on boats and buses in Mexico with my parents, and had spent hours lying on our carpet in Woody Creek watching *The Jeffersons*, *M*A*S*H*, *Hawaii Five-O*, *Kung Fu*, *Fat Albert*, and *Sesame Street*. The places beyond, like the television shows I watched, were far from White. In my head, the world was far from White.

Before we left Aspen, marriages were struggling, drugs growing more addictive, Hunter had lost his campaign for sheriff, and with that, Aspen felt increasingly hostile to my parents and their friends, who were "longhairs" and peace lovers. Colorado's politics were Republican-dominated and probably felt more so to my parents after Hunter's loss. They'd made phone calls and knocked on doors for the campaign, hoping the "greedheads" would quit arresting hippies, subdividing the hay fields, and let people be.

However, in that state to the north of us, Idaho's politics were split evenly across party lines. Idaho seemed free and wild, humble and romantic to my dad and mom. It looked like a place they could raise children away from the glitz and enforced conformity they wanted to leave behind.

In 1975, in the midst of an economic downturn, my family sold our eighty acres, left Woody Creek and our place at the end of the valley. We packed up our dogs and cats, put our stuffed animals and furniture in a moving van. Mom's wooden sculptures of naked men and women rode along as we drove our two battered cars north along the Rocky Mountains to a creaking guest ranch on the Salmon River—in the dead center of libertarian, live-and-let-live Idaho. The ranch had a hot spring pool but no TV, not even radio, nothing to counter the racial Whiteness, the straightness of what was then a vast and isolated spot amid wilderness that stretched for as many as fifty to a hundred miles north and south up the center of the state.

The nearest town was fifteen miles upriver and had a population of forty-seven. Dad hoped to grow and raise much of the food for his new restaurant. People would come by car and stay in a cabin or a room in the big guest ranch lodge.

Raising chickens and vegetables, milking the cow, making the beds, cleaning the chamber pots would be done by our family and by some assembly of other families working on the ranch. It seemed Dad hoped that on the ranch we'd recreate the free-ranging counterculture of Woody Creek, far from the hostile government that had made Aspen feel increasingly foreign.

Yet, as Mom unloaded horses and Dad unpacked boxes of mixers, knives, pots, and pans, White Nationalist Richard Butler also moved to the state. In the North, near Hayden Lake, he began to dream into existence a militarized compound, arming himself and plotting out the lines of a White separatist nation to be built through violence in the Pacific Northwest.

High in the mountains, three hours from the nearest hospital or movie theater, Cree grew tall and together we roamed pastures, mountainsides, and forests, playing in the ten rooms of the lodge and six small guest cabins. So insulated were we that it would be decades before we understood the place and time where we'd landed.

At ten and eleven years old, we would now be raising chickens and rabbits for Dad's new restaurant, working to feed guests, hiking, and reading—something I'd finally figured out and had come to love.

Cree and I set out across the fields and forests that made up our 120-acre ranch. We found an ancient dump filled with antique bottles, cliff faces, ancient trees, wildflowers, bird nests, and salmon who'd migrated upstream from the ocean to spawn and die in the riverbed. While sometimes the black draft horse Zelda was put to work skidding logs down the mountain from the forest, mostly the land around our ranch seemed untouched. I imagined its plants and animals existed much as they had for hundreds or even thousands of years while the Sheep People and the Salmon People of the Newe Shoshone lived there. Forests went on and on, unbroken into the distance, and were home to night creatures, strange plants, toads, pika, mountains goats, rubber boas, and a sort of quiet I'd never known.

That summer, our hair long now and worn in braids, jeans on, tennis shoes on our feet, Cree and I determined we were brave enough to camp out beyond the ranch in the forest all by ourselves. Day packs on our backs, we set out one evening with Cree's black dog, a tent, two pork chops, sleeping bags, matches, and metal grate for cooking our dinner over a fire. Having crossed a bridge and wandered up the valley out of sight of the ranch, we set up our tent on the bank of Warm Springs Creek, a river that drained a huge portion of the White Cloud Mountains, a set of peaks that rose to twelve thousand feet and stretched untraversed by any road or highway for more than forty miles.

When dusk fell, the roar of the river kept our minds off the sounds of animals in the forest. We set up our tent, lit our fire, and began cooking our pork chops, turning them carefully with sticks, hoping the garlic tucked into tiny cuts in the meat didn't fall out. Grease dripped. The meat browned and grew firm. Ready to feast, I looked up at a set of rocks above our campsite. I kept imagining I saw movement. Cree's black dog looked up at the rocks as well. I started thinking about the scent of our meat.

By the time we'd finished dinner I felt as if a pair of yellow eyes were staring down at us from above.

"Maybe we should burn the bones so nothing smells them," I said casually to Cree.

I had long loved the dark and had repeatedly chosen the solo role of being "it," roaming yards and pastures in Aspen trying to catch friends who tiptoed loudly between the "base" and the shadows of trees in quivering, screaming pairs. Their task was to avoid me lying in wait, silent and invisible in dark corners, along lightless trails, in tree wells, or far out beyond the house lights during our neighborly sessions of nighttime base tag.

Cree however, like Mom, had never been at home in the dark.

She said something like, "What do you mean *so nothing smells them*? Do you see something?"

On our arrival at the ranch, my dad, clearing trail, had come back reporting sign of a mountain lion upstream, across the river from where we had just chosen to camp.

"Well, there could be a mountain lion," I said.

That did it. We both worked ourselves up, staring into the dark with our puny flashlights, searching the rock face above us for a set of eyes. We packed our tent, left our pork chop bones in the wet ashes of the fire, and ran all the way down the trail, along the dirt road, and home.

When fall brought flashes of color to the river canyon, Dad enrolled us in the Stanley Elementary School. Our two-room schoolhouse would be an old, curved, metal Quonset hut. I'd be one of only two kids in the sixth grade.

Getting to school most mornings required a two-mile walk along a dirt road on the banks of the Salmon River in darkness. At the bridge where our road met the highway that led upriver to town, we boarded the eight-seat Suburban that served as our bus. On the bus Cree and I curled up together and slept the half hour all the way to town.

As harsh as walking two miles in the dark and cold might seem, it was often magical. When six-foot salmon were not thrashing their way upstream or spawning in the river below the road, river otters would play on the river ice. Cree and I sat on the edge of the road more than once, nearly missing the bus while whiskered creatures climbed the bank and slid down on their bellies into dark pools through holes in the white snow and ice.

We saw weasels and more kinds of water birds than we knew names for. We surprised owls, hawks, eagles, coyotes, foxes, porcupines, deer, and elk. On the road, tracks of bobcats, pine martens, and mink meandered.

I could imagine a whole universe of creatures—plants, animals, and insects—living out their lives invisible to us and all humans, deep in the forest and mountains. And there on a river, set between two of the nation's most vast wilderness areas, we now lived.

The wild of Idaho wasn't the wild I'd understood in Colorado. It felt infinite. It seemed to exist more for its own sake—for the sake of the otters and the mountain lions, not for us.

One day in our second year on the ranch, deep in the men's bathroom of the sprawling ranch lodge, a tight braid swung from my shoulder across my chest. I pushed it back. Panicked peeping rose from the newspaper-covered floor. A clutch of mouse-sized ducklings and fat-bodied hatchling geese ran in circles. They paused. Eyes stared up at me, heads cocked, deciding if I was predator or parent. I squatted on the fake brick linoleum and stretched one arm over their low plywood pen, fingers coaxing them toward me.

I was twelve now. For the next few years, my sister, only eleven, would work the front half of Mom and Dad's new restaurant while I worked the kitchen. Cree opened wine bottles and handled drama. I churned butter, made custards, chopped vegetables, picked and washed wild watercress until my hands ached with cold.

On that ranch, we would grow into teens, Cree wearing her hair down, bending at the waist to flip it back, adopting role models from among coworkers on the wait staff who were twice her age, women who shaved their legs and wore makeup. I, however, remained unclear on the reasons a person would shave their legs. I pulled my long, straw-thick hair back, tight and out of sight. When I grew breasts, they came with a vengeance, unwelcome and unwieldy. But that was a year away. On that afternoon in the lodge bathroom, I was gloriously flat-chested. My task was raising ducks and geese for Dad.

It was spring. The restaurant, cabins, and lodge were closed for the slack season and it would be a month before guests would come again, needing to use the bathroom stall or the big porcelain urinal that hung on the wall above my head.

From the bathroom floor the ducklings peeped. I herded a group of them up the ramp toward the lip of a plastic tub. One jumped into the water; the others followed. They paddled their feet and swam for the first time in their short little lives. I smiled.

I was to feed them and seven geese, clean out their dirty newspaper bedding, and, in warmer weather, take them outside for visits until they were big enough to live in the pasture. These would be my ducks and geese, and I had completely put out of my mind their actual fate. It was like that of the chickens and the two pigs my sister and I had foolishly named. All of them would end up on the ranch butcher block and eventually in the restaurant where my dad would painstakingly demonstrate to me how to cut skin from muscle and meat from bone.

The ducklings bobbed in the water, circling until they grew tired. Each heaved itself onto the wooden ramp that sat propped to give them a route up over the sides of the tub and back down to the newspaper and their food below.

I sat up on my knees and reached into the pen to scoop one of the ducks into my hand. Its bill was flat and soft on the bottom. I pulled the bird close to my chest. It slowly settled from its panic and sat blinking, turning its head to look up at me with one of its eyes. Leaning against the wall, I stroked the odd down, touched the curve of its bill, the warm skin in the webs between its clawed toes. The duck ran its bill through the down on one wing, preening.

I was in love. I thought then that I'd want be a parent, have something to care for, to talk to, a mind to share the beauty of things with, to show how nature and science worked. The complexity of the world was infinite. I loved that fact but had no one to talk with about any of it.

I gently set the duckling on the paper next to the others. It was late. I'd be back in the morning to sit with them, change their paper, and give them food.

When morning did come, I was the first to open the bathroom door. It swung inward and the sound of peeping rose, oddly solitary. All I saw then were the bodies floating, all the ducks but one, motionless in the plastic tub. The ramp had fallen. After swimming and struggling for hours into the night, my ducks had drowned.

The scream that came out of me wouldn't stop. I ran. For days, everything drained out of me. I lost confidence, lost certainty. The images kept coming back, all of it my fault.

That was when the nightmares started, dreams about delicate beings I was charged to protect—human babies, animals, anything—and invariably I would lose that thing; it would die or morph into something else, something sinister with teeth or simply a creature I didn't recognize and failed to care for as any person knew they should. I blamed myself over and over. I could not be trusted. I was incapable.

That memory of my floating ducklings ate deep at the core of my chest. For decades, I couldn't touch or see it without feeling my insides caving in.

At Stanley Elementary School, a blond kid younger than me pumped his legs, riding his swing above me into the sky. Mountain peaks rose, snow-dusted. Kids played behind thin windows cut in the curved corrugated metal of the Quonset hut.

The blond kid shouted, "My dad says . . . " His comment drifted down to me and out on the air to the town around us and its forty-seven people.

Inside Mr. Bradshaw's classroom, only ten of us made up not only the third and fourth grades but the fifth and sixth, as well. We were mostly ranch kids or kids whose parents worked for the national forest fighting fires, counting cows, building fences, making sure hunters killed only the wildlife they had permits for. Idaho was not a rapidly growing place. In the center of the state where we lived, people worked hard for little and often made do by chopping wood, growing food, hunting, and preserving fruit and vegetables for winter. Stretching all the way from Utah and Nevada, north to the Canadian border, our state was twice the size of equally White Kentucky where Hunter grew up. Yet it had half the population.

The blond kid's voice lilted, almost as if he were singing. "My dad says, if he ever sees a Black person . . . " Here, I cocked my head to listen. Had this child's father never seen someone Black? Had he lived his whole life in a town of White people and never traveled far enough to see the true span and complexion of humanity?

The town nickname for my family and the other families on the ranch was "The Robinson Bar Hippies." My parents owned this name, Dad with his long beard and gender-bending hair, all their free-spirited travel, radical politics, and well-worn cars.

I had studied my blond classmate, how he loved to run. He was fast and had a joy about him in spite of ideas at home seeding themselves into him. At age twelve, I still hadn't grasped the depth of the bigotry around me, that we'd moved to a town and state where some still believed disgusting things about what they deserved because they were White.

The blond kid went on, voice matter-of-fact: "If he ever sees one, he'll shoot 'em."

The word "shoot" took a moment to register, rising in the air, up over the swing set like a bullet at the clouds. I had heard classmates say racist things. In Colorado, in second grade, a classmate had used the N-word. I don't believe the slur went unnoticed by my teacher, Mr. Fuji. But here my teachers were White, the town was White, the sheriff and people running our capital were White.

Violence flowed from somewhere unseen. I backed away from the swing set, imagining a shotgun, like my mother's, in his father's hands. What was it about being Black?

I felt shame for this boy. I felt so much shame I didn't tell Dad what I'd heard.

Winter deepened. Feet of snow stretched, covering the land. Over town, peak after peak rose, jagged in glaring white. These peaks were the edge of the Sawtooth range. They towered over the wide basin where our school sat. Drifts buried sagebrush hillsides, at the edge of the Frank Church Wilderness, which spanned hundreds of miles of mountains in the middle of the state.

Following a cross-country ski track behind my dad and my sister, I looked out across the white, drove my ski pole in and balanced, sliding one leg forward. Gliding, I shifted my weight from one foot to the other. Sun blazed in the cold. Breath billowed. Frost formed in Dad's beard. Turning upward along a ridge, we climbed until my arms and thighs ached. Motors whined below. I looked back to see snowmobiles fly the wide meadows in the valley bottom. The engines screamed. Something in the white moved ahead of them, black dots, the shapes of coyotes, running. The machines sped, closing the gap. The running figures vanished under the machines. I looked away, white light burning a hole in the snow.

What place had we moved to? So much wild and beauty and so much ugliness. I tried to grasp that people killed on purpose, not to eat but for some other reason, a reason I did not understand.

3
THE IVORY ROOM

1979–1982

Stanley, Idaho

One late winter morning, I lay in bed. The slanted ceiling fell toward low walls. In the hallway, someone was walking the creaking floor, past the blue room and yellow room. The creaking continued. It was Mom. Long black hair pulled back, pale skin wrapped in a robe, she stepped in through my door and moved to sit on the edge of my bed.

I was wintering in the rambling upstairs of our ranch's old guest lodge. When the snow fell, passes closed, and the restaurant shut down. Cree, my parents, and I would each pick a bedroom from the long line of low-ceilinged, attic-style rooms on the lodge's second floor. The rooms were named for the colors of their bedspreads or wallpaper. The pink room. The ivory room. The yellow room. The blue room. That winter I turned fourteen, I was living in the ivory room.

My mom was still not that mom who'd come in for a chat just any morning. She'd be out harnessing a horse or standing by the bathhouse in her felt hat talking to Edgar, her raven, a gift from her best friend, also named Pat. Her husband had lifted the birds from a nest a hundred miles away. But this morning Mom was here. She was moving to sit on my bed.

That was not normal.

"Nicole, I need to tell you something . . . ," she said, looking oddly awkward. "I've fallen in love." She paused. "With a woman." My mom, afraid of nothing, looked uncomfortable. "I'm a lesbian," she said.

I blinked a few times, wished I could push the covers back and rush past her. While sitting on the edge of someone's bed next to them may be a way to reach out to them, it's also confining.

All this was more parent-like than I gave Mom credit for. I studied her face. My dad had probably made her come in here—or Cree, who'd come to see herself as our parents' confidant and psychoanalyst.

"OK," I said, hoping she'd leave.

"Do you have any questions?"

I felt an uneasiness, a shame that I didn't want on me. It fell from her face and hands onto the ivory bedspread. I didn't want it. She didn't want it. I needed her to be done, to wrap it up and go.

There was no internet then and I'm not sure I knew what "gay" meant. Basically, I was unsure if there was something different about "gay" as opposed to just "sex." Both words seemed to cause upheaval in heavily Mormon Idaho. This was different from Woody Creek. In Idaho it seemed, kids didn't see their parents naked. Their mothers didn't carve wood stumps into the shapes of penises and anatomically correct male torsos. They were not given copies of books like *Where Did I Come From?* or *What's Happening to Me?* At school, rarely did a teacher talk about anatomy, puberty, or sexuality.

I knew I had little shames of my own, both imposed on me and of my own blundering. I think, in my mom's voice, I recognized hers. I wanted nothing to do with it.

I had no idea then, but quickly it would be clear that, to my peers and to their parents, gay was gross. Gay needed psychiatric help. Gay had to do with the Florida orange juice lady, Anita Bryant, and it had to be kept away from children.

With Mom sitting on the edge of my bed, gay almost seemed to have a color, one it seemed I should fear. I didn't want it on me. I didn't want it on my ivory bedspread. I wanted her to stand up and go back down the hall to her own room, the one she shared with my dad. I wanted to smooth out the wrinkles where she'd been sitting and go back to reading my physics book, thinking about gravity, dimensions, and subatomic particles.

When Mom finally stood and left, I listened to her steps fade down the wooden hallway and I knew for sure that I didn't ever want to be gay.

As a teen, I looked away as best I could, tried to deny the looming loss and change in my family after my mother came out. I skipped the dinner where my sister confronted Mom in front of Dad about a phone call and the affair Cree suspected Mom was having. I was fourteen. I shut myself in my room with books, took to pulling my long blond hair back tight in braids and walking alone up mountainsides and along creek banks, focused on patterns in the way trees grew, how rocks are ground smooth in water, how salmon swim from the oceans to die in the mountains on our shores, their molecules and nutrients spread by coyotes, raccoons, and birds across the land.

Dad wrote poems, mourned the loss of Mom. He told me he considered her his best friend. By the time ninth grade came, he'd left for California, reinvented how he cooked, and started a third restaurant in a place where he met goat cheese makers and gardeners. He'd drive an hour to fish markets in Berkeley and hired a woman named Mrs. Herb to raise edible snails.

I followed him when I could, spent parts of summers prep-cooking in his intense and artful little kitchen. Dad and I sautéed, danced by the gas stoves, walked in redwoods, traveled with his new partner, C Rose, a bold, feminine contrast to Mom who chided me about my eating habits but never told me I was fat.

Mom had a way of parroting her father or mother, fixated on what she'd been told about how girls needed to be slim, how a certain shape was necessary to achieve some feminine, one I'm not sure even she understood. She pushed Cree and me to diet.

"You can never be too rich or too skinny," she'd say.

In November, as I entered ninth grade, openly gay city supervisor Harvey Milk was shot in San Francisco. I heard jokes about Twinkies, pulled from the killer's "Twinkie Defense" where the assassin blamed his urge to kill on eating too much junk food. But, at school, no one called out the tragedy of the political violence and fear that gay people in San Francisco must have felt.

My mom, then in love and struggling to find her way in her first lesbian relationship, set my sister and me up to spend the winter in a rented house in Ketchum, a two-and-a-half-hour drive from our ranch. Our high school sat nearby, just outside Sun Valley, a small ski town, not that different from Aspen.

Since my dad left, Mom spent most of her time on our ranch with her lover, Pat, an equally bold, generous woman who loved horses and owned a ranch near Sun Valley. I started ninth grade and Cree started eighth grade alone, theoretically mature and well equipped after years of practice working, living in ranch cabins, and being trusted to adult on our own. Mom visited on occasion. Otherwise, she left us free to roam.

My mom's raven was one of three hatchlings. Each was a tennis-ball-sized creature, all belly and scraggly down, mixed with black pin feathers, a huge, wide black beak, and hooked tongue. Before my mom left my dad, we raised all three wild things in that same bathroom where I opened the door to find my ducklings floating in their tub. I knelt on that same linoleum and stuffed hamburger into raven beaks, changed newspaper, cupped the dark birds in my hands and set them to sleep in my lap.

Two of the three survived. Mom kept one. Dad named the female bird Edgar Birden. She fledged awkward pin feathers, soon sleek and shiny. The size of a small cat, she had great black claws, sharp, and curved. When she flew and landed on my arm, her talons dug in.

When I sat outside, she would perch on my shoulder, nestle her wing into my neck, preen the dander from the gleaming plains of her feathers, then rub her hooked bill along my cheek.

As much as I loved this bird, Edgar was my mom's raven. Mom would call and the bird would answer in Mom's voice.

"Talk. Talk, Edgar. Talk," Edgar would say, lighting from the sky to Mom's arm while she sat horseback, riding her gelding, Gillian, with Pat, the woman she loved. Up through the pines and fir, over the roar of Warm Springs Creek, the two would travel into the wilderness.

Mom was gone from Dad by that point, in the way I'd one day be lost.

Each morning, Mom made her way from her bedroom to the wire enclosure where Edgar roosted at night. She'd talk to Edgar, and the bird would make soft mumbling sounds, wipe her sharp beak gently across Mom's skin.

After Mom came out, Dad moved away and our ranch sat ready for sale. Mom's lover left, returned to her family, trying again with her husband and two kids. The world, once not kind or understanding when people came out, simmered at the news. Mom found herself alone. Our family had scattered. The ranch lodge settled. Boards creaked. At night from all sides, unbroken wilderness pressed.

I imagine Mom walking the pastures, doing chores with Edgar then, the raven flying from fence post to rooftop or riding Mom's shoulder, claws set gently in the skin and thin cloth of her shirt.

When the emptiness of mom's bed grew too stark, when vodka, the wild, and Edgar's touch couldn't fix all that ached, Mom bought a plane ticket for the East Coast, where her own mom and gay brother lived.

Edgar was left without her. The bird was set loose from her enclosure so she could hunt on her own. She waited for Mom. I imagine her sitting on the windowsill outside Mom's bedroom pecking at the glass, flying the pasture and river from the barn to the house and old lodge, waiting for Mom's voice to call, waiting for her red truck to kick up dust on the river road.

By the time Mom came home, weeks had passed. Edgar was gone. Maybe in her loneliness Edgar joined the flock of unpaired birds who ride the air over the river canyon, roosting in the rocks, hunting mice between the cactus, downriver.

Ravens can live fifty years. For much of her life Mom looked for Edgar, driving the highway and dirt roads in her truck until the ranch sold. She bought a cafe, twenty miles east in the desert, downstream. Whenever a raven took shape in the sky, she'd stop what she was doing, stand and call Edgar's name.

Starting when I was in ninth grade, Cree and I took on high school alone. Deep in the grove of aspen trees that made our half of the three-bedroom rental feel like home, the two of us cooked ourselves dinner in the toaster oven, shopped on an account at the grocery store, bought clothes, and did our homework. We made it to school and home each day, me at the wheel of the family's '72 Datsun station wagon.

Weeks passed without so much as a visit from Mom. She had a new partner and seemed happy. A hundred miles away, the cafe the two created had become a queer oasis in the Idaho desert.

One day Mom did appear. Her red pickup roared into the gravel drive and she strode into the house, black felt hat on her head. She seemed changed really. She wore lipstick and her hair was shorter now, shoulder length, blunt cut. She sported jeans and a polo shirt with the collar turned up. Still, she wore boots. Walking in with her duffel bag, she paused and stared at the area that made up the kitchen and living room. Books and clothes lay on chairs and the couch. Dishes filled the sink.

"This place is a fucking mess," she said. "I want it cleaned up. Now."

Cree and I looked at one another, a glance that set us both off.

"When you actually live here," Cree said, "you can tell us how to keep house."

Mom laughed. Cree put one hand on her hip and met Mom's eyes. She was the taller of the two by then and proud of it.

A large part of me was thrilled being left alone, having few rules, reading books, letting my own conscience be my guide. But I didn't navigate the world quite the way Cree or Mom did. I was trustful, to a fault. Trustful people, some theories hold, are often happy people. They're also gullible. My head housed an excess of empathy. I had rooms of it. The imagination flowing from my prefrontal cortex—that brain tool of conjecture and anticipation—was humongous.

I was a daydreamer. Hiking creeks that led into the wilderness alone or raising my hand in English class, I lived with some odd faith that everything would work out. I could see beauty or promise almost anywhere.

By contrast, at age three, Cree's neural factory of invention, left too long unchecked, had started imagining monsters. Where my brain was hopeful and trusting, Cree had long seen impermanence, conspiracy, and obliteration. To me, she was towering and formidable, a master of human complexities, dynamics between people, signals of confidence and success I didn't even contemplate. But the world around her sent sinister messages, kept her weary, on alert.

The ease of life that I felt was not for her.

My senior year, Meg arrived as a new twelfth grader—tall, artistic, and outdoorsy with laugh dimples and fine, straight, shoulder-length hair. She'd been sent away from eleventh grade in very Mormon and religious Salt Lake City, partly because her parents caught her smoking pot and thought Sun Valley, cocaine capital of Idaho, a more wholesome environment.

Ever ready for adventure, Meg landed squarely in the middle of my idyllic high-school-without-parents-world. In my lonely little mind, she replaced the boys I'd been following into the mountains, unsure if I was in love with them or just envious, longing to *be* them, live in those lithe, breastless bodies, stroll the halls worshiped by boys and girls.

Meg saved me from feeling I didn't belong. We read books by existentialists. We wrote papers, and I quietly imagined raising children with her—not the sex, just the family part, traveling, building a house together, cutting wood, growing a garden, growing old.

Seated next to Meg in our tiny high school senior seminar, I'd questioned the point of human existence, decided I needed a purpose, a goal.

In my mind, physics and biology filled every void, painted beauty onto the vast wondrous expanse of the universe as I knew it. But if there were no agreed-on point to human life, if we were all just onlookers to the wild, to illusions of subatomic forces, just silly beings thinking the world existed for our benefit or in a box in the third dimension, if happiness was all that was positive within our illusion—then it seemed a person should live to multiply happiness. We should live to make *other* lives better.

4
RADICAL

1983–1986

Berkeley, California

By my junior year of high school, I was counseled not to go to the University of California, Berkeley. "We don't recommend Berkeley for freshmen," I was warned. I wasn't even supposed to apply.

I could have gone East but New England felt old to me, colonial, crowded, oppressive. I loved the defiance of going to Berkeley, in spite of the warnings. I would pack my blue Datsun wagon and go carrying theories about evolution I wanted to prove or disprove.

Cree had to stay behind in Idaho. My constant companion and ally through all our years navigating Mom and raising each other in ski towns and the wilds, Cree was a high school senior. Without me, she was left to board with a family who took in ski team members while they trained for the Junior Olympics and cross-country ski races in the West. We were vastly different from each other. My awkwardness embarrassed her but our bond had endured. I had no idea how hard my leaving would be for her.

Through my first weeks on the Berkeley campus, I stayed alone in a borrowed apartment above a massage parlor. I walked out into the city on foot, through traffic, walking for miles because walking was the only way I knew to know a place, study the plants, the scent of the air, the kinds of trees that grew, the insects, the water. The place was lush. It felt as if that world of the Bay Area bloomed year round. The air was wet and cool. Often, fog rolled over the city in the night, wrapping the place in opaque curtains, leaving the sleeping street people damp on the sidewalks, the trees dripping in the mist. I'd heard it never snowed.

I had never lived near the ocean. I'd only lived in places so high and cold that fruit did not grow, not even apples. I'd never lived where humanity dominated the landscape. I'd never lived where every inch of land gave sign of human hands, human industry, structures, migration, propagation, waste. The green was beautiful, the span of humanity around me felt kaleidoscopic. My understanding of the vastness of human experience broadened. My skepticism about what was "normal" grew. I dove into every experience headlong.

Only an hour away, my dad's new restaurant thrived. My mom, back in Idaho, was running her artsy American-style cafe with my stepmom, Polly, a cook, gardener, and climber of mountains who was always well dressed. The cafe's dining room, long counter, and chromed art deco stools sat downriver from our old ranch. Mom planted a lone aspen sapling in the yard near the septic tank and, when I visited, I pulled cheat grass and tumbleweed, making way for the cactus, evening primrose, and wild rice grass Polly hoped would grow.

In Berkeley, I was an incoming freshman in the spring semester. Navigating classes on a campus of thirty thousand people tested my shaky ability to manage human interaction. I signed up for courses in psychology, anthropology, neurophysiology, the history of the Asian American experience, Black history, Indigenous peoples' history, and plant physiology. I took cellular biology, theoretical physics, primate behavior, cognitive linguistics, and graduate seminars in neural function. I studied with George Lakoff and thought about consciousness. I invented a major in the evolution of cognition. My thesis, "The Evolution of Hierarchical Structures in Living Organisms and Human Evolution," focused on overpopulation, greed, altruism, and the breakdown of compassion in the human struggle.

In a social anthropology class, we studied population doubling time, the number of years it took for the number of humans to double. My sense of peace was uprooted thinking how, in fifty years, twice as many people would walk the earth. Already humans failed constantly at feeding, clothing, housing, and caring for each other. We would need more of everything—twice as many houses, twice as much farmland cut from the wild because we'd have twice as many mouths to feed, minds to educate, bodies to heal, and cars in the streets.

I knew that few people in developed countries, especially in cities, knew how to live independent of grocery stores and power plants. Skills to do this seemed like something people should have.

In Idaho, Mormons or members of the Latter-day Saints (LDS) Church were preppers. By church instruction, the tens of thousands of members of their Idaho "wards" and "stakes" stockpiled food to prepare for the end. I knew nothing of Mormon beliefs but I bought a twenty-pound bag of black beans and fuel for my camp stove. I studied computer programming, practiced sewing, first aid, and methods for canning, drying, and preserving food. In summer, at Mom's place in the desert, I accepted gun safety lessons and, in Berkeley, semesters of art classes schooled me in pottery, woodworking, and welding.

I dabbled at the far edges of politics, went to lectures, including one where Hunter Thompson came to talk elections, gonzo journalism, and political reporting, arguing the uselessness of political parties. I, too, disagreed wholly with President Ronald Reagan and hated the Cold War and the idea of countries pointing atomic weapons at one another. I'd seen images of the missile silos in the Nevada desert. I'd seen *Testament*, *The Day After*, and other movies about nuclear annihilation.

My first semester ended. I flew to Fairbanks, Alaska, to spend the summer working for the Bureau of Land Management, training to fight fire while living in a tent frame off an Air Force base at the edge of the bush. I hitchhiked rides on small airplanes. On the night of the summer solstice I slept under an aircraft wing on a dirt airfield, above the Arctic Circle where the sun never set. I was lonely and understood nothing about dating or how to broaden my relationships beyond friendship.

Back in Berkeley the next semester, for the first time in my life, I saw two women kissing. Though my mom was gay, I'd never seen her kiss a woman. She was not physically affectionate around me, and I had no curiosity on the subject at all. I had a job working as a personal care attendant and my own studio apartment. I had joined the crew team. My long hair pulled back in a braid, thick junior varsity sweatshirt covering my breasts, I slouched in the team van with the other rowers, listening to my Walkman. It was then that the women appeared on a street corner at my right, one of them in bright white karate *gi*. Arms laced and twined, bodies locked against each other, they leaned in, mouths lost in a place far from that street intersection.

A teammate who worked as coxswain on our boat, a woman I found mysteriously adorable—one who joked more than once that she loved me—watched me sit up in my seat, turn, then stare at the vanishing couple for as long as I possibly could. Someone whistled or laughed and I looked around the van at the dozen sweaty, muscular women I spent my mornings with. I saw them suddenly for who they were: a team composed mostly of queers and lesbians who competed against other largely queer teams, racing in long, tortuously narrow boats, crammed one behind the next. Each of us was trained to pull on an oar with all our being, dripping sweat, staring at the bra straps, traps, and deltoids of the rower in front of us. We followed the count of the small woman in the bow who shouted, "Row," "Row," "Row," until we moved in perfect unison.

The revelations from that day, all the feelings and images of the two women, I promptly put out of my mind. Still, the sensation was there, an invisible undercurrent I carried everywhere.

Meg, my best friend from high school, visited. I took the lead and we bounced, dancing a polka at a Roches concert. She returned to Seattle. I said goodbye.

I made the pilgrimage to see the unflattering queer sci-fi cult classic *Rocky Horror* on Shattuck Avenue. After an Allen Ginsberg reading on campus, I wrote a poem about watching the poet read, his heels pounding to the words "Ass. Ass. Ass," while the straight couple in front of me made out.

This was the Bay Area, the gay center of the American West in the early 1980s. Five years had passed since city councilor Harvey Milk's assassination and two decades had unrolled since the uprising at Compton's Cafeteria where trans women in heels—done with years of harassment and terror—threw bottles at police. My arrival, though, was in the midst of the AIDS epidemic. The virus was claiming a whole generation of gay men. Sunken eyes hung in doorways. Wasting and mourning softened the edges of everything.

I immersed myself in my classes, taking twenty-four credits a semester, wading into my first political protest by accident. Overnight, Reagan had invaded Grenada. Streets filled with protesters. The crowd grew quickly to thousands, more people than had lived within twenty miles of me my entire life. On all sides, people shouted, then began to clap and chant in unison. I'd never felt a human force like that. I put my hands to my ears. The bodies flowed so I waded deep into that power, a leaf on a human river.

In my daily university life, long hair pulled back and a men's suit jacket buttoned over my sweater and breasts, I'd bike the few blocks from my barren apartment to campus, dipping in and out of activism. Near campus, I'd stand scanning posters on Telegraph Avenue, searching for protests that moved me.

I marched miles in chanting crowds to Livermore, California, where a lab was doing nuclear weapons research. I drove south of the bay, pulling my rusting wagon up to the edge of a field outside Watsonville, joining a crowd to support striking cannery workers. I heard civil rights leaders Dolores Huerta and Cesar Chavez speak. I showed up when asked, lent my body briefly to the organizers and the cause. I learned chants in Spanish and African languages. From my safe distance, I watched movements unfold.

One day, between the towering financial buildings of downtown San Francisco, the crowd of protesters ahead of me stopped. I'd come to support striking longshoremen, dockworkers refusing to unload cargo from South Africa, a nation staggering under the weight of apartheid. A dark gash formed in the street ahead. I pushed forward in the crowd, trying to see. Light glinted off plastic. Cops carried shields, long black batons, vests, and full riot gear. The air thickened. We all paused. On either side stood students I'd met on the street and in the train crossing the bay. Some of us stepped close enough to smell the officers' shampoo, the bite of their cologne. We looked into their eyes, the rows of fixed eyes, staring forward, the sets of jaws, the grip of all those black leather gloves on long batons.

There, especially in the faces of the smaller officers, the slight men and few women, something ominous burned. In those eyes some accumulation of fear, hatred, or pain was welling up. They looked out and we stood watching.

When our pressing on the shields grew too great, or perhaps when some signal came, they moved, some taking their batons in two hands to push us back. I felt the chill then of how much comfort and shelter I lived in. This was not a college campus. This was a place police ruled, a place where violence was routine, where the power of arrest, jail time, and the threat of prison could disappear a person who had no resources.

A dull crack close by sent the mass of bodies around me backward. Billy clubs rose and fell. One kid ahead of me fell to the pavement. Others scattered. Blood dripped from those I'd just met. A man my age who'd been standing, marching beside me, curled just out of reach, a small officer swinging a stick down on him. He was bleeding where his head had already taken a blow. He screamed.

Another blunted, bloody blow landed. The crowd surged backward but officers still swung and that bone breaking sound repeated, the billy club hitting a head, an arm, a curled body, until we were all running, some helping others who couldn't run.

I was raised around people who called cops "pigs." Hunter did.

Owl Farm, the house where the Thompsons lived, sat just off the paved road, so the sheriff might pass and slow. On a good afternoon, Juan and I would sit on the deck with Hunter and he'd suppress a smile and threaten to pick me up by the ears. Or that's what he'd call it, squeezing my head and pulling me up so my toes left the boards. Hunter was raised in the South, in Kentucky, and had once lived in the Bay Area. He read, wrote, traveled. He'd watched civil rights marches and Vietnam War protests decay into tear gas clouds, people falling to night sticks, police water cannons, and rubber bullets. The words "pig" and "swine" laced his vocabulary.

To our parents, cops enforced wrongheaded norms.

Often left unsupervised on the streets of Aspen, my friends and I would grunt, snort, or even squeal loudly from the sidewalk when an officer of the law passed by.

In December 1984, campus police cars lined the street, and chants echoed off the university's administration building. Officers in brown uniforms huddled around their cars gesturing at more than thirty students seated cross-legged on the sidewalk, blocking a set of double glass doors. The woman I'd passed in the van, deep in a kiss with her girlfriend, sat there in the middle of the blockade, her long blond hair and army jacket unmistakable. By then I knew her name, Andrea Pritchett.

I was someone who stood in the crowd at the rallies, maybe held a sign I'd painted, and shouted "Amandala" and "Aweto." I understood South African apartheid in the way a person who'd listened to student speeches and read a student newspaper might.

Somewhere people lived in shantytowns inside "township" reservations. They left their scrap-built shacks each day with a street pass to go out and work for next to no pay for people with lighter skin and European ancestry in the "Whites-only" cities—because that's the world those in power envisioned for them.

On a curb, I waited, watching administrators huddle as the line of students settled, unwilling to move. The police milling on the street broke onto the lawn, eyes on those blocking the sidewalk and doors. The crowd chanted for divestment, for selling stocks connected to White South Africa.

For decades, TV and radio reporters had covered anti-apartheid rallies on many campuses. It seemed as if every decade the issue surfaced and US policymakers squirmed a bit but did nothing.

I hesitated on the lawn between myself and the police. Handcuffs dangled from belts. None of the officers wore riot gear. Calmly, they scooped up one protester by the arms, carrying him across the grass, leaving a gap in the line blocking the building entry.

The gap bothered me. My own waiting bothered me.

For once, I had a way to do more than carry a sign or march and chant in the crowd.

I'd spent my brief life pushing the limits of things, foolish things, from hitchhiking on freeways in California to hopping small planes with strangers in Alaska, tromping foolishly ill-equipped over crevasses on glaciers and up mountainsides. I did things that could cost me my life. My luck was abundant, my privilege thick. Trust had served me well. I could handle brief confinement. I wasn't afraid of a minor criminal record. I could find a way to pay fines.

I stepped across the lawn toward the pavement and spun round to face the police. Sitting down in the gap between two others, I planted myself in the way of the doors.

It wasn't long before I felt a hand on my shoulder, heard the words, "You're under arrest."

Twenty-two of those on the sidewalk around me resisted arrest, kicking, struggling, or going limp. Some refused to give their names and were also hauled by bus to Santa Ana County Jail. Sixteen of us didn't resist. We were taken to the campus jail. They collected our fingerprints and scheduled us for court, charged us with "willfully and maliciously blocking a street and sidewalk." Up to that point, I'd never even had a traffic ticket. Carefully, I'd avoided even having a social security number.

The hours we waited for booking in our tiny campus cells were not hard time. The cage-like rooms were clean. Some of our jailers seemed sympathetic. Court dates were set. We were let go.

Long before my case was heard, a coalition of groups of color organized a blockade and sleep-in. Hundreds of us slept on the steps of what we called Stephen Biko Hall. The pressure mounted. Students constructed shanty towns on campus. University administration sent their brown-shirted officers to pull people out of sleeping bags, from big cardboard boxes, and from between palates of wood built to look like shacks. Soon, they arrested hundreds at a time.

As my own arrest weighed over me, I watched the news, went to rallies, took a rock climbing course, and applied for wilderness jobs in Idaho. And still the protests and arrests went on. Between classes, I listened to Angela Davis speak. Joan Baez came with her guitar, sat with us on the steps, warm thigh against warm thigh. She sang protest songs, nudging us with her elbow to join in.

"Not guilty," I answered to a judge in May 1985.

Part of the thirty-eight of us huddled briefly. We'd all entered the same plea.

Dad made the one-hour drive to stand at the back of the courtroom on the day of our arraignment, eyes sparkling behind his beard. He paid my court costs, said he was proud.

Our charges, though, were dropped because, since our sit-in, thousands of students, activists, and celebrities had been arrested in occupations on the plazas under the knobby magnolia trees.

At one point in the series of campus sleep-ins, a university paper covered the aftermath. I shuddered seeing I'd been described as a "buxom blond." I wasn't a leader of the movement. I did small tasks. I'd swept the steps of the plaza with a broom after others had rolled up sleeping bags and left for class. Yet in a newspaper someone had taken time and word count to describe me by my breast size and hair color.

Aloud in our lecture hall, my computer science teacher read lines from the articles about my arrest as part of the "UC 38" and the protests that followed.

"Buxom blond."

In those words, my body felt alien, libelous. I wrote poems about my breasts and read them in workshops. As coeditor of the *Berkeley Review* I published poetry by queer poets: Thom Gunn, Robert Pinsky, Frank Bidart. Their love poems were sad, sexy, powerful. Still, their lives existed in a dimension unimaginable from my own.

Within a year, though, I cut my hair, moving on to sleep with the next in a growing line of fairly feminine men. I had breasts and all the parts. Oddly, it seemed, I was never quite feminine enough. Relationships dissolved.

Alone, the old carpet of my room rough against my thighs, I pushed aside all the images of nights in bed fumbling with some lover. I knew the longing for companionship, but in the flesh I was unsure what desire was supposed to look like, unsure what to do. Something felt broken and unlovable in me. I wrote disorienting poetry, inhaled science courses, drank tea, and studied people in coffee shops.

Social niceties mystified me. I needed more than cues and innuendo to suggest I was welcome or to tell me to leave off and move on. My journals of the time were filled with tiny writing, hundreds of pages of obsessive relationship angst. I was insecure and hard on myself and was also a shitty friend because I shuddered at attachment and neediness, even from people I cared about.

At a party, college punk mingled with artsy gothic. I talked with a poet whose work I liked. She was dating a writer I admired from the Rhetoric Department.

"Actually, I'm bisexual," she said, batting long, heavy lashes. Her name was Elizabeth. I adored her and her poetry. With the lash batting, I felt a barrier rise, a shyness in myself, a need to run. Eric, her date, seemed solid. He was a feminist, smart, adventurous, well read. I slept with him, took mushrooms, went sky diving. For nine months, we dated.

It didn't occur to me how the shame I'd heard in Mom's voice had affected me, how I'd avoided ever telling Meg I would have lived with her, grown old, raised kids. I was that body spinning at the border of an event horizon, mindlessly skirting an invisible singularity, a window in space time, an entire universe of queerness I would one day call home.

At the end of two years, I'd prodded at concepts of altruism and selfishness, genetics, neurobiology, and child development and had earned enough credits for graduation. I struggled to organize my thesis, though, or even imagine an order for it. Everything that required a specific order eluded me, left me a wreck. After an assessment, the Disability Counseling Center described me as having next to no visual-sequential memory. Nothing in my head occurred along a straight line. While my mind could flip complex objects in space, being able to remember formulas, spell words, and keep track of time was outside my realm.

To spell something, I wasn't able to picture the letters in a word; I could only hear letters said aloud out of a dark place on the right side of my head. The science of myself was confounding.

I longed for Idaho, missed the space between people, missed vanishing into the wild as I'd done as a teen. I missed the unknown of how a trail might unfold, a creek bending to reveal pools, boulders the size of polished cars, trees with branches that fit my feet and hands, lifted me all the way into the sky.

On May 13, 1986, my breasts buried deep inside my varsity crew sweatshirt, I sat high up in the seats of Berkeley's Greek Theatre. I looked out at the crowd. Below me, from the center of the curved tiers of stone, Bishop Desmond Tutu looked up at us. The university was negotiating "partial divestment," saying it planned to sell stocks, pull its money from banks and oil companies whose dollars flowed to President Botha and his apartheid government. Bank of America and other universities and retirement funds followed Berkeley. Across the ocean, Nelson Mandela and other leaders of the South African resistance were still imprisoned, isolated on an island. It would take a long time for apartheid to formally fall.

Tutu looked up smiling, his face reflecting the light. "Hey, hey," he said, "have you seen my children in Berkeley?"

We sweated in the sun and Tutu raised his hands, bowed and thanked us in a way that felt outsized, uncomfortable. Seeing the South African leader's body there in that space so far from his home melted a concern I had about the trajectory of humanity, filled me with promise, made me more certain that people could and would affect the lives of others for the better. The arc of history, I felt certain, would bend toward happiness, toward justice.

5
WILDERNESS

1986–1992

Frank Church—River of No Return, Idaho

Requirements for the job of fire lookout were few. Even after I reported my arrest on the government application, the forest hired me. Roy, my boss, eyed me. He'd driven four of us up to Twin Peaks fire lookout, a twenty-by-twenty-foot building that sat at the top of a rocky 10,196-foot mountain. This post, one of more than ten in the forest, was closest to town by far, just an hour from Challis, up a steep, sketchy dirt road.

Roy was a skinny guy. His olive-green Forest Service cap matched his uniform and sat cocked on his head. Against a backdrop of peaks and sky, he grinned at me as he spoke. "Ladies," he said, "make better fire lookouts."

I suspect he hoped he was annoying me. I'd earned a reputation in the required three-day fire school because I'd objected to some sexist slight and had been taken down by a fellow trainee who rolled her eyes at the guys and leaned in my direction: "Stop your senseless bra burning. We're all sick of it."

From that peak where we stood, the entire south half of the Frank Church—River of No Return Wilderness stretched around us to the west. A roadless area of 3,700 square miles, it filled the center of the state. Almost void of houses, towns, electricity, and human civilization, it lay just twenty miles north as the raven flies or hours on dirt roads over peaks and passes from my mom's cafe.

Roy showed us how to read degrees on the circular fire finder in the center of the glass building. This was meant to help us describe the direction of a fire or smoke. We would pass our readings on to dispatch using a battery-powered, two-way radio.

Roy was training an entire crew of green lookouts that year. Each of us was about to be assigned to live on a peak, twenty to forty miles apart, some in deep wild, far from the outside world. Those lookouts would travel to their station on a string of pack mules. Once there, each of us would haul our own water and cut our own wood for heat and cooking. Two of us would be stationed on roads where we'd be flown in by helicopter. We'd be isolated until the snow melted and a truck could reach us for resupply.

I blinked sarcastically at Roy, braced for his explanation of exactly why women made better lookouts. On our forest, with the exception of one timber manager, every fire boss, forest manager, district ranger, fish and game biologist, range manager, wilderness manager, road, pack and trail-crew member was male. Women clerked offices and lookout towers. That was about it.

Roy smiled, enjoying himself. "Ladies handle solitude better. You all stay busy, *knitting* and such. You don't get as stir-crazy."

I didn't understand the stir-crazy part until he told the story of the guy on Sleeping Deer Lookout, years earlier, who'd called in an emergency from his forest radio one night. In panic, he told dispatchers that people had driven the long road to the ridge below his mountain top and had climbed up, trying to break in. "Please hurry," he'd pleaded. "Send a helicopter." It was night so all the forest could do was send a truck, three hours from the nearest guard station.

By the time they got there, several windows in the twelve-by-twelve lookout building had been broken out. The unfortunate veteran who staffed the place was found screaming to himself in the bushes on the mountain below. Law enforcement could find no footprints around the lookout. All the windows on the building had been broken from inside.

In solitude, apparently, a person's suffering had a tendency to take up residence. The stories of people unable to last on a mountain alone were many. If I had demons, I hoped they were not cruel ones. I felt pretty sure that those I did have had been exorcised into my journals long ago. But

I had to admit, that wasn't something a person could know about themselves until they'd spent weeks on end utterly alone.

Roy assigned me head lookout. Only twenty-two that year, my one summer in Alaska waiting around to fight fires qualified me as having "prior government experience." I'd used radios, had ridden in small planes, had already gone through fire training once before.

I'd do regular radio check-ins, keep track of the others, from Pat Charlton in his first year of college to Jody who had gray strands in her long hair and laugh lines around her eyes. One person would serve on Twin Peaks, in the building where we were training. That person would live there above ten thousand feet and, though it was a treacherous drive, could reasonably make the trip back to town on weekends when fire danger was low.

For the three months ahead, before the snow began to fly, Jody, Pat and I would live isolated, Pat most completely, but all three of us would sleep, eat, and work more than seventy miles from radio dispatch and town.

If you ignore the sound of it, traveling by helicopter is like floating, like being weightless. Rising off the ground at the helibase outside town, the machine cut a great arc in the sky, climbing above Twin Peaks and the ridge that served as the wilderness boundary. We floated above jagged lines of mountaintop. Scree slopes dropped below us, great chutes of loose stone shaped by gravity and a thousand years of falling rock. Twisted limber pine dotted the high places. Creeks cut through canyons. Lakes hung in glacier-carved basins on the sides of mountains.

For ten years I'd lived at the southern border of this wilderness and had never actually seen it, its size, shape, and low-key beauty. It wasn't an expanse defined by snow-capped peaks. It held huge stretches of forest and sage-covered hills, unscarred by roads, houses, or structures. It was a window into the land before Europeans shaped it for our needs, upended its solitude and its wildlife irrevocably.

I bent to look ahead through the curved glass. Far off on the horizon, one pointed peak stood alone. A giant cornice of snow hugged its shoulder and clung to the shaded cliff on its north side. A white building with a green roof and wooden catwalk circling it took shape. Its massive window shutters were still pinned down. Painted rocks on the cliff edge marked the one flat spot the helicopter could land.

The machine's landing gear touched down. Below me, the cliff face dropped into a frozen lake. Vaguely, the thin scratch of a dirt jeep road wound its way out from under a half-mile-long snow bank, then along the side of the valley below. I piled my gear by the four stairs that led to the catwalk. Andy, the mustached station guard from the valley below, shyly unlocked the door and shutters then gave me a tour of the sixteen-by-sixteen room. He hooked up a small tank and lit my propane refrigerator and stove to make sure they still worked.

I stood and waved as he and the pilot flew off, left me there to live in the eighty-year-old hut with its four walls of glass and outhouse perched on the cliff. This was a goodbye that would last until the snowfield on the road below the peak melted and the road could be driven again, who knows how many days or weeks away in the future.

As the sun dipped toward the horizon, I unpacked my two boxes of books, put jars of salsa and cans of food on low shelves. The room had grown cold. I lit a fire in the rusted wood stove and I unrolled my sleeping bag onto the mouse-bitten twin-sized mattress. The mattress rested on wire springs and a heavy metal bed frame. This was bolted into a heavy copper grounding wire. It made the bed look suspiciously like an electric chair. Following the wires, I could see that everything metal in the single room was wired together and connected to the wires that wound out of the lookout into the ground. Also wired in was a lightning rod, bolted to the peak of the roof, designed to conduct electricity around the building and into the rocks of the peak below.

In a lightning storm, I'd be sitting on a mass of rock on the top of the highest point in a four-hundred-square-mile area.

That first night I spent curled in my sleeping bag, I looked out as the sky faded toward black. The valleys fell into shadow, then vanished. I lay on the mattress listening to the sounds, knowing I was in a place too far for anyone to save me. Ears straining, the silence magnified the movement of large rodents beneath the floor boards, whispers of motion in the trees, cracking branches, and clunks as hooves hit logs in the basin by the lake below. The silence and the sounds terrified me.

I buried my head in the covers trying to stop myself from listening. When I peeked out, the stars were an overturned bowl that spun not just overhead but level with me to the North, South, East, and West. The Milky Way blazed, a brilliant river, branching through the night with its light.

I'd always loved the dark. The wild had never scared me. I'd grown up with black bears and bobcats passing at the margins of our yard. And I'd listened to my dad's Arctic stories of being herded by a pair of wolves training pups to hunt and of the time a grizzly stood on its hind legs, trying to get scent of Dad and his companions as they crossed the tundra. Like the wolves, the bear had likely never seen White men, only the Inuit who still traveled and hunted as they had for tens of thousands of years. Circling them slowly, standing again and finally catching scent of them, the bear recognized human sweat or perhaps gunpowder and dropped to all fours, loping away across the muskeg to the horizon.

Not knowing what animals breathed in the dark on the mountain around me kept my mind churning. Logically, I knew I was safe. Most of all I felt my smallness and the distance between myself and humanity. My adrenaline coursed every time a new noise made it through the thin windows and heavy cloth of my sleeping bag.

Night seemed to refuse to end, but with the sky's first faint glow in promise of morning, my puny survival felt miraculous. Having fears turn to nothing made me elated, invincible.

The place made me humble, too.

One evening, picking my way down the ridge below the lookout where the trail zigzagged between rock spires and tall lightning-struck limber pine, I turned back home to find deep-set paw prints covering my boot tracks. Looking closely at the dirt, I could tell a mountain lion had followed me downhill and now could only be somewhere on the rock outcropping just above me, looking down.

Breathing gently, I focused on how, if the huge cat wanted to eat me, it would have already. Something kept it from making me prey, pouncing with its teeth and claws. I took one step, then the next, climbing the ridge back toward the lookout, gently, feeling an odd unspoken truce, a blurring of self that made me part of the trees and the animals of the place, a life that existed as the others did, doing what I did just to live, my quiet presence of little threat, walking, reading, and looking through binoculars for fires in the rain, dark, and snow.

Soon, with each mountain thaw and as the rivers swelled and the ridges greened, I returned home for my seasonal job. In the seven summers that followed, I never tired of the quiet and growing sense that I was small.

In my second year, Meg took a job on Twin Peaks on her own college summer break. That year, I chose Little Soldier Mountain, a low lookout far from the road, deeper in the wild. Only the peak to the North, where Pat Charlton would be, was more remote. On my new lookout, coyotes hunted and ravens floated on the grassy ridge that ran south to a long line of other ridges, connecting little peaks, one to the next, sixteen miles and thousands of feet of elevation up and down by trail or bushwhack.

My lookout team that second year watched by day and, when lightning storms struck, by night as well. I lived in an older building, perched over a small lake, twelve miles by trail, high above a guard station and the pools and rapids of the Middle Fork of the Salmon River.

One night, a towering thunderhead floated from the West toward me. Thick white bolts dove out of it from the sky to the ground. Light flashed near the tower where Pat was awake, gas lamp on, like me plotting strikes on his map. Simultaneously the ground shook, white light snaked down and the sky opened up. On tiptoe, I gripped the circular metal fire finder on its high pedestal in the center of the room, trying to get a reading on a tree that had caught fire downhill, only a quarter of a mile away on my own mountain. An orange glow flared in the dark. Through my binoculars, the flames threw up sparks and the fire blazed. Already I smelled smoke blowing toward me in the wind.

Fingertips on the fire finder's metal rim, I focused on the fire. On the storm side of the lookout, it was hard to see. Rain hit hard against the glass. Then the room went blank. I lost consciousness, wrapped inside white light and sound. My arms shot out, muscles clenched, legs stiff. I woke, standing, screaming in the center of the room.

Lightning had hit the lookout, discharging into the grounding system, spreading through the connected metal objects, diving into my fingertips, up into the neurons in my brain, seizing my legs, lungs, and heart, then pouring out somewhere, maybe back through my fingertips, down the thick metal wires, into the rocks and the core of the mountain beneath me.

I blinked, felt the ache of everything, the hum of me. I had been of the clouds and of the mountain. I had stood in the space that connected the two.

The fire glowed. Just a single old snag on a rocky slope near the ridge. The next day, a helicopter came and I spent the night watching the tree's hollow center throw a tower of sparks into the sky. By the second day, the fire was out and I was left alone.

Lightning soon became like an adrenaline I hungered for. I walked out onto the ridges in storms, staying awake into the wee hours, nose pressed to the glass in the pitch black, waiting for flashes, veiny threads of electricity that flowed to the peaks and valley out of blackness or wove in elaborate root-like branches, undulating overhead.

I watched towering clouds set aglow from beneath, watched immense charges of energy tear through the air, felt and smelled the flash and simultaneous explosion of thunder, felt the mountain shake, watched bolts turn twisted limber pine into towering pillars of sparks and flame.

From Little Soldier, I began hiking out overnight on the rare days fire danger was low enough I'd get time off. I packed light and, in one day, crossed the thirty mostly trailless miles from Little Soldier to the peak I could see on the horizon where Jody had been stationed that year. As the hours passed, the walking found a rhythm in me. My long torso and solid legs were built for the trail.

The next year, after a fire season so severe the sky turned dark and the sun so red I couldn't see even the nearest mountain through the smoke, I began asking for a job where I could fight fire or do something more productive than wait while, around me, the forest burned.

As I graduated Berkeley and, in a year, finished my teaching degree in San Francisco, my bosses thought I'd be a good fit as the forest's first wilderness ranger, a solo set of eyes paid to crisscross half a million acres of the Frank Church Wilderness on foot. I'd check outfitter hunting camps for violations, inventory thousands of miles of trails, and look for illegal motors, wheels, hidden caches of food, gear, and equipment. At times I'd be the forest's human presence in places meant to stay free from human machines and technology, their sound and trace.

I was sent to a two-day law enforcement school. Working on that side of the law felt uncomfortable, though I was being trained to defend the wild, not institutions bent on beating protesters or driving nonconformists from the streets. The male trainers called me "little gal" and quickly pegged me as the hippy-liberal do-gooder I was. Most special was being called "commie spy." I got this name after I turned out to be fairly efficient at tracking hidden tarp-covered caches of food, which drew wildlife and made bears grow habituated to humans. I found spark plugs, strings of electric lights, latrines on creek banks, and trash buried in pits around the camps of the forest's less conscientious hunting guides. There in the land of minimal government, I was, to some, the embodiment of federal prying.

Central Idaho where I lived was just sprouting a new type of armed, anti-government militia then. Local people, many of whom loved the land and the wild as I did, felt it was being taken from them by the restrictions inside wilderness. Some in Custer County saw work like mine as dangerous.

Though I'd been raised locally, they saw what I did as government intrusion. Some objected to my creeping along trails in my green federal agency uniform, taking photographs of tree roots scraped raw by poorly tethered horses, scattered toilet paper and waste, outhouse holes dug next to springs. In lands where horses, mules, boats, and feet had long been the only means of entry, a few now claimed the use of generators, carts, and motorbikes as a traditional way of life. They didn't believe the place was better off silent and remote or that solitude, the mountain goats, and wildlife would be at risk or grow scarce if wheels, motors, and engines used the trails and crossed meadows and mountainsides the way they were still allowed to in millions of acres of forest outside that designated wilderness.

At the Clayton Mercantile, upriver from my mom's place where I spent days off, the woman who homeschooled our neighbors led a militia group that met regularly in the town's store and cafe. I'd see the rows of cars parked out front as I drove past headed for the backcountry.

This group was one of a growing number that was arming themselves, connecting with each other from one small community to the next. Organized strategically under the Wise Use movement, they could get funding funneled their way by paid lobbyists or anti-environmental leaders like Ron Arnold. Arnold's art was making environmental groups look radical and well funded while he got local people to help him tear down regulations so logging and mining companies could operate with fewer strings. He dismissed concerns about the long-term impact of mines, factories, and clearcutting on air quality, water, health, and wildlife.

Some, including candidate for Congress Helen Chenoweth, whose campaign headquarters began serving as a drop spot for donations for a new group pushing antigay policies, stood at the center of this budding movement in the Western United States. Chenoweth took corporate money and became a voice for fears that the Western way of life was under attack. She made national news when she claimed that armed federal agents were flying black helicopters and spying on ranchers, outfitters, and locals trying to earn a living in the wild.

More people armed themselves. Richard Butler on his compound in North Idaho was recruiting then, marching, training, working to create for his KKK-affiliated Aryan Nations, a White autonomous homeland, hostile to all but the straight White Christians he gathered around him.

One afternoon while checking water quality in a canyon near private land, I saw a boy my age crouched in a bush with a rifle. His family lived off-grid. To him, my green uniform must have looked like a sign of some sort of federal raid. My boss, standing next to me with a notebook, put his hands up and apologized. We backed away slowly and the boy vanished.

I redoubled my efforts at learning survival skills. I was mostly a vegetarian but knew shooting was missing from my checklist of survivalist skills.

"I don't want to own a gun," I told Mom. "I want to know how they work, how to hit something if I need to take one away from someone." In the gulch back of her place in the desert, she brought cans, clay pigeons, and we set up targets. She handed me a small rifle.

"Point it at the ground when you're walking!" she called after me. Lifting the .22 from my hands, she unlatched the safety, stuffed foam plugs in her ears. Shouldering it, she leveled the long barrel to her eye and scattered the tower of cans.

I built another tower and she handed me back the gun. It was small compared to a rifle that could kill a deer or elk, but when I raised it up, it still felt heavy in my hands.

"It's going to kick on you. Press it to your shoulder," she corrected, grabbing my elbow. "Squeeze slowly or you'll lose your aim."

When I pulled the trigger and hit a can, she grinned and opened a beer.

"All right, man." It was hard making Mom proud of me.

My skills were adding up. Populations were doubling. In my mind, scenes from the movie *Terminator II* played out. I imagined myself as badass Sarah Connor, traveling through time to defend the compassionate from an army of robots at the end of civilization. If oppression ever rose to power, I wanted to be the resistance.

6
MERCURY

1992, OCTOBER

Nevada Test Site

Increasingly, in the desert outside Challis, Mom's cafe and relationship with Polly were struggling. Aside from Joe, the handsome seventy-year-old gay rancher who'd sold Mom her cafe and lived on the ranch down the hill, Mom was alone and she was drinking more than usual.

Boise, Idaho's capital, was a three-and-a-half-hour drive from her place. When I took work there in the winter, the city felt sprawling and vastly different from Custer County where, since my last year at Berkeley, I'd spent my summers, staying in a trailer on her place when I wasn't working in the wild. For most Idahoans then, even though Boise was no more than a large town of roughly a hundred thousand people, our state capital felt urban. The nearest big cities were Salt Lake, Portland, and Missoula, each about an eight-hour drive away.

Boise's streets were tree-lined, its downtown unglamorous, culturally monotone. Neighborhoods were fairly mixed politically; older Republican couples lived next to young people who'd moved to the city from rural areas for jobs or college. Downtown lay close to wild foothills, the whole city tucked between the central Rocky Mountains and the farmland and river canyons of desert and Oregon an hour away.

Settling into Boise to help teach kindergarten, I still didn't let myself consider that I might be queer. That was Mom's path. Not mine. I was like Dad. I, too, loved science and wilderness. Chaos made sense to me. I was still trusting and cared for humanity. Summers in Idaho's backcountry left me free of pressures I didn't have words for. For me, people remained hard to understand.

When I finally bought a house in Boise, it lay tucked under a hundred-year-old white pine, surrounded by a meadow, which I nurtured, letting the tidy lawn grass grow, seed heads rippling and rustling in the wind, just the way they might have on the slope below Little Soldier Lookout. Holding onto that part of myself, I dug into city life, hosting big dinner parties and protest-planning meetings.

Being an activist, believing I could make the world a better place, fit my nature. I had the privilege to do it. My dad had helped me with the down payment on my house so I had a mortgage and roommates but no landlord who could evict me over objections to my politics. I had no college debt because I'd gone to state schools. For graduate school I'd earned a teaching fellowship that let me work and covered more than my tuition.

I spent many nights up late with a glue stick, making posters or pasting together the monthly "Green Reader" magazines I helped write and publish. I'd be on the phone or in potluck dinner meetings, later grading my students' papers at my dining room table while my roommates slept.

In 1992, I began volunteering for the Snake River Alliance in Boise. There, I raised funds and traveled yearly to Washington, DC, with other activists, warning about nuclear weapons and educating members of Congress about radioactive waste.

Though most of us who loved the desert west didn't see where we lived as a wasteland, our part of the country had long been considered of little use by those in the nation's capital. While leaders like US senator Frank Church had worked for years to protect wild roadless areas as designated wilderness, others sent trainloads of radioactive waste to be buried or even pumped into groundwater in the volcanic lava flows near Craters of the Moon National Monument in the southern part of the state.

In the fall of 1992, my brown station wagon hummed the narrow highway, a day's drive south of the Idaho border. Big, with strong thighs from firefighting in the wild, my dishwater hair cut in a bob, I pulled off into a dusty patch of desert lined with rows of cars. Yanking my Walkman headphones from my ears, I swung my feet to the ground.

I'd spent that spring of 1992 as one of many unpaid lobbyists walking the halls of the US House and Senate offices in Washington, DC. In groups we dressed informally and met with senators, telling stories about the weapons factories and chemicals buried in our communities. We asked them to commit to ending nuclear weapons testing and to stop the shipments of radioactive waste to Idaho and desert states in the West.

Bleary, I stood, watching dust rise and heat blur Newe, or Western Shoshone land. Flat and seemingly unscarred by roads, the distance unfolded in brick red, sage green, and gray all the way to the horizon. Behind me, bordered by hundreds of miles of barbed-wire fence, the Nevada Test Site stretched to the north and west.

There in the desert, in the twelve years before my birth, the US had detonated a hundred nuclear bombs in open air. Under the cloak of the Department of Energy, government spewed radioactive dust and ash toward Colorado and Idaho and to the east beyond. Protests had forced the tests underground. By the time I arrived at the site that October, the Department of Energy had exploded nine hundred more bombs in deep shafts, creating caverns of glassified and collapsing radioactive sand and rock. All this had made that part of Nevada one of the most contaminated nuclear sites on earth.

Over ten years, fifteen thousand people, including movie stars and celebrities, had been arrested in acts of civil disobedience there in the desert. Persistence mattered. When the Civil Rights Act passed Congress in 1964, it was the result of fourteen years of civil disobedience that forced White America to confront the reality of racial discrimination and the stories of those affected by it. It was protest that had pressed Congress and two presidents until the cruelty grew too vivid and politically risky to ignore.

There, at the Test Site in 1992, powdery earth hung in the air over kitchen tents and porta potties. I spent a day in training, ladling out vegetables in food lines, washing dishes, picking up trash.

Curled in my sleeping bag, I woke before dawn to find Corbin Harney leading a prayer in Shoshone as the sun rose through the dust, gleaming off barbed-wire fences. An elder with deep lines in his face, Harney spoke for the protests he'd set in motion and for the Newe land beyond, buried in layers of fallout.

Five hundred of us settled into groups of ten for planning small protests and acts of civil disobedience. I ended up in a group with Germans and Swedes, with men and women from Latin America and Australia. The ten of us mapped out what we'd do. As dark fell, we'd break into the testing facility and cross nine miles of desert on foot, reaching the Department of Energy town of Mercury at first light. There we'd pass out fliers to workers or tape them up on walls, proposing that the place be converted to an immense solar power plant, offering safer jobs and an end to nuclear testing.

That is what we planned to do.

The sun set and a fine powder coated everything, every inch of us inside and out. We dressed in our darkest clothing. Some in the groups around us wore bandanas over their mouths. I half wished I'd brought a Geiger counter and half felt relieved I hadn't.

Probably because of my experience in the backcountry, I was assigned the role of scout. When darkness came, the moon rose. I'd be the first to crawl through the metal culvert under the highway. The pipe led into the site where we'd been told Wackenhut military police, the 1990s equivalent of Blackwater, roamed the desert with rifles, in something called a Humvee.

I bent to peer into the culvert. It was large but not so large we wouldn't have to crouch down. I grabbed a stick for rattlesnakes. Our flashlight-lit scramble under the highway and barbed wire into the site was brief. We put out our lights, whispered, then emerged from the pipe, ready to rely on the moon.

I told our team to scuff their feet a bit, follow single file behind me. That way we could reduce our chances of someone stumbling on a rattlesnake.

Away from the light of camp and the road, the moon shone near full, glistening off the skin of saguaro and giant barrel cactus. Armored with long spikes, these towered larger than any of us. Here—where people feared radioactivity and where wire fences and federal laws kept the ground safe from trampling feet and dune buggies—plants grew as they would have five hundred years earlier when the Newe cared for the land.

The night became an ocean of serrated blades and needle-like daggers. Shallow ravines wound below us, and ridges rose against the stars. The dark stretched to the horizon but for one single distant orange light. This light was the town of Mercury, a cluster of buildings almost ten miles away. We'd been told the town held warehouses, part of the weapons-testing machinery of the site. That orange light was our destination.

We walked for hours, nine silent bodies behind me, single file. We paused at the sound of a motor. The distant voices of other groups echoed. Many in their own groups of ten were on their way into the site.

On a rise above us, on the plain between the highway and Mercury, a watchtower loomed. A high-pitched sound carried down, red lights blinked, and we realized the guards had night vision goggles. In whispers, we agreed to crouch low when we heard the whine the goggles made, searching as we ran in the dark.

Headlights swept the faces of saguaro. Still, we snaked together, darting from hollow to hollow. Beams lit ravines and brush-covered hillsides above and below us.

Past the watchtower, we crouched, held our breath, as above us on the hill, a team with their own plans to reach Mercury was caught. In headlight beams, they were handcuffed and arrested by Wackenhut in uniforms. Machine guns lay strapped to the soldiers' backs. On a dirt road, jeeps flowed, filled with men dressed in military desert camouflage. Cornering protesters, they rounded them up.

For hours, we evaded the Wackenhut, trying to cross the plain to reach the light. Mercury grew closer, turning from a beacon to a tiny cluster of blocky buildings towering against a now pale sky.

Humvees rolled over stands of sagebrush and cactus. A cluster of protesters was caught within forty feet of us as we lay in the dust, breathing as quietly as we could. Scrambling up, we ran a ravine bottom, headed for a wall of chain-link and the buildings beyond.

But headlights hit us. Loaded Humvees roared. We ran as two jeeps came at us.

Our group had agreed that the Wackenhut were not our enemy. Security contractors and site workers had no power to decide whether nuclear testing should stop. Our hope was to catch the sympathy of the public so they'd press Congress.

We ran dust-coated and tired. Engines bore down and men shouted, "You're under arrest!"

We stayed in place then, respectful, joking with the guards as they stowed their rifles and stuffed us into jeeps and vans, our hands tightly zip-tied behind our backs.

We never reached Mercury that night but others did. As dawn drew streaks of pink across the sky, we looked back. Someone unfurled a white protest banner from the top of one of the buildings. We grinned as its letters glowed in the sunlight.

The protests and five hundred arrests made national news. As we found our way home that fall to towns and cities around the globe, nuclear tests scheduled for the months that followed never happened. Having listened to Corbin Harney and other activists, perhaps members of Congress could finally picture their own wild places designated as wastelands or sacrifice areas, whole industries promising safety while quietly poisoning air, water, and soil. Testing, as that desert had known it, came to an end.

7
BIGOTS

1993–1994

Boise, Idaho

Long before I traveled to DC, I found myself inside Idaho's Capitol building. In the cool stone depths I listened to the hush and echo of the halls with their marble veneer and formal staircases. As part of a group worried about water quality and forests, I met state lawmakers and glimpsed a world where people shook hands and wore ties. They projected a sense of class and gender that felt strange, even uncomfortable.

In 1993 I moved from working as a volunteer to being a paid organizer for the Snake River Alliance. With this, I left the Forest Service and wild to live full-time in a community of activists in Boise. Though my job lasted only a year, organizing felt as if it would move me closer to a place where I might make the world a more just and happier place. Thinking I could teach kids to question the world and educate policymakers, I gave up a life and an existence that, for seven years, took me into the mountains and fed my sense of wonder.

On a midsummer day, standing on the granite compass rose, deep in the Capitol, reporters crowded in with cameras and notepads. A dry, thin man named Kelly Walton announced that his group had collected enough signatures to put their antigay state-ballot initiative up for a vote in the fall election.

In suits, a group of men and women from four Christian groups smiled and nodded, their feet ticking on the inlaid stone. Somewhere, boxes of petitions sat, certified, in the secretary of state's office. The group had just four months to persuade half of Idaho's six hundred thousand voters to support a measure that would effectively turn a set of biblical beliefs about queers into law.

Because Mom was gay, I convinced myself I was an ally. No one around me back then talked much about gender. Like race, gender was presented as a binary, something finite, an either-or. You were either male or female, White or not. All my life, the culture I lived in washed over the absurdity and biological impracticality of both these ideas. A whole nation and generations of people were expected to accept the power or lack of power that came when they were assigned a race and a gender at birth.

In 1994 Idaho was fairly libertarian, with a live-and-let-live attitude. Cultural attitudes toward gay people were neither universally hostile nor welcoming. In general, Idahoans didn't know much about being gay. At that point, comedian Ellen DeGeneres had not yet come out as a lesbian so people like me from very rural Idaho had next to no positive examples of queer people on television or in the media. Boise, the only city with a Pride celebration, had held a rally, parade, and picnic for four years. I'd never gone.

Though I didn't know it, no laws kept LGBTQ Idahoans secure in their jobs, rental agreements, or business relationships. The risks that came with that left many afraid to object. They, like me, stuffed themselves into heterosexual relationships or married as expected, giving birth to children, aging in genders that were neither fitting nor comfortable. One day, I'd glimpse the beautiful queer underground that's everywhere, a network of quiet lives, often unseen even by families, friends, and coworkers.

Invisibility has its costs, though. It causes stress, creates strains. In 1994 it meant that, to the average Idahoan, gayness was still foreign, an unknown, easily turned into something scary.

All through the late fall of 1993 and into the desert heat of the next Boise spring, I'd climb out of bed, greet my roommates, feed my twenty-year-old Siamese cat, Wren, then bike the few blocks to the office of our state's lone all-volunteer LGBTQ organization. The group's name was Your Family, Friends, and Neighbors. As part of the unspoken underground, even our queer rights group used a code name and avoided the word "gay." We affectionately called some of the work we did that summer "bigot busting" because it involved going out in pairs as volunteers to search for zealots and paid canvassers gathering signatures for Kelly Walton and his group, the Idaho Citizens Alliance (ICA). We'd sweat in Boise's concrete downtown or at concerts, standing as close as possible to a person carrying petitions. We'd warn those reaching for the pen how signing would help haters force our state to discriminate.

Some religions were antigay; others weren't. At the time, state and federal law tended not to be explicitly antigay. In 1994 Idaho law didn't mention gays at all. Even our state's "infamous crime against nature"—or "sodomy"—law threatened straight and gay people alike with five years to life for consensual oral or anal sex. Straight couples, too, could go to jail for getting it on in some way that was not completely missionary style.

Though it sounds all too familiar now, Walton's initiative was a first for Idaho. In plain language, Proposition 1 used the word "homosexuality" and proposed to censor any positive images of queer people from library books and class discussions. It hoped to cut queers from government programs and public television, ban cities and counties from passing nondiscrimination policies, and prevent the state from spending money "promoting homosexuality." Under law, every person in every part of government would be forced to act as if queer people and anti-queer bigotry never existed.

Essentially, Walton and the churches standing with him needed to believe that being queer was a choice. If they could make people believe that, then they thought they could stamp it out with a law.

That year, tall, soft, round, and dressed in loose cotton pants, I stood from my theater seat, tucked my hair behind my ears, and slipped from the darkness into the lit hallway. I was a volunteer ticket taker at our local art theater and was logging my third or fourth time watching the sexy lesbian film *Go Fish*. Grabbing my counting clicker, I took my assigned station in the hallway, by the trash can.

"That movie's pretty hot," a voice said from the hall behind me.

Cheeks reddening, I turned to see a head of permed curls that could only belong to Evie or MaryEvelyn Smith, a woman I recognized from the office of Your Family, Friends, and Neighbors. She smiled and, with her exaggerated swagger, wandered up to stand beside me, elbow on the trash can top where my ticket taker supplies sat. Except for my mom, Evie was one of the first lesbians I knew. She was probably hoping to debrief on the movie's fantastic sex scenes or something about politics. Unsure if I was ready to talk about the movie, I ducked into the theater to sweep trash from the floor, feeling oddly neon and bare.

This feeling grew comforting though, an arrival of sorts. With it, I had to acknowledge in myself a line I'd drawn, a realm where thought and fantasy had never been allowed to go. Over the past seventeen years since my mom had come out, the line had worn thin. The shame I'd once heard in her voice had quieted. The smoothing of that ivory-colored bedspread had stopped.

It would be stupid to deny how much I loved the film, all its skin, sex, and women's bodies. This was also true of gay male love stories I'd seen in the theater. I didn't even try to reconcile myself with the sexual complexity of this. I simply felt longing and desire and set aside all thought of the gray and complex-identity that it would take me decades to find words for.

By the time Kelly Walton and his ICA had gathered their signatures, I'd joined the statewide No On One Campaign against them as one of seven paid staff. Heading the campaign were icons of the queer community, two couples I feared disappointing but very much came to love. Jen Ray Rohlfing and Mary Rohlfing and John Hummel and Brian Bergquist had spent years engaged in queer organizing, art, strategy, and community building. They were funny and saved us from getting grim when it got hard. Our campaign manager and our fundraising director both came from Montana. Two years earlier, I'd finished training as a community organizer in a weeklong program in their state. Montana had fight and union organizing power of a kind Idaho seemed to have lost.

Across the border and the canyons west of us, Oregon was about to fight their own version of the same voter question. It was not promising that the initiatives in both states were nearly identical to one passed a year earlier, in increasingly liberal Colorado.

Summer began, and isolated queers and allies in our rural swath of the West had just four months to convince half the voters in our state to vote no. At a forum broadcast on TV, two men from the ICA ranted about "the dangers of anal and oral sex." One of them spent nearly half an hour repeating the words "anal" and "oral" into his microphone.

National groups from DC brought in pollsters who told us a majority of Idaho voters didn't care about discrimination. As White and isolated as Idahoans were, they likely didn't understand it. Like people in Stanley, they saw feminism, racial diversity, and being gay as "problems" cities had to deal with. If their neighbors were gay, Black, or Asian American and those in town knew them personally, they didn't let go of stereotypes but made exceptions to them.

"Yeah, that's our local lesbian couple. Their cafe has great food."

The stereotypes Idahoans spent lifetimes absorbing from family and television still likely caused some majority to believe, and even express, racist and bigoted views. Like all of us who grew up in White, homogenous rural places, I'm pretty sure my neighbors thought that discriminating on purpose was something only other people did.

Communities that lived off the land viewed government as far away and foreign. Not every Idahoan was extreme in their thinking or belonged to militias. People worked hard, often at several minimum-wage jobs, but were still poor. They hated paying taxes because they were not doing very well. It was a very Idaho attitude to think that when government got involved, things went wrong. In the campaign's polling, only one message seemed powerful enough to persuade our libertarian populace to vote no on Proposition 1: A no vote would help keep government out of our lives.

We set up phone banks, created a database, and started calling households.

The out-of-state LGBTQ organizations did not expect Idahoans to defeat the referendum. Our campaign was expected only to minimize the damage. We'd represent LGBTQ people as wholesome, sexless, and family oriented.

Over the entire nine-month lifespan of a campaign, avoiding the words "gay" and "discrimination" and sticking to persuasive messages about government intrusion was going to be rough for queer activists. No one really loved it, especially the gay men, lesbians, bisexuals, and gender-nonconforming people who lived openly. Many had just come out after whole lifetimes of being invisible so they could keep jobs, buy groceries, and be safe.

By October, we had a path to win, but it meant we needed at least some of the religious conservative vote. Fundamentalists weren't going to swing our way. Some, like Kelly Walton with his many kids, believed in withholding medical care from their own children, letting "God's will" determine the outcome of seemingly everything—except where queers were concerned. To them, we weren't worthy of the biblical "love thy neighbor" or "do unto others."

Our best option was to somehow appeal to the Mormons whose churches dotted the bottom half of the state. In every town there, slender spires pointed fingers at the sky. While it was a very White religion, its missionaries worked in countries all over the globe. They encouraged immigration of converts and stood out for their welcoming and openness to positive immigration law.

Mormons have a complex history in the Western US. Just as Walton's proposition targeted gays, Idaho's first legislature targeted Mormons. At statehood, lawmakers banned polygamy in the constitution. For decades they banned Mormons from voting as well. On some level, many Mormons understood what discrimination was.

As an adult, I'd never kissed a girl. Crushes were a normal state, often an excruciating one. I was a swimmer on the surface of the sea of love. I was doomed, it seemed, never to dive down. Instead, I channeled all my angst into work, into my huge job, employing my scattershot focus and odd sense of detail. All of us on the campaign stretched. Around me, straight allies spent long hours on folding chairs in our phone banks. Volunteers, long-closeted, braved first dates and came out.

One afternoon, deep in the campaign, I invited a volunteer, dark, curly-haired Devon, to my house to rip wooden yard sign stakes on the table saw in my attic. Rough-cut beams angled close overhead. Spiderwebs hung. Our arms brushed one another. Devon felt muscular, soft, and socially confident in a way I wasn't.

Standing in the flying sawdust, we flirted, skirting the edge of awkward small talk. In my skylit attic, sun slanted. Our mutual admiration felt fragile but hours passed. I glanced sideways at Devon's eyes and face glowing and movie scenes started flashing.

Over dinner, we leaned in. Devon's lips found mine. Warm fingers found my waist. My self-consciousness melted until it was just me in my skin. Making love to someone in a body like my own was easy. I knew what I liked, what felt good on my flesh and at the core of me. Being able to touch and be touched the same way in return had a symmetry and safety to it I never expected.

We dated for weeks and to me the longing felt like love.

"This is not exclusive," Devon said in bed, then over dinner, and again as we rode in my car. By October, Devon was gone on a preplanned trip to Asia. I mourned, wishing I could fly to Vietnam as well. I loved to travel but was deep in the campaign and had to stay.

By then, the Idaho Citizens Alliance was running ads accusing our campaign of trying to steal Black people's civil rights. In Idaho living rooms, the TV ads played. Weight tugged at my mind as a Black woman in one ad implied granting gay people rights would deprive her and others of their hard-earned freedoms. The message suggested that rights were rations and that creating new antigay laws would protect Black people from losing their share.

The ads made queers seem evil in new and unimaginable ways. Demoralized as we were, volunteers still showed up, the phone banks slogged on, asking voters to bring friends, to stop censorship and government intrusion by voting no on Election Day.

Soon, up on the Salmon River in Challis, the library fired an artist and trans librarian, Sophia Margeaux-Winegarner, a fellow firefighter. We had floated together over wilderness in helicopters, hauled chainsaws, and wielded Pulaski axes, digging fire lines on ridge tops. Sophia savored dressing as herself in the wild, donning poodle skirts while paddling the back channels of the river, pink gowns in alpine meadows, miniskirts and go-go boots while walking sagebrush canyons. She was let go for a variety of reasons after wearing a dress at a party in town. Someone had complained such a thing wasn't gender appropriate. They said Sophia's choice of clothing made the librarian "unsafe around children"—as if a skirt and pair of heels could turn a bookish gal in cat glasses into a predator.

The ads and rhetoric of the antigay campaign focused new cruelty on queers, and four local high school teachers were suspended from their jobs for using the word "gay" in the classroom.

Now the media was covering stories like these.

Evie, with her short perm and swagger, sat with me in our office licking envelopes and told me how, in 1977, seven female police officers were fired from Boise's Police Department for being suspected lesbians. They'd been targeted with wiretaps but had sued and won. Years earlier, in the summer of 1955, paranoia about communism and homosexuality had spread through the federal government, and Boise city police began arresting first underage male prostitutes, then consenting same-sex couples. Decades later, the men were still forced to live as sex offenders. Some had died by suicide.

Election Day barreled toward us. Walton's ads kept playing. A parade of people appeared at our maze-like campaign office offering to call voters. Donation envelopes flowed in from small towns. Long-lashed volunteer Javier Smith and my interns typed thousands of names into our computers. Once we raised enough money, the campaign shot a last-minute television ad that targeted Mormons in southern Idaho, explaining how our communities had a common enemy: Walton and the Christian Right. Funders of the initiative were the same kind of extremists who made the films *The Gay Agenda* and *The Mormon Dilemma*, which mocked Mormon beliefs and made the LDS Church look like a cult.

On Election Day, November 8, 1994, at 8 p.m. the polls closed and we folded up our street-corner rallies and phone banks, urging our last supporters to vote. We gathered in an aging ballroom, kitty-corner from the Capitol. In a blue-black 1930s dress from a San Francisco thrift store and a pair of punkish platform shoes my dad had bought me, I waded into the evening.

On the TV in the corner of the campaign ballroom, anchors chatted and the vote count flashed. We huddled, watching the gap between the yes votes and the no votes as it narrowed, then grew again, alternating with the brutal national election news. It wasn't a good omen when Helen Chenoweth, the gun-loving, conspiracy-minded, Wise Use Republican candidate for Congress, won. With that, Idaho no longer had a single Democrat in DC. Nationally, it seemed Newt Gingrich's antigay ideas had only helped him. The fear that he and the extremist churches stoked in states like ours would soon help him take over the Republican Party.

Another hour passed, our own numbers grew too close to call. We drank around the TV, waiting until flash bulbs blazed. By just three thousand votes, queers won. The Mormons had mattered. We toasted, and the evening transformed into a stop-motion blur of hugging, bouncing, laughing, and crying.

I rarely drank, so my mind hummed with the alcohol, and I danced. I thought of home in the mountains and realized I believed people in Idaho were essentially good. Minds could change. Someday minds *would* change, laws would change.

When I was in high school, after Mom came out, Dad and I went to the movies, in California. We saw *The Rose* and when Janis Joplin's husband found his wife sleeping with a woman, Dad put his bearded face in his hands and, in the dark of the theater, cried.

My gentle dad. As a teen, when he and Mom moved away and Cree and I spent our four school years together, I didn't even drink or party, partly because I hated the prospect of Dad finding out and being disappointed in me. Worse than any spanking, grounding, or stern word, his disappointment had always been the thing I dreaded most.

I'd already put off having the talk through most of the campaign, waiting until I was at least sort of in a relationship to broach the topic of my sexuality. Being gay and identifying as a lesbian felt like it fit better than the vast continent of conformity I had tried for so long to occupy. But even these words were wrong. Even if my own gender had been simple, a label would have been difficult. My gender wasn't simple, and I'd been dating a trans man in a world before he could describe this to himself—before trans identities were something those around me talked about. Technically I was not in a lesbian relationship. In my grasp for a comfortable term, I'd come to say I was "gay," especially in places where I couldn't use the term "queer" because it was shunned or still seen as a slur.

I wanted Dad to understand me in the most basic of terms. And yet, there I sat, gripping the receiver, struggling to dial the numbers on the phone.

Dad had remarried but still came to visit, sometimes on his own. He helped me with rewiring the old house, built a stone barbecue in the yard, lay floor joists in my attic.

Mom was on her third and final lesbian relationship with my bookish stepmom, Sharon. She and Dad were civil. He never spoke against her, even vaguely. Mom's friendship had always kept his life interesting. At her wildest, Mom still turned over tables in every room she entered, grinning as objects and people came spinning down, leaving her in the center, drink in hand.

She'd always been a lot like Hunter. You'd never see the man's awkwardness through all the flying objects, cocktails, and blotters.

Coming out to Mom was easy. Sitting side-by-side in her faded, red-to-orange '74 Chevy pickup, mountain canyons zoomed toward us and away through the glass. She turned to me with a shit-eating grin.

"Alllll—riiiighttt," she said, drawing out each word as if she were cheering a sports team. One more for the gays. Go Queers. And that was kind of it. There was no deep talk about how I arrived at dating people of my own gender or why I'd spent those years in heterosexuality. I evaded her questions about sex and we kept driving, flying into the river canyon corners as we had done since I was ten.

The phone rang. Dad picked up, voice warm. Even when he was busy, he was always excited to talk. He asked about my plans to travel after the campaign.

Too much chatting would make what I had to say harder.

"Dad, I've met someone."

It was all about the pronoun I used. I was gay, had been dating someone named Devon. I was going to Malaysia and Thailand and the two of us were going to travel from there to Australia.

On the other end of the line, no questions, no congratulations. Silence.

Over the course of twenty years, I'd tried in every way I could to be heterosexual, to measure up to what I understood of my gender. I was barely aware I'd spent a lifetime avoiding even thinking about making love to a woman. My own attractions were elusive. I suspected I liked those more in the middle of gender, humans neither at the GI Joe nor the Barbie-Princess end of the extremes.

"Neee-cole," Dad said through the phone line, his distaste loud. "I'm surprised you're attracted to *young ladies*."

Shame poked at my insides. Those words made my coming out sound so lewd. I'd slept with more than ten men, at least one graying and almost twice my age. Devon was just a bit older than me. I suppose it's hard being asked to think about your child having sex with anyone. Still, I didn't expect disgust.

I braced for his next words, worried this might change who Dad and I were to each other. I said the only thing that came to mind, "Dad, it's not about that. It is about *who* you love, *the person*."

He didn't hesitate then. His voice dipped in regret. I heard words I needed to hear, "You're right. I'm sorry."

Dad. As he aged into adulthood, his own life had already been weighted with the death of his mother and the loss of his mentor and trip leader Art Moffatt on the Canadian barren grounds. He lived far from the wild but still walked in redwood forests near his house and, in spring, sometimes drove north across Oregon to sleep in his tent at the edge of the Malheur Refuge where he'd wait for the migration of the herons, teal, buffleheads and other diving birds.

On the day when I was twenty-two and sat eating lunch in a meadow in the Frank Church Wilderness, I carried with me a certainty that Dad had wanted a life for me filled with mountains and the wild. Sitting on the bank of Lightning Creek, my boots unlaced and my lunch on my lap, a jet flew over, setting loose a sonic boom. Out of the roar a low sad tone rose and then another from the trees right behind me, one voice layered over the next, sounds so deep they dug into my chest. I knew the sound. In our dining room in Woody Creek, after dinner one night, Dad had put a record on his turntable, a recording of wolves, that sound he'd heard in the Arctic at night. He needed Cree and me to hear it.

In the meadow, my fingers in the long grass and trees casting shadows on all sides, the sound of those wolves' voices rose and fell. I felt humble in their presence and restraint. That humbleness grew in me like a thread of power and wonder.

PART 2

LOVE

8
CAROL

2000–2003

Boise, Idaho

I was thirty-six. Hair still cut in that dishwater-colored bob, I went into the world of love open-armed. I saw the good in people, knew most meant well, no matter how scarred the world had left them.

In the six years since I'd come out, Ellen DeGeneres had come out on national TV and our rural neighbors and their kids in tiny towns had some familiar gay human to hold up as an example, someone to laugh with and whose fame suggested the world was loving, even if the laws in our state were not. I dated only two women and another trans man. One brief relationship, which started with nights dancing under a disco ball, devolved into fleeing, filing police reports, and leaving events I'd organized rather than calling 911. A judge wrote a protection order for me.

Still, all my failures at relationships hadn't made me hesitant.

Carol played on the same soccer team I did and had an artful legal slide-tackle, a mop of short blond hair, and lithe, fast legs. After watching for weeks, I didn't know what to make of this boyish human with large light-colored eyes, a person whose smile hinted at a stockpile of unspoken monologues and dialogues. I could have asked about where the humor came from, but I didn't. I just studied that slight half smile, the quiet, muscular swagger, and love for understatement and dramatic pause.

Carol was a veteran, had survived a raucous four-year tour in the Air Force, stationed one hour from Boise in the sleepy desert town of Mountain Home. We sat near each other at activist meetings and Women's

Night coffee house events I organized. We were comfortable with each other. I read poetry. Carol liked the skits and the music, but something about poetry was a problem.

"You want to take tickets at the door tonight?" I might ask.

"Maybe," Carol might say. "Will I have to snap my fingers for the poetry?"

"Not if you don't want to," I'd answer.

"Do I have to listen to the poetry?"

"I'm reading tonight."

"Does that mean I have to listen to the poetry?"

My family didn't joke around much. We didn't tease. I wasn't used to it.

"Why? Don't you like it?"

Carol grinned. "I just know someone is going to ask me what it means."

One night, out at the Emerald City Club, one of Boise's three gay bars, the desert hummed. Plum trees bloomed. Spring settled warm, and the gay bar turned itself inside out like a flower. Queens buzzed in headdresses. Lights spun. I might have taken Carol's hand, or Carol might have taken mine, as we crossed the sticky carpet through the haze of cigarette smoke, past the two women necking by the pool table. We stepped onto the dance floor.

I looked through the bar's smoke. Carol in jeans and a polo shirt was East Coast, blue-collar conservative. The whole Growhoski family was unreasonably modest. They went to church and didn't grow pot. My childhood, in contrast, was spent in the company of loud, adventurous people, the kind who took off all their clothes to swim and held parties where kids and dogs scattered from the deck into the darkened brush to play.

Carol isn't my type, I thought. And yet there we were dancing.

It wasn't the first song but the second, Madonna's "Like a Prayer," when Carol began to smile. I grinned back and my feet wove into the music. Our eyes met. Madonna's voice rose. We were two gender-nonconforming people without a whole lot of religion. "Like a Prayer" was perfect.

Daring me, Carol circled, matching my steps. Gazes locked, we danced, neither one of us exactly leading or following.

I close my eyes. Oh God, I think I'm falling . . . out of the sky . . .

Carol's arms rose then, and the person I saw unfolded. I glimpsed bravery, leaving home young, years in love with an alcoholic. I saw the scratchy closet that was sex in a dorm during military service, before Don't Ask, Don't Tell.

Time swirled between us, tension rising through the lights and cigarette haze.

In my head at night, from the futon mattress on the floor of my bedroom, I weighed out strategies for fixing the state's lack of queer civil rights laws. I plotted education campaigns, full-page print ads, lobbying, ways to engage queers in changing state lawmakers' minds.

Early spring in the year 2000, Carol was on crutches from a cross-country skiing accident. I was deep in political organizing. We'd spent every day together, but our relationship had stalled at "friends." In pairs and little groups, Carol and my trainees wandered the hallways between the Senate offices. I led pink-cheeked Ollie Shannon, a queer high school student in a loose shirt and pants, up a stone stairway, winding toward the third floor and the chambers of the Senate.

Fixed on the idea of being feminine, I wore a thrift store dress, thinking it would make me look conservative. Polyester floral-print pressed cold at my waist, gaping at the front. I felt air on my breasts and looked down quickly, just as a senator appeared in the elevator door.

Pulling Ollie along, I pushed toward the dark-bearded man with his white senator's badge, asking, "Sir, do you have a moment?"

His face tightened.

Heels tapped at the stone floor. A paid lobbyist in a green name tag, skirt, and nylons walked by.

I was used to hiking in the mountains, teaching kids at an alternative school, mingling with activists, and now I couldn't help but think about my leg hair, how my cleavage was too obvious for me, too obvious for a building filled with religious people. I longed for a jacket, but the senator was speaking. He didn't seem to have heard my question.

"Yes?" he said, shoulders tight in his suit. *Senator Davis*, his name tag read.

Ollie braced, waited for cues as we fumbled, unsure if the senator would pause to talk with us. Ahead of him, the Senate floor gleamed in sunlight. Like the House chamber on the building's other side, this huge semicircular, velvet-curtained space with its curved rows of desks and microphones was an engine of the Capitol. It was here, from oversized rolling chairs, where lawmakers debated and voted to pass or kill bills.

"Can we talk with you for a minute?" I asked.

In the Senate entry, the senator slowed, nodded, and motioned for Ollie and me to sit with him on a small couch. Listed as a bishop in the Mormon church, Bart Davis was a lawyer from the eastern part of the state. He sat stiff, just feet away from us. I felt his stare warp the wood-paneled foyer outside the Senate chamber. Around me, the whole building echoed, seemed to whisper a sort of sinister "Hush . . . hush . . . hush."

I glanced down at the men's shoes on my feet. I hadn't found heels my size and wasn't even sure if I could make myself wear such things.

Visibly sweating, Ollie spoke, child's face round and pants baggy, always baggy, like no envelope fits, as if what's there is too complex, too armored for any envelope or gender. "Senator, did you know it's still legal to be fired in Idaho, just because you're gay?"

The senator's eyes shifted from Ollie to me. From the opposite wall, his picture stared down at us while Ollie spoke, smart and well-rehearsed from our role-plays, diving into the bit about the antidiscrimination law. Davis tensed. He rose in his seat, glaring at both of us on the too-small couch.

His words filled with what felt like anger and disgust. He said, "On your issue, I am your worst enemy." He leaned back then and repeated, "Your worst enemy. Your worst."

Then we were all standing and I was rushing to pull Ollie away from him, out through the glass doors, away from the Senate, toward the circular rotunda and the five stories of air rising under the curve of the building's huge dome. Ollie stood breathing hard, eyes round and scared.

We stared at each other. I shook my head in apology and looked up into the dome whose underside was painted gray-blue and speckled with gold and silver stars.

Five years later, my picture would hang on the wall of the Capitol next to Senator Davis's. I'd have a chair in the grand chambers and be allowed to climb the metal stairs that wind upward, under that gray-blue ceiling. One day, I'd touch those painted stars. I'd stand and lean out through the opening below them, balanced, looking down the height of five flights to the marble floor and the tiny people below.

These days, they let no one like me climb to that high place. The doors to that part of the building are locked and the stairs barricaded. There's nothing to catch a person if they fall—no railing, no nets.

Like my family, Carol's has good queer genes. Two of Carol's four siblings are gay men. All of them are smart-assed and funny.

Standing at the head of the room in the basement of the teachers union hall, I could tell that Carol, like high school-aged Ollie, was not a fan of the role-plays in my lobbying trainings. Both of them were experienced and were supposed to set an example, one pretending to be the lawmaker, the other the activist. The two stood together holding my message sheets and one would giggle while the other would pretend to be serious. Both would look awkward when I glared.

At long folding tables, PFLAG moms, gay men, trans women, and teens wrote their personal stories.

"Focus on the parts of your life lawmakers won't expect," I said. "Not 'I was born in San Francisco,' but 'I'm a teacher,' 'I served in the Air Force,' or 'I have two children.' Choose details that break stereotypes. Make them like you. Make them comfortable."

Carol may have hated role-plays but was surprisingly good at them. There was acting skill there and an edgy humor, as if taking anything too seriously was uncomfortable. Oddly, we fit. I wasn't sure why.

For Carol, early in that spring of 2000, the second of two long relationships had ended. Over beers in brew pubs, while the soccer team we played on mourned its losses, we discovered that our mothers, Pat and Gloria, were born two months apart, in hospitals fifty miles away from each other in New England. Each competed as the only girl in their town's rifle club.

By April and the end of Idaho's annual three-month lawmaking session, Carol and I stood together on the steps of my house, and I didn't care if Carol wasn't my type. Maybe my ideas of type were wrong. Maybe all the pain of previous relationships was a sign I needed to burn down my idea of type.

My porch light lit a warm pool in the Boise night. The constant chatter that is me—the words that spill out to fill every moment when I'm unsure what to do with myself—stilled. I leaned in, pulling Carol's body toward me. We kissed. Folded in that moment of breath, hair, and lips, I let fall fourteen years of failed dating of men, women, and budding trans men. Carol let go of two long losses.

Days later, we cooked and slept, woke curled together in the small bed on the floor of Carol's rented house. The ache in my chest grew and I reached around for those soft breasts, felt the nipples, ran my fingers over each line of muscle, put my lips to that pale skin, and nosed my way between those thighs.

Carol and I settled into committed dating, trading house keys, toothbrushes, and underwear. Carol microwaved boxes of lean cuisine while I made vegetable curry or pasta with chard and goat cheese. Cooking for each other was a ceremony that had long marked love in my family.

We curled together in the sun of my fenced yard. In the foothills above town, we walked my husky-rottweiler, Pinza, while foxes slipped in and out of shadows and young great horned owlets clacked their bills to scare us away. Sometimes on weekends, we'd wind the long road into the mountains to hike the peaks near Stanley. We backpacked the valleys above our old creaking guest ranch where I grew to a teen. I showed Carol the desert and my mom's place, her funky but now-closed roadside cafe, still complete with its counter and long row of chromed, art deco stools.

Our comfort felt solid, but progressive Boise lay in political water heavy with religious belief about gay people and sin. So we drove to Pride in San Francisco, waded into a dyke march set to the rumble of maybe a hundred women, butch and fem, dressed and undressed, rolling in on motorcycles. We held hands, took pictures, felt safe, felt promise seeing how places far from the mountains had offered queers part of the dream.

A year into our relationship, the wide streets of Salt Lake City gaped, empty in the warm October evening. We had stopped in that city on our way to the Utah Canyonlands. It was the first night of our first weeklong vacation together.

The clatter of glasses and hum of voices rose from one of the city's few brew pubs. The bar operated as a private club to escape the Mormon prohibition on alcohol sales in bars and restaurants. We'd just finished sipping our Polygamy Porter and stepped out onto the sidewalk from the darkened barroom.

Behind us, downtown churned with well-dressed families and young men in white shirts and dark ties. The annual LDS General Conference had drawn thousands from the states around. They streamed to and from the arches beneath the towering spires of the Mormon temple and buildings where the words of the prophet had just been broadcast live worldwide. When the broadcast ended, the stillness of listening broke. Families flowed into restaurants. Modestly dressed women in skirts strolled the streets with children trailing along in dresses and ties.

Beer humming in our blood, we watched the light fade as the sun set. On the sidewalk, I gave Carol a peck on the cheek just as a car, low and flashy, pulled out of an alley, into our path. It took a second to register this, but the car was filled with men. The driver revved the engine, inching forward, trying to block our way or play chicken with us on the sidewalk.

I shrank, seeing the bodies jammed behind the tinted glass, imagining baseball bats, fists, and lengths of rope. I saw no white shirts or ties.

Beside me, Carol cursed, "Assholes," and pulled me into the street past them.

Tires squealed. Fishtailing down the empty, one-way avenue, the car bled sound and rubber as it sped away in the direction of the hotel where our truck sat in a lot, six long blocks away.

Unnerved, we glanced at each other and walked, almost jogging, toward the next intersection where, down the street, the car appeared again, tires burning marks on the concrete as it slid into a turn headed back for us. We ran, trying to use the one-way streets to keep the men away. Our feet hit pavement in panic. Arms pumping, tires behind us screamed. The streets stretched out, wide, every block too long. We turned corners until they vanished. Soon though we were trapped on a length of sidewalk, the car ahead of us now, coming toward us.

We had nowhere to hide but a fast food restaurant, so we slipped inside, pushed past diners and children, to the counter. People stared at us, sweaty and out of breath, as we scanned faces, hoping none of the men from the car would come in.

The staff stood unmoved when we explained people were chasing us. We needed someone to call the police. No one did so we left the counter.

Leaning against one another, we peered out through the plate glass, waiting for a glimpse of something moving or lying hidden in the deepening dark.

Shaking, we ran the last few blocks to our hotel, asked the desk not to share our room number, then lay awake, worrying about the stickers on Carol's truck, the clues we'd left spelling out we were queer and were sleeping in that hotel.

The sun rose. We dressed, left, worried we'd been absurd. Maybe we had nothing to fear.

In those minutes while we ran, my long-held sense of safety frayed. Fears swelled and shrank for months after. Threat began to blur itself into the landscape of every town we visited. We flinched when people yelled from cars or threw things in parking lots as we held hands. At remote trailheads, the words "Queer," "Gay," and "Girlz" emblazoned on our car's bumper stickers worked like neon, outing us. We braced for vandalism. Subconsciously, our eyes measured Boise in darkness, calculating vehicle trajectories and rates of speed, homing in on gestures between people, cloaked glances in empty spaces or corners of bars.

We reassured each other, one of us meeting the other's eyes.

"Come live with me," I said over and over.

"I don't want to live in your space, your house."

"I'll move out and we'll both move back in," I said. "It will be our place then. You decide what art goes on the walls, where the furniture goes."

It wasn't until a full year into dating that I said goodbye to my roommate, and Carol and I tore my house apart and put it back together. Carol brought a cat named Bear, a fancy futon couch, a modern table and chairs, stacks of blue jeans, precisely folded T-shirts, and dishes that matched.

We held what we called a cohabitation party, an excuse for a potluck dinner at a long string of tables in our living room where artists, teachers, poets, and soccer friends tossed relationship advice in the air. I knew far less about coupling than I believed I did. I'd never really lived with a lover while still dating them. I'd been the type of person to offer a room to an ex after we'd broken up, or to bring Pinza and a toothbrush with me to stay for months with the person I was dating, while all my things waited, frozen in still life at home.

Part of me assumed I'd have children still. It ached when my nephew was born.

"That's a deal breaker," Carol said.

The loneliness in me, the space made for caring for something small, grew quieter. I had a place in the world as a budding activist, a community organizer. I had Carol to backpack the wild with, to nod patiently at the bits of science flowing out of my mouth.

In not having children, some relief grew, too. In my dreams, I lost children, left them places still, forgot to feed them. Images of ducklings, dead in a plastic tub hovered, brightly lit, somewhere behind it all.

9
PILOT FISH

2003

Boise, Idaho

Carol and I gardened. We built fences, a wood box, and cold frame. We built them plumb and square. I ran the power tools and knew people we met on the street, anywhere we went. Carol could recite song lyrics, lines from documents, remembered the day of the week for a cat adoption, a concert, a fight with an ex, years back in time.

Carol built a castle of routines, feeding Pinza, commuting to an IT job, biking to soccer practice, coming home to shower and help me cook. I typed dates and details for meetings into a beeping electronic organizer that fed me arrival times for strings of meetings and events that kept me believing I mattered, believing that I increased happiness in the world—or at least warded off some suffering, somehow.

I started most days at five, rolling out of bed, pulling on my running tights, and joining my soccer-playing friend Lee in the dark of morning to run Pinza and her dog, Duke, up trails in the foothills at the edge of the city. Afterward, I'd bike from one project or political campaign to the next, sipping tea, performing poetry in slam competitions, reading the newspaper late at night.

When I first met Lee, she served on the board of the nuclear watchdog organization I worked for. Compact, dark haired, and intensely modest, she laughed easily and had a day job at our independent record store. She was as fully committed to her activism, the same way I was. In our volunteer work lives, our paths crossed constantly.

In winter back then, I taught writing, sat with stacks of student papers when I wasn't doing web design or campaign mailers. I walked deep in the halls of the Capitol with volunteers. Our meetings with lawmakers always felt too brief, seemed only to scratch the surface because our teams could only be there a handful of days a year, helping chase down only a fraction of the legislature's thirty-five senators and seventy representatives. Compared with the time Republicans spent soaking up the messages coming from their churches and political party, we were a blip, hardly a force to help them see queer people were human, worthy of respect and dignity.

Somehow, I needed to spend way more time in the Capitol. I needed all of us to spend more time in the Capitol. Somehow.

From the phone in the emergency room lobby, the woman's voice ground flat. She could have been a machine. "Relationship to patient?" she asked.

"I'm her partner. I live with her. You called me."

"I'm sorry. You're not family? Only family in the ER."

"I *am* family."

"Hospital policy."

"I can get her brother on the phone. He'll tell you."

Silence.

I said, "Would you like me to get my attorney?"

I did not have an attorney.

The phone stayed silent then.

"One second, please."

Doors buzzed. A person came from the back to take me behind the doors and white curtains to where Carol lay, face smashed and bandaged, struggling at white straps that fixed that muscled body to the bed.

The nurse told me a neighbor found Carol on the ground, unconscious, bicycle smashed nearby. "We've had to sedate her," he said. He stepped aside to let me pass. "She punched one of the EMTs."

Carol struggled on the bed, voice slurred. "Where's my bike?"

I explained, "It's on the sidewalk, near our house."

Hand in mine, Carol began to mumble oddly, angry, but still knew me.

"Where am I?"

"The hospital," I said.

"There's some damage . . ." the nurse said.

Carol looked up, startled, asked again, "Where's my bike?"

The nurse nodded at me, "Her memory."

"Where am I? Where the fuck am I?"

We explained.

"It's hard to say how long it will last," he said.

For an hour, every few minutes I had to explain to Carol "It's OK, I'm here. It's the hospital. You had a bike wreck. Your bike's on the sidewalk near home. It will be fine."

But it was not fine. It occurred to me the damage could leave Carol stuck this way for life, every three minutes unsure where we were or where that bike was, unsure what happened just three minutes earlier. I pictured our lives so huge, both suddenly folded into a postage stamp of time.

I began to cry. This confused Carol, caused panic.

But as one hour wore into the next, the intervals between the questions got longer. "Where's my bike?"

The span widened to four minutes, then five, then six without, "Where's my bike?"

Then we were in the car driving home. Eight minutes stretched to ten.

Carol didn't remember crashing, leaving the bike, getting to or leaving the hospital, but within hours the humor that had melted in panic returned, memory began to return. In bed I held Carol as tight as I could, shielding the delicate bones broken around one eye.

The postage stamp of time unfolded.

The answer to all the questions was, "You're home with me. You are, at last. You'll be fine."

It was a late night after a Friday-the-thirteenth party, which Carol and I had titled our "Bad Luck Bash." We'd painted our bedroom gray-blue so it felt like a place deep under water, in the calm. Tucked in bed next to each other, Carol's voice broke the silence.

"I don't love you."

We were both more than tipsy, a state that makes me fuzzy and careless in my conversation. It's a state, which—inevitably, after a large number of beers—makes Carol argumentative, humorless, brave in saying what feels wrong.

"I want to break up," rose out of the space beside me.

I stared at the ceiling then one blue wall, feeling water close over me.

We were happy. We cooked and ate, danced, and gardened.

Yes, I struggled with my moods at times, with the way they briefly took grim turns at some point in my cycle. There was stress, too, with my doing way too much at once. But I loved this kind of stress.

"I thought we were happy," I whispered.

"I'm not."

The words struck like little hammers.

We loved each other. We'd built a home, a place for ourselves between our work, soccer games, and many friends—my many friends, my many obligations.

"I'm not."

Had I heard that? Was I so broken I'd not even seen Carol's misery?

I'm sure I left our bed. I don't know where I slept.

I run when hurt. Most of all, I hurt myself when I fail. I have a temper, but that thing is reserved generally for my own fuckups, my own broken shit, not anyone else's. In a tantrum or meltdown when not given space, I will wind up and slam doors, even break things I love, tear out my own hair, bash my head with my fist. This was now. This failing was larger than failing Carol. I'd not even known I was failing Carol, the one person I loved more than any other, next to my dad. I'd had no inkling. I was that oblivious, that messed up.

Days later, I left a soccer party crying. I walked miles home from a teammate's living room where Carol had spent an hour flirting with a pale, blond woman.

In my thoughts still, I would live a lifetime with Carol.

We were a year and a half into our relationship. No other had lasted as long. I failed to understand what it took to keep someone I loved from running away. How could I make other lives better if I was unable to read unhappiness, even in someone I slept next to and hoped to live forever with?

That night, after walking miles, staggering along busy streets, I went to my yard and tore up plants, a long list of everything I knew was toxic in my own backyard. I made a milkshake of these things in the blender, having no idea how painful, long, or slow my death would be. I didn't care. I drove with the milkshake into the foothills, planning to drink it all and be done.

I pulled into the lot on the ridge where I ran with Pinza and Lee in the mornings. The sun was setting. The trail wound forward. I could almost see Pinza's black-and-brown body running along it through the sage. The sky was orange and rich with a light that reminded me of home in the mountains, crossing miles of river canyon alone, legs steely with muscle, stillness stretching to the horizon. I had lived with so much beauty there. If life was so horrible and I had so completely failed people, I could always go out there again and live alone.

The world was big. It held beauty. It was easy to forget that.

The sun warmed me. I sat behind the steering wheel. The cruelty of what I was about to do, to Carol, to my parents, leaving Pinza to wait when I would never come home, bringing into the world so much loss and pain—that was the opposite of love.

I opened my car door, lifted the glass jar in my hands and unscrewed the lid. I dumped the mash of plants and liquid onto the ground, started my car and drove out of the foothills for home.

Still paralyzed by loss, I wanted only to sleep since doing anything became painful. I didn't care what meetings I missed or projects I dropped into free fall by vanishing.

Frightened by how close I'd come, I signed up for therapy where I was asked to consider if Carol leaving me invalidated everything else I did with my life.

Still, my world ran at a slant. Everything happened as if on a tilted plane, off from where it had been, never normal or comfortable, now brutal and surreal. I tried to reimagine my life without Carol but I couldn't. It was too grim and only made me more sad. Though my therapist said I'd heal, I didn't believe it.

I wasn't ready to give up. Carol, however, had moved to a furnished apartment a mile from my house, taking a suitcase of clothes and buying a bright blue beta fish named Sushi. The fish sat in a perfectly round bowl in a perfectly ordered living room.

Still, Carol's furniture sat in my house. Bear, the cat, was there. I fed him, found hope in his presence, and made coffee dates with Carol.

Carol had always answered my every, "Is everything OK?" with, "I'm fine."

But I'd chosen organizing, work, meetings, planning, and events over reserving time for the two of us.

All this—the pace of it all, the frantic part of my life—was who I was, who I'd spent most of my life being. I was all in. Work was more than how I paid the mortgage; it was my reason to exist. How did I separate that from me? Did I want to? Could I if I tried?

Near the end of October, after six weeks living apart, I brought up the issue of tickets we'd bought months earlier and convinced Carol to travel with me to Asia, as friends. The two of us packed and boarded a plane for Kuala Lumpur, Malaysia. In Panang we woke to the call to prayer in the dark before dawn, a melodic "Allahu Akbar" spoken into the sky from a single loudspeaker. The words were layered over the words of other voices, broadcast miles off—other Allahu Akbars chanted by different men in other parts of the city.

We stayed in a tiled guesthouse that had seen better days. We stood as rain fell in sheets through a jungle, boarded a bus and missed a stop so we ended up getting off at a forested roadside, far from anything familiar, unable to speak the language, only able to gesture and fail at pronouncing the name of the town we needed to reach before dark.

Taking a train south, we stayed in a thatched hut and boarded a boat off the island of Koh Tao in a rough swell, plunging from the deck in forty pounds of scuba gear, only to find Carol's air supply needing repair. At forty feet below the surface, three-foot-long, coral-munching trigger fish were mating and defending territories. As a huge, brightly colored male came at us, Carol grabbed my arm and dodged behind me. I flung my flippers out just in time to have the fish turn and bite a hole three inches wide from one of the fins of the woman working as our dive master.

"You're trying to kill me," Carol said.

"I'm not," I said kissing one Polish cheek, adding something like, "You love adventures. These are adventures."

Nonetheless, Carol dove again. And again, off Koh Phi Phi where a ferry had sunk at the edge of a deep-sea precipice. Diving in full scuba gear over the wreck was like flying through a maze of butterfly-brilliant fish, floating into darkness to that place where the depth gaped bottomless below us. We ate curry and rode boats on rivers and tides, wandered markets and trails, finding temples decorated with sleeping dogs and buddhas, abandoned slippers, and squares of fluttering gold leaf.

Still, Carol wouldn't take me back.

In the deep, again and again, we saw tiny, torpedo-shaped pilot fish. These hovered at the mouths of lumbering larger fish, sailing like tiny colorful twins near the spot where the big fish's ears might have been. I imagined the pilot fish whispering directions, the two exchanging ideas about depth, meaning, and navigation, as if one could not exist without the other.

In another thatched hut, on a moldy mattress, we talked about our failings, read self-help books on the ways people express love. As we boarded trains, buses, and boats, we left torn-out chapters strewn behind us in humid hotel rooms, working our way through each book to the end.

Carol needed love in the form of focused time. This meant time where we did not simply exist in the vicinity of one another, but actually shared activities one-on-one. At events back home, this should have been where I introduced Carol to people, took a moment to check in, offer to leave an event if need be. I could, at the very least, acknowledge Carol's generosity and willingness to endure social situations that were often tortuous and lonely.

I listened. Listening is not my superpower. My mind is busy. It wanders into eventualities, causalities. More than once, my new year's resolution has been to listen better.

According to one of the books, I needed verbal reinforcement and physical affection. These two, though they pique my chemicals of happiness, do nothing for Carol. Instead, I needed to slow, turn, focus, and let time spin out on the two of us, keep my mind in one place, settled and still, tied one-to-one—not once briefly, but repeatedly in a shared activity.

This slowing and focusing was against my nature. But I wanted to learn it.

"I'm sorry I'm such a tornado," I whispered into the dark of Carol's absence. "I'm sorry. I'll try harder."

It took time for Carol to agree to give up the tidy furnished apartment and move back in to live in the wild spot where we grew tomatoes, hosted loud parties, and cooked together on a funky electric stove.

As much as I meant to slow, meant to make dates and spend focused time with Carol, the need for a queer presence in the Capitol drove me.

"What group did you say you're with?" a Senate secretary asked.

"Your Family, Friends, and Neighbors," I said.

A pattern began to repeat.

"And what issue did you want to speak with the senator about?"

When I answered, the secretary tended to pause. "I'm sorry, the senator's schedule is full," or "The chairman isn't available. He's booked up."

With gay men, high school students, and PFLAG parents, we put on the latest version of what I thought were Republican clothes and went inside the Capitol without appointments. I trained queers to find lawmakers on their way to committee meetings. I had them practice introducing themselves and telling stories in elevators.

In California, East Coast states, and beyond, people like us were climbing legislative mountains, moving toward full legal equality. They had protections in employment, housing, education—even in being served at lunch counters, hotels, grocery stores, and bakeries. By 2003, heroic county clerks in California and New Mexico were issuing marriage licenses as acts of civil disobedience. We were struggling but I had faith in the courts, in the Supreme Court and its dedication to the Constitution and defending the masses and minorities when we were downtrodden by the cruel. The world was changing, but Idaho was not.

Idaho's legislature had become three-quarters Republican. Sitting beside them on couches or standing in hallways, I heard many of them say discrimination against LGBTQ people didn't exist. To sway them, I needed stories. I also needed the impossible; I needed statistics.

Paid to write and carry out a survey on tobacco and the impact of stressors like discrimination and violence for the Idaho Department of Welfare, I spent a whole summer traveling the state, visiting soccer games, bars, and festivals with young, red-cheeked Ollie Shannon. We traveled to little towns, and I hired Ollie to set up tables, both of us waiting while people sat with pens, pouring over my long questionnaire about cigarette smoking, abuse, hate crimes, and harassment. In less than a year, we got more than a thousand surveys back from LGBTQ people and five hundred more from straight people hanging out in the same crowds.

Half the gay men and trans people marked that they'd faced threats of violence because they were queer. A third had attempted suicide. That was twice as many as the non-queers I surveyed.

These were people of all ages and most lived with the stress of being expected to deny or hide who they were or who they loved at church and work, in custody battles and business deals. After nearly ten years of working on LGBTQ issues, I finally had numbers and evidence of the enormity and universality of the pain. I'd done enough struggling from the outside, hoping something we said in our brief meetings with lawmakers or in the few minutes we had in committee hearings would persuade them to care.

Working from outside of government, all I could do was jam my body into the gears, cast my words into the air, and bring in others to educate them. The next step forward was civil disobedience. But, without a job or housing protection, any mug shots or criminal records from protests would threaten queer activists' rental agreements, livelihoods, and careers. Explaining arrests to future employers would add to the hell. I couldn't ask that of the hundred or so people we'd need to make civil disobedience so noticeable that eyes would turn and laws might change.

I was about to turn forty. I needed a better strategy. Continuing to do what I was doing felt like complicity rather than resistance. Deep in the dark of winter, earth spun, tilting us into the solstice. Carol and I debated, hosting friends at a long table in our living room. The wood stove burned. New Year's Eve passed.

Slowly I realized my own queer friends barely knew what rights they had. Senators themselves insisted wrongly that we were protected by federal law. By the time we reached any point of understanding with one policymaker, they'd retire only to be replaced in the next election by another. These people represented LGBTQ people. Yet they could so easily avoid listening to our stories.

As long as we had no seat at the table, they could all avoid hearing us, even pretend we didn't exist. If one of us ran for office and was elected, we'd sit every working day in a desk next to other lawmakers, in committee meetings, through debate and recess, through side conversations and caucus meetings. We could ask questions of chairmen and senators publicly, not be forced to wait for a moment in an elevator or a public hearing where the audience was allowed just minutes to speak.

Every January, the clock started on the roughly three months when Senator Bart Davis and the 105 elected senators and representatives arrived in Boise to make law. They drove the steep mountain highways or traveled by plane from their ranches and small towns to stay in rented or borrowed rooms and apartments.

In their suits, ties, jackets, and skirts, they climbed the Capitol steps to spend three months writing and voting on bills and drafts of bills, approving rules, deciding how state agencies would spend a couple billion in tax dollars. They'd choose who got taxed and who didn't, what made a person a criminal, and who was human enough to deserve state-sanctioned freedoms and rights.

I'd taken the path of protest before. Working from inside government was a dimension of advocacy I still could not imagine. We were asking a libertarian state to say cruelty was wrong, to intervene and protect us from violence and harm. If lawmakers didn't seem to care about discrimination, I couldn't think of another way to make them understand, except to spend more time with them, to have human conversations I'd never had before.

Even if it was unlikely I myself could ever be elected, maybe the world could be made better if I took on some other role. If I could find a job inside the Capitol, I could be an example for lawmakers. I could put a face to what a queer person looked like, every day.

In January 2004, the Idaho Community Action Network offered me a job as the paid lobbyist for their nonprofit. I dressed up, and Lee, my running partner, walked me down to the musty basement of the statehouse for a lesson in the true formality of the process.

"Pay the fee and join the Legislative Advisors," she said. "The food alone is worth the cost." With her shoulder-length hair down and a briefcase in her hand, Lee had gravity. With my short hair, thrift store skirts, and arty glasses, I didn't.

I was going to be paid to train Latine activists, women in motored wheelchairs, and men who'd lost houses to medical bills how to lobby. They'd all learn how to help lawmakers see the law from their point of view. I would have a voice, too, and I'd wear a green name tag.

The corporate lobbyists I worked beside often knew and were trusted by lawmakers. Many were former lawmakers themselves. I mostly disagreed with the bills they carried. But, with my name listed in the lobbyist directory and my big shoulders crammed into a suit, I circled the statehouse rotunda dawn to dusk, returning to the windowless, lobbyist room with its secretary, fax machine, and excellent snacks.

Those in the club I now belonged to wielded great power. Most knew the law. Leaning against the marble veneer in suits and chatting, they adhered to a sort of civility code. Generally, they set aside issues they clashed over for the sake of camaraderie. Outside the battles in committee rooms, we avoided talking about what we were paid to fight each other for.

Walking the curving halls, gazing up at the fifty or so framed sets of sepia or colored photographs of lawmakers, I learned names and histories. I created allies in the ranks of Republicans and studied the factions, power players, and tensions between them all.

The formality of the Capitol was an odd equalizer inside that White, White place. In there, it was easy to assume all lawmakers were married, Christian, Anglo-Saxon, and gender conforming, even when they were not. When I found the photo of Representative Lenore Hardy Barrett as a freshman, I smiled. Just like her male colleagues, Barrett wore a suit, a pressed white dress shirt, and a striped tie. Face set stern, not a curled strand of hair out of place she wore no scarf, pin, or jewelry except for a single pair of large white button earrings and a bit of red lipstick.

Barrett served on the tax committee and was known for packing a gun, even in the Capitol where there'd never been metal detectors. In committee I found her brusque and funny, focused on lower taxes, small businesses, and a whole lot less government. She lived in Challis and represented Custer County and the huge mountainous district in the center of the state, home to our ranch and my mom's cafe, now mostly abandoned on the banks of the Salmon River.

Lenore knew Mom, vaguely. We talked about home sometimes and found some zone of agreement on tax policy. As the months passed and I earned her vote on bills, I reassessed the pureness of the evil so many queer and progressive people saw in Republicans in the House and Senate. Representatives I'd seen as simple, one-dimensional haters, grew into complex people. They were mink farmers, taxidermists, homemakers, truck drivers, and parents. Some had lost children; others had grown up with little and were now multifaceted in how they saw class, race, and religion, or how they related to people who struggled.

With my green lobbyist's name tag clipped to my jacket, senators no longer seemed frightened to be seen with me. Some invited me into their offices for long conversations. Others, even antigay conservatives, sponsored the bills I was hired to carry, voting for them or offering ideas to make them better. The merger of a telecommunications company I battled against failed in the Senate that year by one vote. For that alone, the year felt worthwhile. I felt useful.

Just weeks away from turning forty, I'd never seen myself as a Democrat. For years, I'd organized for the Greens. One day the senator from my district slipped me an invitation to the Idaho Women's Democratic Caucus. Carol and I decided I should go.

I'd worked inside campaigns, not only as paid staff on the antigay ballot initiative but as fundraising director for a former justice of the state Supreme Court, Bob Huntley. Seven years earlier, he'd run for governor as a Democrat on a beautifully idealistic platform of raising taxes to fund public schools and breaching the hydroelectric dams on the Snake River to save endangered salmon. I learned from him that campaign issues can change minds when they don't just pander to prejudices. He was brilliant and formidable and making fish half of his platform was brave.

Eyeing the living room of the house where the Women's Democratic Caucus met, I felt young. I was probably the only queer person there. The power, comfort, and access of the women around me made me feel radical and suspect. I watched as they passed around a basket of finger puppets someone had brought back from Central America. Barb, one of the leaders from North Idaho, mentioned union organizing. *Yes*, I thought, *maybe some around me were a little radical.* Perhaps clothes, hair, and accessories signaling class and power didn't always reflect what happened in the depths.

My parents' allegiance had always seemed to lie outside political parties. They didn't love Democrats but despised everything Republican, all those ideas on race, religion, war, and capitalism. In Aspen, they'd both worked for Hunter Thompson when he ran for sheriff on the third-party Freak Power ticket. Their brand of politics stood on the side of antiwar protesters, long-hairs, and pot smokers—not on the side of mergers, mandatory minimum sentences, abortion bans, or greed. I couldn't see

Dad or Hunter supporting laws that made the powerful more powerful or ones that forced those without power to live in fear.

As an organizer, I'd seen Democrats, like Republicans, take the wrong side in the struggle. I'd seen Bill Clinton support media and corporate deregulation, the dishonorable military discharges of Don't Ask, Don't Tell. I'd seen cuts in welfare pass into law with Democratic votes and presidential signatures. The party wasn't perfect.

Seated with all those women who'd found their way inside, I had to make a choice. I wished I had more than two choices. I wished the United States portioned political power based on the percentages of votes each party got. I wished US politicians formed multiparty coalitions and a system of proportional representation like many European Parliaments. Instead, we have a winner-take-all system so I had two parties to choose from and two parties only. I'd have to be a Democrat or a Republican.

After all I'd seen in my years in the statehouse and national politics, I knew I couldn't be a Republican.

The basket of knitted finger puppets landed in my lap. Inside lay tiny pigs and horses, chickens and cows. Digging around, I found a gray donkey. I made a donation and took it home, propping it up on my dresser, trying on the idea that I might spend months or years identifying as a Democrat.

At night, I lay in bed next to Carol while lines of debate ran through my head, facts and stories I'd use with lawmakers, ideas for running a campaign to serve as one of them. Campaigns I understood; candidates, though, walked in the spotlight. The campaign around them too often wasn't focused on an issue or cause; it was focused on them, electing them, trusting their work and judgment on the issues.

When our district's long-serving Democratic representative and tax policy expert announced his plan to retire, I had little time to file papers for his seat.

"Do you think you can handle it?" Carol asked, face cautionary, heavy with a sort of cringe.

"I think so."

"They're not going to be nice to you."

"I suppose not."

Carol seemed to be calculating how directly to say the next part: "You can be kind of sensitive."

Emotional. Dramatic. Too exacting of myself. "I know. But I see they're human now. Some will be assholes, others won't."

"You sure?"

"I think so."

I think we saw serving in the Capitol as a simple three-month, part-time job. It wasn't. Even the campaigning part was intense. Fortunately, I didn't run for office alone. I had company. A bunch of us ran zigzag for nine months—with me frantic at the center. I knew things about campaigns because I'd raised money, knocked on doors, organized field strategy and volunteers.

Quickly, the focus turned toward me. Things began to hinge intensely on what I said. I had a decade of practice speaking to media, making all the mistakes, getting some things right. I'd frozen in front of a bank of cameras in DC in 1994 and woken in a sleeping bag on the Capitol steps at 5:00 a.m. with a camera in my face as I listed impromptu bullet points in support of passing a minimum-wage law to protect farmworkers. I'd written press releases and trained spokespeople. I thought I knew things, like how to talk about issues in ways that made people care.

Again, I pulled young Ollie into my organizing. They became my volunteer coordinator. As the first nonbinary person in my life, I'd watched Ollie grow as they graduated high school and considered college. In my race for the legislature, they would do the job I did ten years earlier as a staffer fighting antigay policy on the No On One Campaign.

I hired a gay man with some connections in the Democratic Party as my campaign manager. Perhaps I was a bit unconventional for him. I had opinions, lots of them, about how things would go. I made giant cardboard thermometers to track my fundraising progress and other charts to track how many doors we'd knocked on, supporters we'd identified, undecideds we'd persuaded, and phone numbers we had on file. Volunteers from my nuclear watchdog days, soccer team, and the No On One Campaign worked beside me. Donors I'd met a decade earlier wrote checks and hung out at events wearing my campaign buttons and carrying clipboards with my cluttered volunteer sign-up sheets.

Running for office on a legislative scale depends on door knocking. A candidate doesn't just pay for TV and radio ads, show up to kiss babies, and hope for the best. Nothing I'd ever done involved showing up on a doorstep and talking about myself with perfect strangers, but I liked this part of the work. I liked meeting people, winning them over, listening to them, and learning what we had in common. Platform talking points seemed to matter little compared to work I'd done in the community. People liked what I'd done and promised me their votes.

A year earlier, my trial run at door knocking had been volunteering for a mayoral candidate. I begged Carol to come with me. Suspending all snark and dressed in a polo and khakis, Carol climbed in the car carrying our map and list of voters. We each took half the list and one side of the street. At the first house Carol went to, the voter inside had been asleep and was pissed about the ringing doorbell. Carol wanted to go home.

We kept going and I got into standing on doorsteps talking about city issues. Then I heard a loud moan from the sidewalk. An elderly woman in a wheelchair had insisted Carol come inside. She'd talked politics for half an hour and Carol had listened, hating to disappoint the woman by asking to go.

Finally we were back on the sidewalk. "You stay. I don't like this," Carol said.

"One more hour and we'll go," I said.

Carol growled.

A few lawns later, I was deep in conversation and heard the words "baby killer" yelled in the distance. I turned to see Carol walking purposefully toward our truck chased by someone in a housedress who seemed to sum up all Democrats with one single issue.

Carol was done door knocking, forever.

The November election was nine months off. I had not one but two Democrats to beat in the May primary before I could run against the Republican in the fall. District 19, where Carol and I lived, had once been politically mixed, but in recent years it had become the bluest, most open-minded, liberal district in the state. The foothills with their views and bigger houses were slightly more Republican. The Capitol and all of downtown had been drawn into my district. I carried a clipboard and lists and walked all those streets, asked for voters by name, no matter what party they claimed they did or didn't belong to.

I designed my own literature and scribbled lists of former lawmakers, activists, and small business owners who said they'd endorse me. I pleaded for campaign donations, advice, and moral support. Lee lived in my district, so did Meg and long lists of queers I'd organized dances, concerts, and Pride events with. They all showed up, over and over, for months.

I dug in, set all else aside, and became a soft machine with stiff hair that did little but make phone calls and knock on doors.

Brian Cronin was a young, tidy, enthusiastic, Party Democrat, one of my two opponents. By *Party Democrat*, I mean he seemed to embody the class and certainty I believed the party required. He was running to win.

In two months, I knocked on nearly four thousand doors. Then someone started a rumor that I'd be "a single-issue candidate." This was code. Vaguely polite code. Even though many queers held key roles in the invisible machinery of the party, some thought the party's visible ties to a gay candidate would be toxic to Democrats' hopes of winning statewide elections again.

Though Newt Gingrich was no longer Speaker of the US House, Idaho was still part of his America. His think tanks kept peeling back the American psyche, finding fear an excellent prod to get their voters to show up at the polls. Harvey Milk, Marsha P. Johnson, Billie Jean King, and Ellen DeGeneres had made Americans more aware we existed but, to Gingrich, queer people were not victims. Even Matthew Shepherd, left hanging from a fencepost in Wyoming, was not a victim but, to them, an evil that voters needed protection from.

Our agenda was a crusade, Gingrich said. Our desire for "special" protections would take rights away from straight America. He was trying to make people afraid to serve us in their restaurants and rent housing to us—something they'd already done for as long humans had had housing to rent and food to serve. He called being gay a choice, a moral failing.

Republicans hadn't won a seat in my little legislative district since the mid-1990s. Still, someone seeded the party circles with another rumor that, if Democrats let me win the primary, voters would be so deeply repulsed by the idea of me serving as their lawmaker that they'd stay home in November or vote for the Republican to avoid having a queer person speak for them in the statehouse.

The fear that I'd lose the seat buzzed. Democrats were already a small minority and couldn't afford to lose a single seat. So, I started knocking on every door in my district—not just the doors of registered voters. I talked to people who'd never voted and, when they seemed supportive, I got their phone numbers and registered them to vote. I won over

Republicans, Independents, and people who wanted nothing to do with political parties.

Often people already knew me, knew the work I'd done in the community. I listened to them, absorbed stories, memorized faces, gathered names, pushing all of us forward, day after day, in a ritual of determined exhaustion.

10
CONFORMITY

2004

Boise, Idaho

Talking to voters, it rarely came up that I was gay. I'm not sure it occurred to most people. They didn't know the size of the pink closet in the Capitol or the names of those in both parties who'd served invisibly in the House and Senate before I ever arrived. When newspapers mentioned my name, it came attached to two words: "openly gay." I was *the* openly gay candidate. Ten years earlier, a young, dapper gay man named James Du Toit had run openly but lost his campaign for a seat on the Boise City Council. Now, there was just me.

"For god's sake!" Carol swore.

I ran back into our house to change the shirt under my suit jacket. "I'll be just a sec."

"We'll be late. It doesn't matter. You look fine!" Carol yelled.

"No. This collar's too butch."

I heard a moan. "Please, let's not have a fashion crisis."

Fashion crisis is what Carol called it when I worked myself up, even grew so stressed I cried arranging and rearranging my hair and clothing. I still had short hair but had rituals about the details of this hair. Religiously, I let strands in front of my ears grow long. Rather than side burns, I had thin spit curls. I gelled these so that they ran onto each cheek like curved needles.

The hair on my forehead was styled into another gelled curl that I coated with spiking glue until it became hard and impossible to dislodge. I hated big hair but needed feminine touches, details that made my hair look intentional, even if it was a bit arty for the Capitol. In a stiff wind or when hit by a scarf or a sweater, this curl and the rest of my hair stayed in place. The only way my careful control of it all could fail was if I spent hours door knocking in the rain.

Most my life, I'd worn one earring or even several small ones running up my right earlobe. Dressing myself for lobbying or campaigning, I wore two dangly ones and dressed in low-cut V-necks, with just enough skin showing to disrupt the line of my broad shoulders and take focus away from my strong, blocky jaw.

I refused to shave my legs or armpits. I told myself, the hair on my shins protected me from scratches when I was hiking in the backcountry. I stayed oblivious to the messages about hygiene and femininity and wore long pants or opaque tights, even when my long leg hair stuck visibly through the fabric.

As for my facial hair, my little mustache is pretty prominent. Rather than tweeze or shave it, I bleached it. This meant I spent an hour or so every few weeks mixing white goo that burned my skin but left me with a healthy blond micro stache and a soul patch below my bottom lip. I was, and still am, pretty fond of both.

When in the Capitol or campaigning, I wore shoes with laces and a little heel, sturdy enough I could run in. My favorites were a pair of men's size 9.5 disco shoes from the 1970s. I'd found them new in a box in a thrift store. I wrote a slam poem about them. When I wore them, the song "Stayin' Alive" from the *Saturday Night Fever* soundtrack played as I walked the statehouse and their hefty click reverberated off the marble walls and stairs. Time slowed when I felt them on my feet. Flecks of light from a disco ball spun, speckling the ceiling and walls. My body felt like mine, my stride long and invincible.

All the strict protocol signaling my compliance with gender norms was invisible to me. I couldn't explain why I grew so stressed when I strayed from the invisible comfort zone I'd built. I couldn't say what the insistence on the curls and two earrings was about except that I felt it was safe and expected of me. My mix of skirts and pants mimicked what most female legislators in the building wore. I hoped nothing about me would distract my colleagues as I spoke to them. I wanted nothing neon to blink and remind them I was queer, different, that my existence or the shape of my family might be at odds with their religion or beliefs about marriage or the proper roles and appearance of women and men.

What I didn't recognize was a fear that I'd be unwelcome in the circles I'd spent just over a decade slowly becoming part of. Something in me sensed that while people knew I was gay, they liked the relative invisibility of my gayness. If I didn't obsess with the details of how I looked, if I looked butch, seemed masculine or undecided about my gender, I'd be less welcome. I'd be less trusted to speak for communities that didn't yet have any idea what to do with gender nonconformity, ones that saw failing to conform as laziness, as a lack of understanding, or lack of willingness to do the work of functioning as a professional.

By the final weeks before the election, people I'd met lobbying on tax policy had spent months with me in the rain and snow. Immigration attorneys, environmentalists, high school students, photographers, and people with disabilities I'd worked with in the Capitol had made thousands of phone calls to persuade undecided voters to vote for me.

Dad came from California. Stroking his now tidy, graying beard, he settled into a table with a list and a landline phone. His fatherly voice greeted each voter by name, repeating something like, "Hi, my name is Bruce. I'm Nicole LeFavour's dad. Nicole's running to represent you in the state Capitol this election. Are you familiar with Nicole?" He'd smile through the phone, waiting for the answer, asking, "Can we count on your vote?"

When primary Election Day finally came, teams headed to phone banks and neighborhoods, and my mom went out midday, wearing a sandwich board pasted with election information. She was assigned to cruise the bars, including the gay bar, the Balcony Club, where she spent the entire afternoon talking me up and making friends.

That evening, the first fifty of my 350 volunteers crammed themselves into my campaign office. While the polls closed and numbers rolled in, Lee and two other young female strategists huddled around computers. We all peered at my too-small TV. Ollie fretted. My campaign manager, Zach, and Carol started drinking. Carol made fun of us all, glazed after days of cooking vegetarian chili and directing the hundred people who came to our house to do last-minute work dropping campaign literature on doorsteps.

The Democratic Party had gathered blocks away at an old downtown blues venue, once upon a time a clean, well-lighted place. In our office, the TV screen scrolled through 105 legislative races. There'd be no runoff. To win, I'd simply need more votes than either of the other two candidates.

Brian was doing far better than our opponent, lawyer and former state senator Steve Scanlin. Scanlin had roots in the queer community and, maybe for that reason, had run gently against me. With Cronin doing so much better, I'd need maybe 40 percent to win.

An hour passed. The early results looked good so we locked the office and rolled into the street, headed out as a mob through downtown toward the party gathering at the Blues Bouquet. In my journal, I described us as "a big group—many of whom had been drinking for two or so hours already—queers, Latinos, Greens, enviros." Laughing, reeking with underdog machismo, we filled the sidewalk. In one hand, Carol swung a freshly opened bottle of champagne.

The bar was dark and a bit somber. Brian and Steve weren't there yet so I hugged volunteers, Lee, and the women who'd managed data and voter turnout strategy for me. They would all grow powerful in the years ahead. Lauren would become our city's first female mayor, defiantly flying Pride flags as the world around us grew oppressively antigay.

While the place filled and the final precinct numbers came in, television stations asked for interviews. The daily paper took photos. Amazingly, they had endorsed me. They'd also printed a story favoring Brian to win. Those rumors about my ability to win the general election still circled over us.

That night, Brian didn't win. With Mom's loud, two-fingered whistle and a surge of screams, I felt Carol, Ollie, Lee and all our bodies rise in a sort of slam dance. We leaned together and the months of doors and phones slipped away. We posed for a photo between the bar tables before reporters walked me off into their lights.

In that three-way race, I became Democratic nominee for Idaho's District 19 with not 34 percent or 40 percent but with 53 percent of the vote.

My general election fight was far simpler. Alicia Cassarino, my Republican opponent, was gentle, funny, and hardly a conservative. We debated and crossed paths at forums, shaking hands, trading softballs. When the polls closed on November 2, 2004, and all that could be done was done, Carol and I stuffed overnight bags and headed downtown to a hotel room upstairs from Democrats' election night headquarters.

Early in the evening, numbers came in and my cell began to ring. Down in the Democrats' red, white, and blue ballroom, and in quiet hallways, people shook my hand, nodded their heads, and I did interviews with newspapers and radio stations I'd never heard of. Queer strangers said my win that night felt like a turning point for the state, a glimmer of hope in a culture that had chosen limited government over their safety.

After midnight, television on in our hotel room, Carol and I lay exhausted on hotel sheets and watched a tide of conservative victories sweep the US. Somberly, national media noted only a few progressive wins in a tide of losses. Idaho had elected its first openly gay legislator and Barack Obama had become the US Senate's only Black member.

Focused on policy, I had not thought ahead to the world I would enter. The *New York Times* quoted me on queer representation in red states. I traveled with the Victory Fund, meeting Representatives Tammy Baldwin and Kyrsten Sinema, Houston Mayor Annise Parker, and Dallas County Sheriff Lupe Valdez—all of us elected firsts of some kind.

At home, before lawmaking season began, I caucused with my new political party. My colleagues, the elected members of the House and Senate, granted me committee assignments, provided staff support, aided me through the process. Kind as they were, party powers outside the Capitol still seemed fearful about adopting into their midst a blinking neon sign announcing that, yes, from there on, they'd be the party of the gays.

Arriving at my first pre-legislative event, a tour of various industries in the northern part of the state, Representative Wendy Jaquet, twenty years older than me and longtime Democratic Leader of the Idaho House of Representatives, offered to share a hotel room. We sat on the twin beds and Wendy looked at me, smiling.

"Let's call Jackie Biskupski," she said, picking up the big landline phone she'd just finished using to call and console Democrats who'd lost their races.

Jackie Biskupski was Utah's first openly LGBTQ lawmaker. Elected four years before me, she represented a liberal part of Salt Lake City, much the way I now stood for a liberal part of Boise. I'd met her through the Victory Fund. She worked in a rough, Mormon-dominated legislature, much like ours.

Representative Jaquet understood triangulation in ways I didn't. She dialed the phone. It may have been days or weeks later that we finally got Jackie on the line.

Wendy's voice was sweet, concerned, "Jackie, we'd like your advice." Without small talk, she began a series of questions, something like:

"Jackie, should Nicole bring Carol to public events or is that a bad idea?"

"Should Nicole talk about gay issues to the media? In the statehouse?"

"What about gay rights bills?"

"How should Nicole dress?"

Jackie's answers saved me. She pried an opening for me with something like, "Yes, Carol should come to events." Jackie said it was important for my colleagues to see us as a couple, an example of gay people in the flesh. Yes, I should talk about gay issues, but first I should work on other issues for a bit. Let them get used to me working on things they might agree on. Eventually, yes, I should work on gay rights bills. And wear what other legislators wear—pants, dresses—just look around.

Wendy listened, nodded, and that was that.

For days, we traveled in buses with other lawmakers and it sunk in slowly that I was being treated as an equal. As we stopped at factories, colleges, and hospitals, longtime lawmakers of both parties made small talk and shifted seats, getting to know the newly elected freshmen. The ones I met were curious and kind.

Deep in Boise winter, fussing with my clothing the morning before our first legislative session in January of 2005, I kissed Carol on the lips and set out to walk the ten blocks through the city in the cold. Standing at the bottom of the Capitol's huge stone stairs that first day, I felt the weight of all the people I represented.

Climbing those steps, I felt the hum of all the unknown. I was leaving one dimension of myself and entering another, one where I would be *of government*, where I'd have to remain calm, where I couldn't run from conflicts or organize a rally during a debate to drive home a point. It would be just me and the other 104 lawmakers. I'd have to figure it out, get over whatever it was, get numb to my colleagues' beliefs about queer people, or search for some sliver of shared something. I'd have to scramble to find a way to reach them, a way to work with them, regardless—because that is what I believed serving in elected office was about.

Now I was *the man*, an elected voice for those I served. In my mind, my district trusted me to make voting decisions on their behalf, to explain the reasoning behind those decisions, and to give them my cell phone number so they could reach me if I ever served them badly.

I was assigned to the tax, environment, and judiciary committees. Wendy was more than kind in those assignments. They were powerful committees that addressed complex issues. Each struggled with aspects of justice.

Standing outside an evening reception for freshmen lawmakers at the once all-male Arid Club, Carol and I locked eyes, turned, and walked in together. It's very possible we were the first out queer couple intentionally invited there as guests. The campaign had forced us to navigate a life where gowns and suits were required, where couples were Mrs. and Mr., and where casual conversations revolved around crops, cows, cars, children, and grandchildren.

I smiled. Other freshmen checked their coats. Carol and I turned to meet spouses and lawmakers. Chuck Winder had just been elected to the State Senate. He was shorter than Carol with distinguished Friar Tuck hair and round glasses. His smile was kind. Many years later, in 2022, he would serve as president pro tempore, the most powerful member of the Idaho Senate, and that year he would save families with trans children from a single anti-trans bill. In 2024 he would be targeted by extremists in a primary election, ousted from office with the use of one faked recording and a robocall.

Carol turned to a woman nearby to shake hands. Silver and glassware glinted. Carol smiled, said, "Nice to meet you," but the woman lowered her hand and turned away.

My eyes shot to meet Carol's while coats exchanged hands and bodies pressed close. My look said, *It's OK. We expected this. This is why we're here.*

I'd always been good in emergency situations. I was levelheaded when things caught fire. I hoped my reflexes for calm would hold. I wanted to project dignity.

Weeks later, as I climbed the steps toward the front doors of the Capitol that first day of my term in 2005, I held onto how I'd been elected to serve people I'd met on doorsteps and through my campaign, all of them—people on Harrison Boulevard, and in the Section 8 housing projects, those who opened their doors in their pajamas, others who shouted at me or turned off their porch lights, people from the synagogue, the Islamic center, and the LDS ward—not just queers or progressives. I agreed with the Constitution. I would need to hear conservatives, listen to what fundamentalists had to say. Like it or not, I was the legislator for *all* those in my district now.

Inside, I chose a big leather seat on the floor of the House at the edge of the caucus, on the line between Republicans and Democrats. Unlike most in my party, I'd sit next to a Republican. I hoped to learn something sitting on that cusp. That first day, the Speaker's gavel fell and lawmaking season began. After hours of ceremony, I made myself a cup of tea and walked to my assigned committee meetings, ready for hard stares.

I would be in the company of the House's old guard now, representatives and chairmen who'd refused to speak to me about LGBTQ issues or had strongly opposed heat assistance or tax bills I carried a year earlier. My election had called new attention to the queer part of my identity, and I considered that I might be stopped at committee room doors or silenced when I attempted to speak. I braced for "special" problems or malfunctions of access and procedure.

But none of this happened.

It is true, Representative Delores Crow, chair of the House Revenue and Taxation Committee, came to call on me when I raised my hand in committee by turning my name and title into a long drawn out moan. "Reppppraaaasennntaaaatuvvvve Luuufaaavrrr," she'd say, as if even my name and title were exhausting. These dramatics likely had more to do with how many pointed tax policy questions I asked and less with how much she disliked that I was gay.

In one committee after another, I was offered a seat. I listened to public testimony. I was called on to debate and vote on bills, on drafts of bills, and on agency rules.

Each morning, in the tiny, formal breakfast room, high on the House side of the Capitol, I mingled. The seventy of us trickled in, sat at a few scattered tables. We scooped up eggs and entrées made by our private cook. The only vegetarian in the House, I'd cradle my bowl of oatmeal, scan the room and sit down, often at the big central table next to someone I didn't know.

The day I sat next to Representative Ken Andrus, he gave me his goofy, modest smile. He was a sheep rancher from the southeastern part of the state.

"What's that like?" I asked.

His words were slow. As the second oldest House member, his face wrinkled when he smiled. I'd often seen him sitting alone, getting help with his laptop.

"I like it," he said. "I get out into the hills and walk."

Not an answer I expected. I told him of my years on the trail as a wilderness ranger. We each appreciated the quiet, the vastness of those huge untouched places where we might walk for days as the only human for miles in any direction.

I'd seen his wife in her old-time clothes, smiling at events where Carol and I thought we needed to look fancy.

"I've got ten kids," Ken said.

He was Mormon and knew I was gay. He had a degree in animal husbandry, and I recalled he might have served on a school board.

"I think they got me to run because my last name is Andrus."

One of the state's most famous governors, Cecil Andrus was a Democrat, godfather of the party now. In polling, he was the most popular figure in Idaho politics. I'd met him in the governor's office in 1993, when I'd sat with others asking him to turn back shipments of radioactive waste from power plants and missile factories. If your name was Andrus, even if you were a Republican, it would help you get elected.

I think Representative Andrus had never turned on a computer or used the internet. I helped him and other freshman Republicans with their email. Technology was easy for me, but I didn't know much about Mormons. I didn't know how a political caucus worked or how much independence I'd have to vote my conscience.

In the Capitol, some Republicans I met said outright they didn't think they'd ever met anyone gay. Ken didn't seem to have trouble saying the word. I suspected in all those big religious families, most my colleagues had a son or daughter who stepped outside gender norms. In time, I'd hear those stories. On the three committees where I served, I gained new appreciation for the word "power." Now I gave my opinion on the language of bills. I could propose changes in words that would become law. Sometimes when I made a motion to amend a bill, debating for or against a change of even one word, I could make lives better.

11
BEAST

2005

Idaho House of Representatives, Boise

As a freshman in Idaho's House of Representatives, I didn't sit quietly.

Party leaders and experienced caucus members were supposed to be the ones to stand and debate. They took turns rising before our sixty-nine colleagues and the reporters staged to one side of the House Speaker's big chair.

On a good day, together with glib House Republican Leader Mike Moyle, gender-bending Lenore Barrett, Democrat Shirley Ringo, and several from the tax committee, I would set about killing bills. The group of us took our tax policy very seriously. We led the small business block of the House, an odd assembly of conservatives and liberals dedicated to destroying corporate tax cuts. Most of us disliked these bills because they shifted taxes to small businesses and working people, typically with no guarantee of jobs in exchange.

When a bill we hated escaped the tax committee by a narrow vote, we'd take turns, rising from our wooden desks on the floor of the House to ask the Speaker's permission to debate. I'd get on the phone to a desk across the room. Lenore would stand in her tie, busting out in lines of rhyme, leaning into her microphone, her narrow mouth tight with a smile.

Arguments would flow back and forth, each of us addressing each other in the third person. One moment it might seem we had the votes to kill the bill in question. Then with good debate on the other side, we'd lose them.

Finally, the secretary would give a last call, "Has everyone voted who wishes to vote?" and "Does anyone wish to change their vote?"

The battles that Shirley and I helped lead transcended political party. They split both the Democratic and Republican caucuses down the middle. For me to make progress on queer issues, I'd also have to keep political parties out of it. I'd have to get Republicans to help lead.

Like most states, Idaho had already passed a simple law redefining marriage so it applied only to heterosexual marriages. They did this at the same time other states did in 1996, right after our win defeating Proposition 1.

Before I ran for office, freshman Senator Curt McKenzie, a slight and very serious young attorney with red hair, tried twice to propose bills to further restrict marriage and "marriage substitutes" so the state would not recognize any form of gay union. This was hardly a state crisis needing to be addressed by force of law. Queer couples at the time still had no civil rights protections and no national right to same-sex marriage. Social security and health care didn't follow gay unions and so, in most states, all we got from a wedding was our sparkle and our love.

McKenzie, like most Idaho Republicans, had traveled to national conferences where industry and religious groups offered model bills, suggesting these could earn lawmakers a place in history, saving some constituency from the evils of environmentalism, social welfare, or government regulation. These groups had increasing success inserting religion into law in rural states, testing the Constitution, and expanding their power to use government to their own ends.

McKenzie's bill was the second explicitly antigay bill to be considered by the Idaho legislature. Even worse, it was a constitutional amendment; its power would supersede state law. In 2003 I waited with other activists, dreading the day it would rise up for a public hearing from the dark of the Republican committee chair's desk drawer. But, as the gavel fell and that three-month session dissolved into packing boxes, it never did. It had been "deep-sixed," stuck in Republican Chairwoman Sheila Sorensen's drawer to die.

Back then, that killing move by the committee's chair seemed magical, like a gift. I didn't know then how much I'd grow to hate this power of chairs, their ability to squash an idea without ever holding a hearing and listening to stories from the lives on either side.

After I was elected to the House, McKenzie's constitutional marriage ban faced a new committee chair, one who quickly gave it a public hearing. Though nearly all those testifying spoke against it, the bill passed with a majority vote out of committee and sat waiting for a vote on the Senate floor.

Most disturbing was that, as an amendment to our constitution, McKenzie's bill banned not just gay marriage but civil unions, domestic partnerships, and anything that even looked or smelled like gay marriage. For something meant to exact suffering on LGBTQ people alone, this Idaho marriage ban was written to do harm without ever mentioning queers by name.

To stop a constitutional amendment, we needed twelve of the thirty-five senators to vote no. Only seven Democrats served in the Senate. Getting five Republicans to side with the tiny caucus of seven Democrats seemed unlikely.

In my disco shoes and with spit curls glued to my cheeks, I flew up and down Senate stairs, my shoes ringing. I reasoned with strangers and those I knew from years before. I sat across from Senator Davis, his desk between us, his now clean-shaven face round, his black beard gone. He argued that we should let the people vote.

"Do you think it's a good idea to put the rights of a small, maligned minority to a vote of a way larger majority?" I asked. I was thinking of how Mormons themselves had once been targeted by our constitution and deprived of the right to vote.

The LDS Church was a puzzle to me. I know more now than I did serving next to scores of Mormons, drinking herbal tea with some, watching them stand around me at their desks, crossing their arms during the morning prayer. The majority of my LDS colleagues didn't swear in conversation, didn't drink alcohol or coffee at legislative events. Often, one of their many children would be a page, wear a red vest, wander every corner of the building, waiting on the committee chairs and staff.

When members of some churches ran for office, I might find antigay or racist points on their palm cards and websites. By contrast, overtly antigay positions weren't typical of LDS candidates. The church was heavy on family and didn't exactly seem to hate gay or transgender people. Still, I know we posed a deep theological problem for them.

For Mormons, the problem with us has to do with the very gendered roles for men and women within the church. "Mother" is not a name but a role, an exclusively female role within LDS wards and families. In those same realms, the role of "priesthood holder" is exclusively male. Without both halves of this binary, the faith does not endure, a man does not populate his own planet in the celestial afterlife. Even the assent to a planetary heaven relies on a male priesthood holder using his special powers to summon his celestial wives.

In the LDS faith, everything, from the layout of each Mormon temple to an LDS wife's secret naming, relies on a gender binary. This is still a problem for gay marriage in the church. It is a problem once handled delicately when it came to intersex people and gender transition. The mixing of religion and politics has caused this delicacy to fray.

On the day I watched the 2005 marriage amendment debated on the Senate floor, I sat on the edge of a theater seat in the gallery, just above the chamber where the senators would be called on, one by one, to vote. For months, I had many long conversations over hosted lunches, industry dinners, and office desks. I wished I could count on every Democrat but I couldn't. We needed twelve "no" votes. Twelve.

Gripping the list I'd made, I watched the roll call unfold.

"Andreason?" the secretary called, her voice practiced from thousands of votes in that chamber.

"Nay," said the white-haired Republican from Boise. His voice was firm. It didn't waver. I smiled.

The secretary kept calling senators' names.

"Cameron."

"Compton."

"Coiner."

Nays echoed up from the floor but not enough of them.

Working in alphabetical order, the secretary called "Little." The brisk, angular senator's vote was nay.

Agile and able to launch questions barely detectable as argument on the budget committee and Senate floor, Senator Brad Little stunned me that week with a quote in his local paper arguing against banning gay marriage. Like the other no votes to that point, he was not Mormon. He, it seemed, was leading the opposition to the marriage amendment from the Republican side.

The roll call came to a close below me in ayes and nays. The secretary gave the count: fourteen no votes, twenty-one ayes. Eight Republicans had joined six Democrats. Our state's bill to create a constitutional amendment banning gay marriage was dead.

From their desks on the Senate floor, a few senators looked up at me.

Something like hope circled the chamber. It settled next to me in a seat. I took it home.

As often as I felt I was alone, in that place, at last, I wasn't.

That same year, after many years of attempts, a bill to include people with disabilities in Idaho's Human Rights Act, finally passed both houses to become part of our state nondiscrimination law. Soon this would be the very part of law I'd need to focus on. It was time to write and find support for a new bill that would add four words—"sexual orientation" and "gender identity"—to Idaho law, alongside existing protections for race, color, religion, sex, national origin, and disability.

March ticked by. Geese started nesting on the roof and windowsills of the abandoned courthouse across the street. Still, that first legislative session didn't end as it should have.

The tradition was, when lawmakers stayed too long, the press corps put on their ugliest ties and wore them in the Capitol as a signal we'd overstayed. As the long session turned from days to weeks, I wandered through thrift stores, buying an armful of the ugliest ties I could find. I organized the women of the House to wear them for a day and all but three Republican women joined me. A future White Nationalist lieutenant governor stood with Representative Lenore Barrett, Democrats, Republicans, committee chairs, and freshmen.

My seat mate, Representative Shirley Ringo, helped me tie knots. "What, LeFavour, you don't know how?" she teased. She had a tiny image of a donkey embedded in the gold cap that covered one of her eye teeth. As she grinned, it flashed.

We took a photo, standing in rows, ties dangling. In it, I'm kneeling on the floor in the center. Twenty of us smile, but Lenore Barrett, the one who once wore ties for real, is dressed in a brown jacket at far left. She is deadpan.

On that day, I didn't know how moments like this would end, how it all would end. I saw only beauty, only love—love that would take a long time to understand.

After that first legislative session ended, Carol and I drove west across Oregon's deserts to the coast. As the ocean pounded at the sand and cliffs, and starfish and anemones rose and then sank into the tide, we, along with Pinza, walked the redwoods, where we hovered like ephemeral gnats at their wooden feet. Vanishing into the clouds, these trees grew while the sequoia, which once towered out of swamps near my mom's place, now lay long dead, preserved in stone made from volcanic ash. With every passing decade, the fossils of their trunks decayed, scattering wood-like bits of rock down slopes of cactus and salt bush.

With Pinza curled in the back of the car, we headed south to the Bay Area where Dad still lived. He'd retired, remarried to a photographer named Faith, and had written a book on walking in France.

When we arrived, Billy Noonan came for dinner at their funky farmhouse. Once a candidate for coroner and running mate in Hunter Thompson's bid for sheriff in Aspen, Billy was central to almost every family dinner in Dad's house.

As part of a knot of Dad's friends from Woody Creek, Billy was part of the community they'd all once built and helped maintain as they scattered across the West. Billy said he was proud of me. His white beard and hair trimmed, he'd once sported a black handlebar mustache and had been pictured on campaign posters in a trench coat with a shovel in a cemetery in front of a gravestone. The words beneath the silk-screened image on the poster read "Let Noonan Do It." Dad still had the poster on his wall.

Dad loved Carol. While Carol exuded a devil-may-care wit and sarcasm, I think Dad saw the love and deep empathy at the core.

Though Idaho was conservative and sometimes libertarian to the extreme, Billy, Hunter, Dad, and the counterculture of Aspen in 1970 had been up against a Nazi sympathizer and supporter of Hunter's opponent in the sheriff's race.

In Idaho, White Nationalists had not organized a parade since 2000. The year I was elected, Richard Butler had lost his Aryan Nations compound and had died. I had been part of a "Too Great for Hate" campaign that still responded to racist incidents and used a network of human rights organizations across the state to respond when White Nationalists leafleted a university or neighborhood parking lot. Increasingly, things had been quiet on that front.

By January 2006, and the first days of my second year as an elected maker of law, the Capitol's hush felt warm. I held the power of the previous session's win close. We watched the news as constitutional amendments like the one we'd defeated devoured other state capitals. Making my visits from the House side of the building across to the Senate, I started to feel a weight pressing down.

Senator Little's angular face was hardly set in stone. In his office, blond, strategic, understated, Senator Joe Stegner, one of the two moderates in Senate Republican leadership, tilted his chair back and, from behind his wide, gold-rimmed glasses, described the pressure, the price he'd paid for his no vote the year before, the toll it had started taking—not only on Senator Little but on all the other Republicans who voted no as well.

Some were committee chairs. They could lose those positions of power if Davis and the Senate's Mormon leaders decided to bring out the thumb screws, clamp them on, and turn clockwise. Both Little and Stegner could be voted out of their party leadership, replaced by more conservative senators longing for their seats. Even worse, those who'd sided with me and stood for their gay constituents were warned they'd be targeted in the November Republican primary, just five months off.

I walked the halls every day. I didn't go home when the gavel fell in committee but walked the few blocks downtown for lobbyist receptions and dinners where I could sit next to senators who'd stood with us, listen to their perspectives, remind all of them of the human beings at the other end of every vote on gay marriage. They were being asked to choose between elected office and us, the gay and gender nonconforming, fighting what to them probably felt like the losing side of a brand-new cultural war.

In those ballrooms, clubs, and convention rooms, for the nightly lobbyist events, I put on skirts and chunky heels and strained to blend in, to be a presence beyond political party, a presence that fit in those formal spaces, in spite of my queerness. Sometimes a server would stop, bend toward me, and whisper, "Thank you." A lobbyist or agency director might pause and I might catch a sympathetic eye and return a knowing smile.

While I tried to be everywhere, Carol lived a life of work, meetings, travel, commuting to an office filled with cubicles, coming home to a silent, cold house, lighting the wood stove, walking Pinza, making dinner, eating alone.

On February 2, 2006, I climbed to the Gold Room, a dated, rectangular ballroom, hung off the top floor of the Capitol. That year the marriage ban would start in the House, not the Senate. I wanted to speak to my House colleagues before they voted so I signed in to testify with Lee, Evie, Javier, Carol, and our perennial clan of activists.

Lee had suffered patiently as my friend. For a decade she'd spent an hour in the dark of morning, three days a week, listening to me worry. I'd hear the honk of her car horn, roll out of bed next to Carol, and ride to the trailhead with Pinza and Duke, Lee's white-and-tan pit bull–Great Dane mix.

"You ready?"

"Yep. Let's do this."

We'd strap headlamps on, feet pounding a trail we knew from rote after a decade of runs. In darkness, our breath heavy, we'd meet deer, foxes, and coyotes, and one winter our dogs discovered a series of carefully hidden mountain lion kills in the creek, under willow branches, just off the trail.

Pulling up to the house, under the old pine tree at the edge of our meadow, Lee and I would part until next time, each going home to dress and make our way to the Capitol to take on our very different roles.

As I walked into the Gold Room in the top of the Capitol that day, the chairman and committee formed a grim line behind a table before rows of padded, gold-toned chairs. These sat filled with whispering queers and allies who fell silent at the crack of the gavel. For hours, we stood one at a time, stepped to the podium, introduced ourselves, and testified against the new incarnation of McKenzie's marriage bill.

Even if normally such a large volume of testimony against a bill might stall or spark a push for amendments, the marriage ban slid from that committee on a well-greased track. Our Republican Speaker wasn't a sponsor but his second-in-command was. Four days later, the bill landed on the House floor for a vote, and LDS Republican Leader Lawrence Denny stood from his leather chair and asked for support, explaining the state's need to protect marriage from the threat of people like me.

The secretary opened the machines for the representatives to vote.

I set my finger down hard on my red button and stared up at the lit dots next to the seventy names on the House scoreboard. Votes wavered. Four Republican names glowed with red nos. The year before, there'd been only one in the House. Still, four was far from enough. I knew Republican colleagues who were voting against their own children. With sixteen Democratic nays, we were seven short of stopping the bill.

Killing that amendment would be up to the Senate again. That scared me.

I'd practiced not making votes personal. A person would die in that place if they did, if they looked into friends' eyes and saw only their failures, the lines their colleagues drew to please church or ally, or just to survive through the next election.

I was never a pragmatist. Foolishly, I'd hoped my Republican colleagues' affection for me would translate into votes. I'd hoped it would matter to Lenore Barrett that she knew Joe Anderson, the beloved gay rancher who lived alone and owned the ranch on the river below my mom's cafe.

In the House, when we voted, it hadn't mattered enough.

On February 6, two days before my forty-second birthday I sat in the gallery of the Senate again and watched Bart Davis, Joe Stegner, Brad Little, and the other senators vote once more on the marriage ban. The weight I'd felt from the start of the session hung like a beast, its body draped across the chamber's skylights. The desks and red velvet curtains below muffled the echoes, hid the walls from view.

We needed a nay vote from the Mormon Democrat from the eastern part of the state. If we got it, we'd need only five Republicans this time to kill the bill.

But the church that once saved queer people from Proposition 1, the one that stood against the makers of *The Gay Agenda*, was not going to save us from a ban on gay marriage. Idaho's Mormon population was growing and with it their percentage in the House and Senate. The once gentle hand of the church reached out from its headquarters in Salt Lake. Its complex of LDS businesses, nonprofits, and religious organizations was about to fund campaigns to ban gay marriage in Utah and then soon in California and other states. Families in Salt Lake would be pressed by the church with fundraising appeals.

I looked down at the senators who'd blocked the amendment the year before. Only a few were in districts where they'd still be safe in their reelections.

When the roll call came, I heard an "aye" from Senator Andreason, the white-haired Republican representing a Mormon part of Boise. The chamber tilted.

Then another brave Republican who'd voted no with us the previous year voted aye and I knew we were done.

Dread fell from the beast lying on the skylights.

When the secretary reached the *Ls* and Brad Little voted aye, I cried.

Looking down, I saw the weight in his eyes.

Fear, it seemed, had grown to hold a vast place in politics, in campaigns and political parties. Conscience would not be the guide. This was not a good turn for queer people, not a good turn for anyone voters could be made to fear.

I deal with loss in stages. First, there is a longing to flee, a longing to drive winding mountain roads at dusk, owls in flight over pavement, to the desert where I imagine I'll settle and grow old. Then comes immobility, invisibility, stillness. Finally, my mind starts to whirr. I spin out a strategy of miracles, people I'll conspire with, steps we'll take. I plot out in detail the fine points of moral pressure, unheard of political bravery, stunning turns of allegiance.

12
VEIL

2006–2007

Idaho State Capitol, Boise

Carol squeezed my arm. Below us on the curving marble stair, I saw the four women.

Inside the Capitol, polished white stone gleamed. The building spun in an echoing hum of sound. Voices rose off columns, mixed with the scuff of feet. Music filtered up from floors below. The staircase was packed, half of it cordoned off, three stories cut vertically in two by a long winding line of velvet rope.

From one side of the rope, hands reached, people grinned and leaned in. Someone touched my shoulder, a hand patted my back, strangers in suits, coats, long dresses, tails, and ties smiled and nodded.

But ahead, at the turn, maybe twelve steps down, four women leered up at Carol and me with disgust. In front of us, almost a hundred couples inched forward, also arm in arm, acting out the grand promenade from a Disney princess film that was missing only drag queens.

The Capitol had transformed for the night to host the welcome of a new governor. For the ball, I'd bought a special shirt, a shiny green silk wraparound that I'd envisioned tightening until my breasts vanished. My long skirt, found in a thrift store, was made of polyester velvet. Carol wore a blue silk vest under a jacket with tails.

Standing on the stairs, looking down at my body, my breasts felt as if they were swelling, not caged but ballooning out like Violet Beauregarde in *Charlie and the Chocolate Factory*, inflating and tugging me toward the ceiling and the underside of the dome.

The knot of faces on the landing below scowled. Two years had passed since I'd been elected. I ached to let go of the floor, pull Carol by the hand, rise out of the long line of newly elected and reelected couples, away from my own body, styled hair, and velvet skirt.

It had been twelve years since voters had rejected Proposition 1. As far as I knew, Democrats had never proposed a pro-LGBTQ rights bill. Our party, like Republicans, still believed that the vast majority of Idahoans didn't know queer people and didn't want to think about people being gay. I looked down at the clusters, lines, and crowds of people, their eyes following us. I saw greetings and quiet smiles and felt certain that, even here inside government, the majority were not antigay.

I'd spent two years following Jackie Biskupski and Wendy Jaquet's advice, being the well-behaved queer, sitting in the breakfast room or at lunches getting to know the Ken Andruses, the Lenore Barretts, the Chuck Winders. I'd worked to pass mental health, tax policy, and prison bills.

But the silence had grown heavy. It was time for my colleagues to see that the world needed them to take a side. Their own children had come out. Gayness was no longer foreign, wasn't an unspoken or unspeakable thing.

Winding down the final flights of stairs toward the band, I wanted voters to hear their leaders speak in positive terms about queer people. I wanted my colleagues to say the words "gay" and "transgender" in ways that changed public perceptions for the better, especially here where we had actual microphones and where reporters sat in our meetings, waiting to write down what we said.

Each year since I was elected, I sat with other Democrats for hours in Wendy's caucus and strategy meetings and saw how often our press releases, news conferences, and fundraising centered not on policy but on our party trying to gain power or simply retain the power we had. At about this time, the Democratic National Committee quit sending money to states where they'd been losing elections. The messages, the media, and the campaign funds stopped flowing. Idaho's smattering of secular nonprofits dwindled to a tiny few as progressive foundations also shifted funding to battleground states. We were on our own. Those who once pushed back on the tide of extremist policy and ideas would cease "wasting" money in red states.

In Idaho, Democrats held fewer than a quarter of the seats in the House. We were a tiny portion of many parts. We were the minority to Republicans' majority. Any hope we held of that changing dissolved. Areas of the building set aside for party strategy left the small group of us eating sack lunches in cavernous caucus rooms while Republicans crammed themselves into identical spaces, fighting for leadership titles and all the committee chairmanships. The building was designed to manage power and create privacy and separation, but its architects hadn't imagined the imbalance we faced.

With Carol on my arm, we passed the glaring women, reached the bottom of the Capitol, and stood at the edge of the dance floor. From that spot, the rotunda and two chambers of the legislature rose above us like a creature with two great wings. We stood in the heart, that hollow at the building's center.

The music grew faint, and the formal line of couples dissolved. We hovered at the edge. I felt Carol's hand on my arm. Around us, cloth-covered breasts pressed to chests, powerful people danced, and I heard that word I'd first heard, sitting on that couch with Ollie and Senator Davis five years before. It was a repeated echo of the words "Hush . . . hush . . . hush."

I felt the eyes then. Most followed one couple, a tall upright man with dark hair, stiff and carefully styled. This was our new governor, once the winner of a tight jeans contest. He wore cowboy boots and, in his arms, he held his very new, young wife. "Miss Lori," he called her. Months earlier, as a candidate, Butch Otter and his best friend both took on what they called "trophy wives."

I'd known Butch, from my No On One days as one of the elected Republicans who'd come out supporting our campaign, standing against the censorship and bans on antidiscrimination laws. He'd been far from alone. A decade earlier, many Republicans were still truly libertarian and crossed that party line with us to stand against antigay ideas.

In Congress, before running for governor, Butch had voted against the post-9/11 eavesdropping and paranoia in the national Patriot Act. He'd now have veto power and manage state budgets. He'd run the agencies that were the arms of government. He was a governor I thought I could work with.

I felt Carol tug at my arm and saw a look in those eyes I knew well. It was the Act-Up Carol, the Carol who saw me pause, listen to the "hush," and look cowed by the formal crowd and the prospect of creating a spectacle on the dance floor in front of the governor and lawmakers.

Carol had a way of pushing, bolstering my gut, unhitching my sorry fear that I'd reflect badly on queer people, that I'd hurt our chances of changing minds. At that moment, we stood where likely no queer couple had ever stood. Carol was not going to fade into the crowd and let us be swallowed by the silence.

I closed my eyes.

"OK," I whispered, feeling Carol's glee at the idea of us, small breast to large breast, dancing on the marble below the stars.

Carol had the advantage of distance, a perspective that gave a view into my world from some other dimension. Maybe Carol saw ahead in time. I had so little time then. All I'd done to that point was push against bad legislation.

That night, at the start of my third year in office, I felt Carol's arm around my waist. I led as the music rose and Carol tugged us out into the open. There we spun, repeating our four well-practiced swing dance moves, slowed to look like a waltz. And there, too, danced Governor Otter and Miss Lori.

Carol grinned. We danced and I shook my head, smiling.

Looking through photos from the night, the building seems to breathe, spaces around the governor and another couple widen. Sometimes people are looking beyond the governor and Miss Lori at something else.

Years later, Carol studies those pictures and turns to me, "They're looking at us."

The first two years of my four years in the House were thrilling for Carol and me. I'd stand on stage at a rally or event, looking out at a field of faces, and felt genuine love for the people I spoke for.

I called out from microphone after microphone, "You're beautiful," until Carol teased me for the repetition.

Some of the most humbling parts of the job came from speaking to crowds of people and standing on doorsteps where I witnessed someone's passion or pain and felt part of something larger than myself. I think, too, I loved feeling a part of people's faith in me.

One evening after drinking downtown, Carol and I headed homeward on our bicycles, minds bathed in the juice of Bittercreek, a brewpub always crowded with wooden tables and people we knew, there in the center of Boise, a block from the Capitol. Spring had crept in; lawmakers had gone home. For the moment, the sky was turning evening colors and thoughts of work dimmed.

Feet on pedals we laughed, careening down half-empty streets toward our house with its wild meadow and towering eastern white pine. Before we reached the Capitol, we glanced left and right to find lampposts decorated with white bows of tulle, that semi-transparent netting used for bridal veils. Fascinated, we tugged down one of the decorations, bundling it in our arms, stretching it out. The fabric was maybe twelve feet long and four feet wide and somehow, at the moment, magnificent to us. Some couple must have been getting married in the Capitol. The city couldn't help but notice.

Carol's family lived in Massachusetts, where gay marriage was legal—but only for those who swore they intended to become residents. We'd recently decided on a Vermont civil union and planned to travel there for our wedding. Before the legislative session started, we'd sent invitations. Dad, Mom, Meg, our soccer team captain, Nancy, and all the spouses were flying out for the ceremony. My sister, Cree, her husband, and two kids lived in New York. My badass sailor aunt Sid, my Irish grandmother, and Carol's mom, uncle, and Growhoski siblings would all be there.

Standing on the street with the folds of fabric in our arms, we stood in a window of time where Idaho might acknowledge the bit of paper we were about to be granted by Vermont.

In November, if voters supported it, Idaho's looming marriage amendment would change all that.

In the distance, oversized white ribbons like the one we held, hung on every post, lining the street on either side. Spinning, Carol and I each grabbed an end of the long trail and faced each other, turning round, rolling ourselves tight inside either end like two human spools made for wedding veil.

In Vermont, the night before our ceremony, I watched Carol and Cree at the fireplace, tossing pizza boxes into the flames.

"You'll start a chimney fire," I said, passing them on my way to help Dad in the kitchen.

They rolled their eyes, bonding over a shared dislike for my alarmism.

From the kitchen, I heard a roar in the living room. From the fireplace came heat and a familiar sound from my childhood: the roar of a fire so hot it had ignited the interior of the chimney. As a teen I'd heard this sound in a different dining room hearth, the one in our ranch lodge where guests sat at tables and silverware clattered. With long strides, Dad had walked in wearing his apron and upended a table against the brick fireplace opening, smothering the flames.

Here in Vermont, the little inn we'd rented had a dining room and kitchen that the owners let Dad use to cook our reception dinner. Dad, approaching eighty, was busy making vegetable stocks, prepping wild mushrooms. The chimney's growling intake of breath and the heat blazing into the room could only be one thing. I hesitated. Some part of me still wanted Dad to save us, just the way I wanted him to mediate every worldly injustice and every simple conflict between Cree and me.

I turned to the empty room behind me, yelled, then reached for a table, tipping it up and pressing it tight against the brick. But something still roared above my head, up where the brick chimney ran through bedrooms and out the roof.

I ran with Carol and two Growhoski brothers up the staircase, yelling to the innkeepers for fire extinguishers. We found a window in the attic and leaned out to look at the roof. Bricks careened down out of flames. LeFavours yelled and Growhoskis joked. Innkeepers came and Carol and the rest of the wedding party passed fire extinguishers up the stairs.

By the time the firetrucks reached the inn, the flames had died. My ninety-year-old Irish grandmother sat calmly on the couch with her purse, unruffled, lipstick in place. Mom, cocktail ice clanking in her hand, grabbed my sober gay uncle and Carol's younger brother, Joe. Together they wandered to the drive, leering at the muscled guys by the firetrucks with their overalls and hoses.

On our wedding day, Dad paused in his cooking. My chest-tall niece and nephew fiddled with baskets of rose petals. Up in our low-ceilinged rented room, Carol and I kept grinning.

Our vows were funny.

In that calm, I looked into the blue-gray pools that were Carol and I saw everything inside there leaning toward me, nothing hooded or wavering.

I felt certain of us.

From a bag, we unfolded the train of tulle, that fabric from the Boise lamppost. We spooled ourselves into it, stood shoulder to shoulder, entwined. We practiced our vows, bumped our way down to the living room, still wrapped in tulle, and were joined in union by a justice of the peace.

Under Idaho law of the time, we were as close to being wed as we could possibly be.

That summer when we arrived home in Idaho, I typed my name into the search engine on my computer, looking for some article or reference. On the screen, my name glowed, attached to a website called Pass the Ammo. I wasn't the only one listed on it. Like the other gay and justice-oriented people, I had a page dedicated to me, titled—like the other pages on the site—with words that rhymed with "shoot": "Pass the Ammo, Boot Nicole LeFavour." The gun imagery and way they used the word "homosexual" as a slur was creepy.

I'd been getting media coverage as the lead opponent of the antigay marriage bills, corporate tax incentives, and environmental deregulation. Now I listened to hang-up calls and read occasional hate mail.

I refused to let those things make me afraid. I told myself I wouldn't live like that.

Though it was largely considered a lost cause, before the November 2006 election, I raised $10,000 in a weekend, took photos of gay couples and lesbians with kids, and mailed postcards opposing the constitutional marriage ban to carefully targeted voters across the state. Someone had to make sure something positive was said about us to counter the hate being spread.

The next year, in 2007, the lobbyist for the local American Civil Liberties Union (ACLU) brought a proposal to the Senate to add the words "sexual orientation" and "gender identity" to our state Human Rights Act.

Buried deep in the work of rewriting Idaho's prison sentencing laws, I didn't know about the gay rights proposal until McKenzie tucked it away in what was now his own committee's desk drawer. When I heard about the bill, I went to see him. After working with him for two years, I had a hard time seeing him as the hater he sometimes seemed to be.

"It's not getting a hearing," he said.

"Why?"

He admitted he'd had a fight with the ACLU lobbyist on an abortion bill. "If you want to bring it next year, we can introduce it."

I vowed to myself that when the time came, I'd do the legwork and build support for the bill before the session started. My second term in the Capitol, I hoped to finally dig in and help work on a bill to advance LGBTQ rights.

Idaho is unusual. Unlike Democrats, even first-term Republicans get their ideas introduced or "printed" in the Idaho Capitol. A committee will discuss and vote to give a draft a bill number and then schedule a public hearing for it—even when the ideas stink because they're poorly thought out, unconstitutional, or have no chance of passing. Democrats, not so much. The deep six was the fate of most our bills. Often they saw little but the dark of a chairman's desk drawer.

To get votes for a new nondiscrimination law, I needed to argue that Idahoans' narrow support for banning gay marriage didn't mean voters hated gay people. To prove this, I helped get a question included in a statewide university poll, asking if firing a person from their job just because they were gay should be allowed in Idaho. A stunning 64 percent agreed that kind of discrimination should be against the law.

What I needed next was a Republican face, a name with an *R* behind it as a cosponsor, a brave member of the GOP willing to go out front for the queers.

13
POOFTA

2007–2008

Boise, Idaho

On the summer day when US Senator Larry Craig was arrested in an airport bathroom in Minneapolis, the national media started calling me because he was Idaho's Senator in DC and I was Idaho's out elected official. What did I think of him soliciting gay sex in an airport toilet stall?

During the Clinton era, Senator Craig voted against the 1995 Employment Non-Discrimination Act, a national ban on workplace discrimination. For those of us in red America, the bill would have advanced legal equality to a point it would not reach for almost thirty years. History could have been different but it failed in the Senate by one vote. The bill still has never passed both houses of Congress.

Craig insisted he wasn't gay. I could see why.

"I'm sorry we live in a world where the senator can't be open about his sexual orientation," I said.

Suddenly, it seemed the fate of all gay people had attached itself to my ability to help Idahoans understand Larry Craig.

It was not enough to point out that he'd been caught soliciting sex from a consenting adult and in a place where soliciting sex was a norm, like the Las Vegas Strip or 14th Street in DC. When straight people had sex in bathrooms, it didn't tend to make national news.

Larry Craig was once a member of the Idaho legislature. He was a colleague to almost all the people I was spending my days riding buses with that fall. Hushed conversations had been happening on all sides of me most of the day. No one joked about Craig's claim that he simply had a "wide stance" in the stall or about his denial that he used well-known toe tapping signals to proposition the cop in the next toilet.

That year, Craig's phrase "wide stance" earned a place in dictionaries of queer slang, alongside terms like "light in the loafers," "poofta," and "flamer."

"He's got a wide stance," someone might say of a person attempting to wield power from a closet.

Before the session started, during the fall legislative tour of industry, Representative Scott Bedke leaned toward me across a big plush couch. Behind a pair of wire-rimmed glasses, his blue eyes narrowed. "I don't understand," he said. He didn't want details but wanted to know why any man would solicit anonymous sex in an airport, or anywhere, under any circumstances—especially a man with so much to lose.

It was a fair question—unless you considered how having a long-term relationship, paying an escort, or having lovers on the side was simply too big a risk for a Republican elected to the US Senate.

I looked at Scott, "Imagine you're a gay man. Your dream is to be in politics and it's the 1950s and you're a Republican, so, any idea you have that you can live as yourself is off the table."

Scott nodded.

"You're a man attracted to men. Some men are attracted only to women. They find the idea of sex with men disgusting."

I think Scott was following.

"Some men are attracted only to men and find the idea of sex with women disgusting."

"Yeah," he said. I could tell he was not entirely ready to let his mind go down that road.

"Some men fall somewhere in the middle. Say, though, that you're the kind of man who's attracted only to men. As you build a political career, you kind of have a choice: never have sex again or have sex secretly."

Since college, Craig had pursued a political career. He'd done solid work in the US Senate on immigration. As my friend Ted McConnell, a gay Republican who served in the Reagan White House pointed out, for men of Craig's era and aspirations, being gay wasn't an option.

Paying someone to have sex with him, face-to-face, opened up the possibility that an escort could earn far more through blackmail or by exposing the senator to aid people who didn't care for his politics.

"Scott, think about it. You're a gay Republican in Idaho. You want a political career. What are your options—besides anonymous sex and a setup where the person never sees your face?"

Future lieutenant governor and Speaker of the House Scott Bedke nodded, or shuddered, but seemed to comprehend.

Weeks earlier I'd told him about the bill I was circulating to add LGBTQ people to the Human Rights Act and asked if he'd cosponsor. He'd said he wanted to "shop it around," meaning he'd check to see what others in the building thought. To me, so used to hearing a flat no, this had me flying, for weeks.

That year, Idaho's Capitol sat gutted and hollow. Bart Davis worked logistics for the looming remodel, relocating legislative operations inside the too-small, vacant County Courthouse across the street. The place had an abandoned jailhouse in its turret.

Whisked from our velvet cocoon, the entire House and Senate landed not in a building painted with gold and silver stars on its dome but in one with a two-tiered chamber for the House of Representatives and a steep staircase lined with murals—one of them depicting White men in pants and shirts preparing to hang a long-haired, shirtless brown man with a noose.

Idaho's tribes were consulted on whether the mural should stay in place or be painted over. They opted for leaving it where it was with an interpretive sign, a daily reminder to us as we passed of how foul our history was and on whose land we made our laws.

I buttoned my jacket, looking down at my shoes.

I stood outside Senator Bart Davis's office door. It had been seven years since he sat with Ollie and me on that tiny couch. "I am your worst enemy. Worst," he'd said. Knocking on his office door was something I did regularly now. The questions he asked were often deep. At times there was an irony in his answers—a knowing, calculated irony. He had great power in that building. He knew the limits of it and how and when to wield it.

Sitting stiff in the chair across from him, I watched his eyes flash. His black beard had not returned. "You'll need an exemption for religious organizations," he said. He meant adding gay people to the Human Rights Act would be impossible without special language, language never required when "disability," "race" and the other protected classes were added to the law.

The 2008 session started. In the temporary balcony of the House, I turned to my computer, working on an entry for my blog *Notes from the Floor*. Technology was helping illuminate what was happening inside the place. For the first time, a video feed of our lawmaking was being broadcast to the outside world.

Behind me, candy clattered in a dish and low laughter burst from the male freshman Republican "back benchers" at their desks. There in the back tier of the balcony, past the candy, in the last seat against the wall, Curtis Bowers cowered.

This freshman had been shamed not just by queer groups but by sitting Republican legislators, for an antigay tirade he'd published in a local paper. In it, he'd described homosexuality as a tool in a communist plot to overthrow the US government.

With his editorial, I feared his words might incite anger, even violence.

In his nonlegislative life, Bowers ran a restaurant. For years, Carol and I had eaten his fondue. It was a favorite place for birthdays. We'd gone at least twice for our anniversary. The servers had been kind, taken a photo for us, smiled as we held hands across the white tablecloth.

I walked to Bowers's desk.

His seat was squarely in a corner. No one would stand there unless they had something to say. He looked up.

"Your editorial—I'm sorry you feel that way about gay people."

I expected a long response but he didn't offer one. His editorial had been something right out of John Birch Society materials.

"If you've got questions about gay people," I said, "I'm willing to talk."

I wanted to change his mind about us. That was my level of optimism. Yelling and shaming weren't going to change the way he felt or voted.

Bowers, however, avoided me, skirted rooms so we never actually talked. And he didn't last. Appointed to fill a vacant spot in the House, he lost the next primary election, replaced by a more moderate Republican.

That year, in the time before the Capitol expanded and we shut ourselves away in our own offices, I had conversations with two representatives who whispered about their brothers. Both had been gay men who'd died of AIDS when they were young. These two Republican House members were friends and sat just seats away from each other and yet never told each other about their brothers.

Somehow my colleagues didn't talk among themselves about their gay family. In their homes, I realized, queer people like myself were still secrets that brought on shame.

I carried my bill draft to the Senate State Affairs Committee. Good to his word, Chairman McKenzie put it on the committee schedule. The language I had was simple, five pages. It would add four new words to Idaho law, "sexual orientation" and "gender identity," plus a tiny paragraph exempting the Boy Scouts and religious organizations. I did not include definitions for "sexual orientation" and "gender identity" because in my experience letting straight lawmakers spend too much time thinking about gay sex never went well. Our bill's subject was employment, housing, education, and the sale of goods and services. When the Idaho Human Rights Commission needed definitions, they agreed to let me add language saying they could refer to federal law. With that they'd testify in support of the bill.

My colleague Senator Tim Corder was upright and gentle, a Vietnam vet elected the same year I was. Whenever Carol and I invited Republicans to dinner at our house or I organized social gatherings downtown for the dwindling remains of the nineteen members of our class of lawmakers, Tim was part the group.

I'd come to respect him after debating against him at forums and on TV on the issue of marriage. His vote against wasn't based in hate or disrespect but more on how he saw marriage as part of religion, as a contract with God, not the state. He had a sense of humor about the ironies and, over coffee, he confided how, in the war, one of his close friends was gay.

I explained the bill I was hoping to pass. "Will you cosponsor with me?" I asked.

He smiled. "Maybe," he said, in his often understated way.

After many more discussions, he agreed that if I could get other Republicans to sponsor with him, he'd put his name with mine on the bill.

A Basque representative from the House and Senator Coiner, a well-educated, bearded Republican rancher from Twin Falls who had a gay son, joined as cosponsors along with two other Democrats. On the day our draft was scheduled for consideration, Senator Corder stood and presented it to the committee. As a straight, Christian, former Mormon, his explanations were artful. Even when he referred to being gay as a choice and "lifestyle," he was convincing.

Six-to-two was the committee vote, with Chairman McKenzie miraculously a yes. Only Senator Davis and tough old Senator Darrington, both members of the LDS Church, voted no. Even with my exemption for the Boys Scouts and religious organizations written into the bill, it seemed Davis was troubled.

On that day, our draft became Senate Bill 1323. Aside from the Human Right's Commission's attempt to include us in hate crime laws after Matthew Shepherd's death in Wyoming in 1998, this would be the state's first bill to advance LGBTQ rights. Now it was ready for a public hearing where lawmakers would hear our stories, ask questions, and glimpse life in Idaho through other eyes. If our hearing went well and our bill earned five votes, it would pass the committee and then need to pass the Senate and House.

I've always seen bills like birds, rising out of a committee room when passed, settling on the floor of the House or Senate, fleeing through the double doors of the foyer, crossing the massive space of the rotunda, under the gray-blue dome and the painted stars, off to a committee room on that other side and then down to that chamber's floor for a final vote.

By my count, all I needed was one more Republican yes vote to get the bill to the Senate floor. I held myself carefully, afraid to make a mistake or set an example that would do harm. Still, in nearly every room, I was the sole model of queerness, the one face for the bill that they saw.

Kissing Carol goodbye, I walked blocks through the winter dark.

I sat across the desk from one senator after another, as they leaned back in squeaking wooden chairs and I leaned forward, glancing sideways at the photos of them with dead deer or their families.

"It isn't government's job to tell me who I can and can't hire," I heard repeatedly.

Straight, White men who'd grown up in the same religion as most of their community tended to be vague on what happened if you were gay, Black, brown, Muslim, Jewish, or a woman in their towns.

I'd answer gently, "But sometimes an employer thinks a whole group of people are sinful, dirty, or incapable and don't want to give us jobs. How do people support themselves, their families then?"

The chair would creak as the senator shifted, smiling, "We don't need any more protected classes. If I'm fat or ugly *I* might not get that job, and I don't have some law protecting *me*. Why should you have some special right I don't?"

I'd answer honestly. "The term *physical characteristics* should be added to the bill, too."

"Then you've got everybody in the law. Why not just say, 'Don't discriminate against anyone,' just say '*All* people are protected'?"

I'd counter, sitting upright, disco shoes on the marble below my seat, "But somebody always thinks some group of people are an exception. What if a store owner thinks gay people like me are horrible and they think the law can't possibly have been meant to protect us? What if they're firing people specifically because they are who they are: women, transgender people, those of LDS faith." I almost always included Mormons. They preferred the term "Latter-day Saint" and I think they understood why I included them. Tensions existed still in many communities. Religion was an important protected class.

"A law won't change that," the senators might say.

"Saying it's wrong, though, is something our state better do. Otherwise we're saying we agree people deserve that kind of harm."

Republicans had written our existing Human Rights Act. It had functioned for decades. They'd created the Human Rights Commission as a buffer, as other states had, protecting businesses as much as employees every time a discrimination case was raised. We wanted to add just four words to this law.

I felt certain I would get yes votes from Senators Little and Stegner along with the committee's two Democrats. I needed one more yes.

"Small businesses with fewer than five employees *are* exempt," I told Senator Davis when he and Senator Stegner sat in their office, seeming to grill me.

I suspected we could get Senator McKenzie to be our final swing vote, in spite of his being quoted in the Nampa paper supporting Representative Curtis Bowers's bizarre antigay editorial. He'd already voted to introduce our bill in committee. I needed to find out if he'd changed his mind about queer people. He wasn't a bullshitter.

Senator McKenzie's office did not have the weighted, Victorian formality of Senator Davis's office.

"Representative," the secretary nodded to me, "You can go in."

Curt, red-haired and slight of build, sat behind his desk. I took a seat. He was about my age and was not Mormon. He leaned all the way back in his chair, hands behind his head. He had questions, was open to discussion, but not ready to promise a vote of any kind.

"Can we agree this might someday be necessary?" I finally asked, my fingers flipping through my paper copy of the bill.

"Yes," he said, nodding.

"There will be a time?" I breathed gently, as if a loud noise might erase this concession.

"Yes, there will be a time."

My confidence grew. I had changed minds. I knew how those in the big black leather chairs around me saw the issue. Once McKenzie scheduled our public hearing, the testimony would be powerful. I could answer their questions and get their votes. We were ready.

14
POWER

2008–2010

Boise, Idaho

The 2008 session rolled forward, nearing its end. I checked again, then again with Chairman McKenzie's secretary, scanning the agenda on the committee room door. I reminded queer allied groups and activists in what we called "The Coalition" that McKenzie had grown more positive about our bill.

I was waiting. Time kept passing. Weeks passed. We all grew tense, impatient. I'd done the work, months of getting sponsors and votes. Still, many around me doubted the level of support I'd found. They questioned my vote count.

Leaving my desk on the House floor, I folded myself into the vertical glass cube that was the building's old phone booth. Pulling the door closed, I breathed for a bit, then used my cell to check in with Carol. A friend had offered to lend us a house on the Oregon coast, a place we could walk for miles in the rain or fog with Pinza. When the session ended, we'd go.

Climbing the stairs again, I found McKenzie in his committee office. The secretary made me wait. Shuffling through papers, Curt was evasive, wouldn't give a date, a plan for people to testify. "I don't have an answer for you." He glanced toward me then looked away.

"Votes look promising in the House." I said. "I've been working hard." I hoped he'd feel my urgency. Our Democratic caucus had swollen in the last election from thirteen to nineteen. We'd need just seventeen Republican yes votes there.

But winter faded. Groundskeepers began mowing laws. Staff brought packing boxes, set them in rows in the basement. Bill deadlines passed while I waited, checking again and again for our hearing.

All too quickly, down on the House floor, the white-shirted high school pages did their parting skits. Before I could make a last frantic run across the building to visit Senator McKenzie, the new Mormon Speaker lifted his gavel from his desk, bringing it down in a single thunderclap. The session was over.

As lawmakers emptied desks to go home, we held a tiny rally of protest outside in the cold. Members of The Coalition stood in a circle in front of the aging courthouse with its jail and ugly mural. Lesbians, attorneys, staff, and faith leaders held signs and spoke to the media. It was staid and sad.

I'd failed while doing everything I could think of to do. I had votes. I had solid Republican sponsors, faces for the bill, and they never even let us testify.

"Fuck them," Carol said.

"No. I have to figure out a way."

We went to the coast for quiet, walked Pinza in the fog, stared into tide pools, lay in the sand dunes, listened to the surf and rain.

Back home, I comforted myself with how, weeks before the session ended, I'd filed papers to leave my seat in the House and run for Senate. If I won, from there, I could be more effective. The Senate, I thought, would be a better fit. I'd serve next to Bart Davis whom I'd come to suspect had more roles than just leader of Republicans in the Senate.

I visited with my cosponsors. We'd be ready. From that new angle, I might grasp more firmly the nature of power in that place. I'd do everything that had to be done.

Unfortunately, that summer, half of The Coalition had very different ideas about what strategy we should use. Most had lost faith that a bill to protect queer people had a chance to pass. From creaking metal chairs, some said we needed to put the definitions of sexual orientation and gender identity back in, even if it would "make lawmakers uncomfortable." They argued that Republicans needed to get used to seeing the words "homosexuality" and "bisexuality" and adjust themselves to the neon and uncomfortable part of our existence.

Over the years, I'd done uncomfortable education work. I'd shot photos of lesbian and trans friends looking like a rural straight couple and had taken out full-page ads in our local newspaper. The ads highlighted the sweeping scope of Idaho's sodomy law and the penalty of five years to life in prison for consensual oral sex. In big bold letters I asked Idahoans, "Is your sex illegal?"

In trainings I'd long said, "Great to make the powerful uncomfortable when they've got time to sit with their discomfort and learn from it, adjust, desensitize. But in the middle of voting on that policy? No." On the House floor, discomfort made those with the microphones reach for the red button. They'd vote no.

I felt years of careful preparation slipping. I had friends in that room, leaders whose organizations had been defunded, who'd grown used to losing because, nearly every time they walked up those steps to push Idaho forward, they met a new higher wall of party-line hostility or a chairman's desk drawer. The way I clung to optimism was out of place there. I'd seen and heard stories from lawmakers I couldn't share. I felt a level of hope I couldn't make them feel.

My Senate election campaign felt minor compared to my primary race four years earlier. I spent most my effort helping elect Black human rights leader Cherie Buckner-Webb to serve in my vacant House seat. Cherie would be an ally with strong conviction and a powerful persuasive voice. Again, Carol and I ran literature drops out of our house and served Carol's vegetarian chili to hundreds of volunteers walking neighborhoods to turn out voters in the November cold.

Election night, Carol and I celebrated as this time I won with 71 percent of the vote. In December 2009, high up in the temporary statehouse, I raised my right hand and, with the other thirty-four newly elected and reelected Senate members, I swore once again to uphold the constitution. Hearing the words in the mouths of staff and colleagues, the title "Senator" felt heavy. The white badge I now wore was supposed to mean an elevation of status for me. It's stunning how untrue that was.

Although the November election had made Barack Obama the forty-fourth president of the United States, Idaho's Republican primary elections had eliminated many moderates. The tone in the Capitol had turned on edge. New tensions bit at both parties. Some force was rising. Since the final marriage battle, we all felt it.

Under stress, things fracture.

Senator Brad Little had left his Senate seat to run for statewide office. He was now our lieutenant governor. He would stand at the dais in the center of the Senate and his only vote would be to break a tie. A carefully groomed Christian fundamentalist, future Congressman Russ Fulcher, took Little's place in Republican leadership. Senator Stegner was suddenly the lone moderate there. He'd have to reason his way to decisions with Fulcher, Senator Davis, and the Senate's most powerful member, our devout Mormon president pro tem.

Not helpful was how I was a freshman again and the Senate committees I was assigned were brutal. One was the Joint Finance and Appropriations Committee, which met daily, endlessly, from 7 a.m. to 11 a.m. I missed serving on the judiciary and tax committees, where we shaped laws that directly affected justice and people's lives. There, the language of bills mattered. There was power in a comma or difference between "may" and "shall," "and" and "or" and in the words within a definition.

Assigned to the Committees on Commerce and Health and Welfare, now, four days a week, it felt as if the sky was falling. Bills passed I knew would do harm. My colleagues' libertarian streaks had many feeling hostile toward using government to ensure the well-being of their constituents. Too often their compassion was saved for industry. The job of social welfare, some argued, should be left to churches. But, newly elected to the Senate, I had no seniority, no choice in the matter of where in the building I'd serve, what issues I'd spend two years immersed in.

Somewhere exists video of my presentation of The Coalition's queer civil rights proposal to the committee that year. It's not pretty. My face is puffy, the color of paste, my hair slicked back. Senators probe and I respond. They dwell on the definitions. As I suspected they would, they ask me to explain the meaning of the words "homosexual," "bisexual," and "heterosexual." Sexuality is ridiculously easy to weaponize. On the video, senators stray far from the stated definitions and propose absurd alternative meanings for each of the words.

When it was time to vote, Bart Davis was missing from the room. One of the committee's two Democrats was missing, too. Only Stegner and the committee's one remaining Democrat voted aye. This time we would have no chance at a public hearing. Not even a chance. Before the bill could even be introduced, we were done.

Not as obvious to me as it should have been was the lurking presence of a tall man with wild white hair. Seated in the back of the room was Cole Community Church pastor Bryan Fischer, media-savvy, organized, and connected to Colorado's antigay American Family Association. He was deeply racist and anti-Mormon. Two years earlier, he'd suggested that gay Americans were communists and Nazis and that the Holocaust had been a plot of the gays. In his dress suit, Fischer sat on one of the wooden chairs in the audience just feet from Carol and the director of the Commission on Human Rights.

After the vote, in the stairway above the mural of the men with the noose, a public television reporter interviewed Fischer and me about the need for a law to say that discrimination is wrong. Fischer implied LGBTQ people were ill-intentioned, that our troubles were imagined. He had likely worked the committee's senators in advance.

Even if we'd been prepared and even if The Coalition or I had worked the issue all fall, that committee was going to be a tough place. Powers from outside the state were busy whispering to lawmakers. They targeted money at races to force out Republicans whose votes they didn't like. Without the moderates, none of the policy I cared about was going anywhere until Democrats won new seats. So I helped my caucus. I took time, raised money, worked on strategy and messaging, and traveled to help Democratic campaigns.

I made errors in understanding the nature of power that year, failing to see the allure of title and hierarchy for some I served with. In the House, I had more than pulled my weight on policy and party campaigns, and Wendy appreciated me for it. Still, one powerful member of our Senate Democratic caucus found ways to make me suffer. A new rule he authored affected only me. It allowed only party leaders and senators from outside Boise to meet with voters as part of Democrats' statewide Pizza and Politics forums. I was grounded, and for the first time in my years in the legislature, I stayed behind as my colleagues toured the state.

Maybe my queer presence sucked media attention from party events and messaging. Maybe my blog posts being printed in the daily paper and reporters covering my positions on issues of poverty and race annoyed leadership, muddied the rigid hierarchy of partisan government.

When I asked if the new rule that prevented me from traveling the state was about my being gay, our assistant leader told me, "Well, you're not one of the pretty people."

Not wanting to cause a scene or project a lack of unity, I spent that session newly isolated from elected Democrats. I was left busy through winter's predawn mornings and nights, drinking tea by the light of my computer screen, struggling alone to read bills, answer letters, and see an end to the heavy committee schedule my leaders had assigned.

For the first time, I was sliding backward, slowly, nails grinding to nothing while I tried to stand. For almost six years in the media, I'd been the most obvious LGBTQ person and at times even the most visible Democratic face.

Even though as a lawmaker I was no longer supposed to be a community organizer, I could not do what needed to be done without help from others. It was time to bring the community into the ring in greater numbers, make young queers our poster children. They could break stereotypes and add depth to the way lawmakers saw us. In conference rooms, with new message sheets and long role plays, I trained Emilie Jackson-Edney, a gentle trans leader and military veteran with flowered tattoos. I gathered students and allies to talk to TV, radio, and print reporters.

I knew well that in a rural state like ours, dominated by mountains and canyons, it wasn't easy to reach people with traditional media. Vast swaths of Idaho still had no TV reception and were information and technology deserts. People turned to newspapers and newsletters and, unfortunately, listened to conservative talk radio shows. For corporations and national organizations, email and talk radio were ideological funnels. They stoked voters' hatred for government regulation, welfare recipients, immigrants, queers, and anything that would make corporations more profitable and religion more central.

To have any chance of being seen as human in my colleagues' minds, we needed lawmakers to see that queer people lived all over Idaho. Pouring over lists and making phone calls, we started to organize in all corners of the state.

One night, I stood at the door of my annual campaign fundraiser where a queer celebrity panel of judges scored dueling drag queens with numbered placards, Olympics-style. It was early and half-costumed queens streaked by in padded girdles, breasts, and hairnets, carrying headdresses and whole racks of perfumed props and gowns. Out on a balcony by the cash box, I greeted people and offered up my elaborate sign-up sheet with its million tiny check boxes.

"I'll just sign up for all of it," said a woman with straight white-blond hair and long eyelashes. She picked up a pen and introduced herself as Mistie Tolman, saying she'd been wanting to meet me.

Mistie was a political science student, a young mom to four kids, and a many-times-removed descendant of LDS prophet Joseph Smith. She and her partner joined what I called our "Safe Schools Fair Employment Working Group." Mistie matched me in optimism and dedication. She grew essential to my sense of hope as we strategized how to win new votes and prevent the House and Senate from again deep-sixing our bill.

Winning the support of conservatives was now our only option. Marking off names in my legislative directory, I made rounds of the offices, introducing Mistie and others when I could. I wrote no one off. I tried to persuade Senator Fulcher, the manicured Christian who'd just joined Republican leadership. He was kind and polite but wasn't going to help. I visited new Republican members and longtime colleagues from the LDS and Tea Party camps. Some of them took time and shared stories about gay family members.

By my count, I nearly had the votes I needed on the floor of the Senate and a promising half of the House. It was a problem, but I believed, not a huge one, that the head of the Senate, president pro tem Bob Geddes, was a hard no.

That December, when lawmakers were back in the Capitol for presession caucuses, I pushed hard to elect towering fellow Senator Edgar Malepeai as our Senate Democratic caucus chair. Caucus chair was like a whip, the wrangler for our minority leader. Edgar was a government teacher. His family was from Samoa. I would grow to admire him deeply as he spent that year tasked with disciplining me for our Democratic minority leader.

"Shit," I'd whisper, getting a text from Edgar.

He needed to meet with me. Often it sounded urgent.

One time I accidentally outed a candidate from Pocatello in the *New York Times*. Other times I upset Democratic or, one time, Republican leadership, and it was Edgar's job to scold me and make me promise never to do whatever it was again.

He and I would walk out of the statehouse at the end of the day, have a glass of wine near the Capitol, and I'd apologize. My transgressions were generally not things I'd ever need to repeat. Edgar would nod, almost apologetic himself, and we'd move on to other things. I loved him dearly.

Before session started that year, deep in the Capitol, I fidgeted on my side of Senator Davis's desk in his new two-room office suite off the curved hallway that circled the Senate chamber. Around the room, well-dusted items were arranged at ninety degrees in relation to each other. The building the senator had spent three years remodeling was now grand. The marble gleamed. In the committee rooms, elevated platforms would hold lawmakers while those we governed would watch from seats below. New hallways led to back exits and private elevators built to let us skirt lobbyists, constituents, and the media.

Across the desk, Senator Davis smiled, still trying to look stern. "Why should we include gender identity in the law?" he asked. From his tone, this felt like a lesson, practice for something I needed to be ready for.

My strategy to that point had been to pair the terms "gay" and "transgender" in every sentence, as if they were one word, inviting no questions.

I thought about the press release I'd written and faxed out with Emilie Jackson-Edney earlier that year. In it I described gender as a spectrum, not a set of two boxes. Mistie, Emilie, and a group of us gathered downtown at noon when the sidewalk cafes were full. We donned a memorable lineup of beards, skirts, buzz cuts, and wigs. Together we embodied a span of human concepts of self, a sort of gender gamut as we claimed pavement between life-sized cardboard cutouts of Barbie and GI Joe. Shoulder to shoulder, twenty of us spelled out how closely we identified with stereotypes of butch and fem. Carol and I jostled for spots in the dead center.

I wrote a gender identity quiz and added it to my website.

Our now liberal, queer city framed in the window behind him, Senator Davis scowled. I fumbled trying to answer his question succinctly. He seemed to have been pondering the question himself. He wondered if one could simply decide a law applied to only part of a community. He seemed not to parse queers into gay and transgender. He talked about gender identity much the way the Supreme Court would, nearly a decade later. In 2020, gay people, the court would suggest, were not fired typically because of the idea we slept with someone of the same sex, but more broadly because our behavior, relationships, and often our appearance "defied gender norms."

Footsteps and voices rose in the hallway behind me. I could see Senator Davis's secretary at her desk through the open door. In so many words, the senator was saying, sexual orientation and gender identity were interconnected. Leaving one identity out of our bill as some argued we should, legally would leave most of us on the tracks to be hit by the train.

He wasn't finished.

"I think you'll hear it, so I'll tell you first," he said. I watched his face as he spoke. "I told constituents at a meeting in Idaho Falls I supported including gay people in the law. A reporter was there."

I stared at the eyes below his dark brows, trying to gauge hidden meaning. He was so stern but I'd seen him take hugs from the uniformed pages, had seen him smile when he was caught being generous or kind. This was not a joke, not a test. The story had run in the Idaho Falls paper. He wanted me to know.

A tension that had eaten at me for over a decade fell loose. My eyes filled. I pictured the day I'd first met him, his words from the black chaise to me and to Ollie, "I am your worst enemy." His voice had dipped then, as if, for the first time, he'd met evil incarnate. "On this issue . . . your worst enemy, your *worst*."

When Bart Davis voted with us, others would follow. That year we would have an opening to pass our bill, at last.

Weeks later, beneath manicured lawns, the Senate committee corridor echoed. Layers of whisper ran under lines of skylights.

"I can't," Tim said looking down at his strong hands, shaking his head.

Senator Tim Corder was my dear friend, the one who'd debated against me on marriage, whose surviving friend from Vietnam was gay.

I needed Tim as a cosponsor. He'd presented our bill artfully two years earlier in Chairman McKenzie's committee.

I looked at him, some part of me mirroring the way he shook his head slowly from side to side. I wasn't sure what he'd said.

The opening gavel had fallen. Partisan camps had gone to their corners once again to caucus and map their agendas for the three months ahead.

Deep in the white marble, I had an office for the first time, one of the few windowless ones, and I'd set about decorating it, hanging photos and bringing in the disco ball that had hung over the Women's Night events I'd organized when Carol and I first met. That ball made me smile. It had hung in the air, flashing light over more years of fem romance and queer love than probably any object in the state. And it now sat lit on my desk, decorating the walls and ceiling with little squares of light.

In the hallway, the echo pressed at us. Tim looked up from his hands again and I sensed I didn't want to hear what was coming next.

"I can't do it this year," he said.

Fear hummed behind my eyes. "What do you mean?" I asked.

He was my hardest working ally, the one who talked problems through with me, kept tabs on other sponsors, stuck with me when I grew frustrated or failed to understand the difference between a person's belief and their willingness to vote to support that belief. I couldn't lose Tim.

"I just can't this year. I can't sponsor."

I stared at him. Of all people this made no sense. "Why?"

"I just can't."

"You have to tell me. What happened? What do you mean?"

"I can't tell you. Stop asking." He looked down again. "I'm sorry."

I had drafted the legislation listing four Senate Republican cosponsors and four Senate Democrats. I'd listed Bill Roden, a deeply respected former Senate Republican leader. He had helped author our Human Rights Act decades before. He would agreed to be the proposal's main sponsor and contact person. He'd present the bill in committee.

Months earlier, Joe Stegner, Tim, and two other Republicans had been willing to put their names on the bill. One was white-haired Senator Andreason. The previous year, as leadership moved to the right, Andreason told me he didn't care what they did to him: I should list him as a sponsor. I did.

Now the session had begun, and when I went to his office, Andreason looked at me, head up, eyes unblinking. Like Tim, he said he wasn't able to sponsor. Suddenly, he was no longer a yes.

"Why?" I said.

"We can't." Again, the old senator didn't blink. Eyes wide, he just stared at me.

We, I thought. *We*.

What deal had been cut? I had the votes in committee, perhaps even the votes on the floor. After years of work, I had Davis and McKenzie's support and now it seemed suddenly my sponsors, every one of the Senate Republicans, were barred from adding their names and supporting the bill.

Even Bart became evasive and stern. This would be an election year. Every two years was an election year. As a sort of consolation, he said to me, "Next year will be better. You can try then."

Sitting in his office in the child-sized chair across the desk from him, I cried. I tried to reason. I grew stern. I raised my voice. But I'd become invisible again. They all needed not to see me. I wandered from committee to committee making pointless motions, stabbing at what, I didn't know.

That year, 2010, was the year after Arizona's legislature passed the most outrageous of anti-immigration laws. Businesses boycotted their state. Courts intervened. In the interim, anyone brown enough to look even vaguely like they might fit stereotypes of "undocumented" or "illegal" lived in fear of police and their neighbors.

At a backyard party, immigration attorney Maria Andrade's dark eyes shone in the firelight. She shook her head. "We'll be next," she said. "You watch. They'll bring that bill here."

I nodded. Idaho, we all feared, was about to bend to the national wind, enter that era of racial profiling, detaining people at random—coworkers, classmates, passers-by—without process or cause. It would be terrorism in legislative form, a bill meant to make a state inhospitable, meant to apply to one group of people and drive them into hiding or over the state's borders, away.

But by some miracle, in the months that followed, not a single proposal on immigration appeared on any agenda in Idaho's House or Senate. Not a sign of those ideas from our state legislature, the lawmaking body that was, increasingly, the first or second to push the envelope of cruelty—the first to pass the latest nick in *Roe v. Wade*, the latest expansive twist in the Second Amendment. We could be counted on to trot out the American Legislative Exchange Council's extreme corporate and religious playbooks, to draft whatever was most environmentally damaging, misogynistic, or marginally constitutional.

I have no way of knowing what deals were made in the caucus meeting the Republican senators held when the session started that year. Why wouldn't Republican friends tell me if their caucus had cut a deal? If it were true, it was a violation of the constitution, which specifically prohibits one party alone—the majority party in this case—from deciding the outcome of lawmaking from behind closed caucus doors.

A summer passed. The next year, in 2011, those same Republicans, men I'd counted as friends, shook their heads again. They said one after another they couldn't cosponsor. All of them in the Senate, without exception. Again.

Winter dark still hung in the sky above the Capitol. In the budget committee room, high up in the building off the central dome, twenty of us sat on our elevated stage behind our polished desks and microphones. High on the wall, a new ornate clock ticked.

Shirley and I sat in a row with a handful of Republicans and two other Democrats. As just four out of the committee's twenty members, it was painful for us to make policy there. I missed the tax committee in the House and how, once, we had debated outright and voted for what was fair. Privatization was taking hold. Now, glossy magazines and weekly newspapers flowed into our mailboxes from think tanks in Colorado and DC, even one from the Democratic Leadership Council, a tool of monied interests who argued that Democrats should embrace corporate solutions. What I once loved about the nuance of the legislature—the exchange of perspectives and possibility that the best ideas might win—was slipping away.

A seat on the gleaming dais of the high budget committee was coveted. Every hour in that place was counted out by the soundless tick, tick, tick, and the growing drip, drip, drip of millions of taxpayer dollars as they shifted from preventing emergencies to increasing the comfort of those who seemed to need it least.

Occasionally, a group of us went rogue and killed a budget, like the one for the state lottery. One day we debated the fate of the entire Women's Commission, an office staffed by a single individual. That person's role was to collect data and submit an annual report to Governor Otter on the state of women, suggesting how legislation and government spending could better serve that half of the population.

On that day, I voted yes, and together with eleven other ayes, the Idaho's Women's Commission ceased to exist. In the decade to follow, as a pandemic raged and religious extremists forced women and girls into pregnancy, no one in state government—no one—would track the decline in women's pay, the increasing burden of childcare and home schooling, the disproportionate number of unhoused women, the suicides, and the numbers of teenage mothers.

And that was a simple budget.

I was expected to work on complex budgets and grew to know too well the consequences of cutting them: pollution monitoring would cease, caseloads for probation officers and social workers would grow, meal programs would be gutted, teachers would be buried in overflowing classrooms, people would wait in police stations instead of finding treatment for whatever mental health struggles, whatever use, abuse, or addiction problem they needed help getting out of.

During these budget meetings, I had nowhere to go but to sit watching the committee—sometimes even those in my own party—vote yes, because tax cuts never left enough money to serve everyone. By my second year assigned to that committee, I'd fully draped myself over that guillotine many times with no effect.

When a budget passed through our hands, it moved to the Senate floor.

I'd stand at my microphone, waiting to be acknowledged, knowing I'd feel dishonest sitting quietly, even one time when I knew what our choices were and who had been expendable with each shift in the numbers, each tick of the clock.

Standing at the dais in the center of the Senate, Brad Little, with his perfect head of hair and sharp eyes, would raise his head to meet my gaze. Once leader of the struggle against our state's marriage ban, he himself had once sprayed the Senate with pointed projectiles that few seemed to recognize as anything but questions. But he didn't debate bills anymore. As the years passed and he became governor, increasingly, he would choose to comply.

From the dais he said, "Senator LeFavour."

I pulled the microphone toward me, its thin, black, flexible arm bent, the foam cover grazing my lower lip. "Mr. President, to debate the bill."

By rote, Lieutenant Governor Brad Little, serving as president of the Senate would answer back, "The lady may proceed."

The lady. Sometimes that was funny.

"Good senators," I might argue, "Today, I ask you to consider the consequences as our state again fails in providing enough mental health and substance abuse treatment for those in crisis. . . . This bill means fewer treatment beds, longer waiting lists, more overdoses, more incarceration, family loss, and despair. Cuts mean more people wind up in our prison system, costing the state more, not less, per day. . . . Good ladies and gentlemen, we can vote no, go back and provide greater support, or vote yes and decide this loss of lives is acceptable."

Here, Senator Davis might rise, or I might be gaveled by the Senate president for lack of decorum. From the floor, legislators are never supposed to do so much as suggest our colleagues are intentionally doing harm.

Unlike battles and debate in the House, the Senate's formal procedures made it so that every time I made convincing debate against a bill, Senator Davis would rise and ask the Senate to take a break and "go at ease." Then Democratic and Republican Leadership might huddle with the bill's sponsor. Sometimes Bart would motion with his finger, and I, as an opponent of the bill being considered, would stand with the knot of formally dressed senators to one side of the dais, asked to help decide how we should proceed.

Frequently millions of dollars rode on one bill. One time we were debating loosening regulations on nursing homes. I nearly killed the bill, nearly had the votes to stop it. Nearly. But then Senator Davis moved we go at ease.

Again and again, Bart would make motions to delay a vote on imperiled bills before us and lobbyists would be gifted with a day or two to twist arms or pepper senators with niceties and junk statistics so the legislation would pass.

This was Senator Davis's job. The pillar of power he stood on required it. Besides his conscience, he had other masters.

Day after day, my eyes would scan the room of senators and I'd begin again to describe the costs, the losses, the crisis, first in one budget, and then, ten minutes later, in the next. Some days my caucus voted with me, and other days I was asking just too many nay votes from them. The rain was falling and their powder wouldn't stay dry.

Gun powder, I guess. We each had only so many bullets as well. I roamed that place then with an empty firearm, my powder so sodden that having bullets wouldn't have done me any good anyway.

Besides Edgar, who truly saw me, my caucus in their frustration often caused me pain. I could have left to escape what I now saw was the nature of power. I could have offered my seat to someone else, given others a chance to run for the glorious Senate. But I had two bills, one on bullying and the other to include us in the Human Rights Act. I couldn't leave until the Supreme Court or those in DC solved our queer rights problem—or until I'd passed both into law.

So, when March came, I filed papers and I ran for a second Senate term.

15
BODY

2011

Boise, Idaho

That next December I had surgery. Carol's insurance covered the radical breast reduction, one so extreme that when I lost weight, my doctor panicked, scolding that I wouldn't have enough "mass" left in my double D cups to make the procedure "medically necessary."

Carol and I stood in the brightly painted yellow kitchen in our same old creaking house.

"I'm going to get my breasts hacked off," I said grinning, repeating the phrase, bouncing. "Hacked off."

After the string of appointments we endured, suddenly Carol sounded uncomfortable. "Yours can't be smaller than mine."

Those words seemed to suggest that our breasts had some subtle relationship to our gender roles, to our relationship to each other. I would have never guessed.

"You won't leave me, will you?"

I heard sorrow somewhere in the lilt of those words. The question seemed so odd, so unrelated to anything to do with breasts or surgery. Why ask that?

"Of course not," I said, not even vaguely contemplating how much Carol saw of my layers of self-hatred, my disgust with my body, and how changing its shape might change me.

Oblivious, I pulled Carol into a long hug.

The post-surgery did not go smoothly. As soon as I got home, the mass of stitches where my left breast had been turned a sort of orange color. The tissue, pocked like a grapefruit, swelled tight—the breast seeming to grow back with a sort of twisted humor. It began to burn with fever and ache.

This meant I had to endure weeks of antibiotics through an IV and a Sunday office procedure with no attending office staff or assistant. This lack of staff meant Carol had to hold clamps and bits of surgical tubing for an hour while I protested loudly over failures in sterile technique. The surgeon stuck a drain tube into an open portion of the wound on my chest.

Daily, I walked from committee, out of the Capitol, to sit with chemotherapy patients. Barely grateful—as I should have been—I'd walk back to the Capitol, climbing up through the rotunda to debate and vote on the Senate floor. Soon the swelling stopped and my skin faded to the pale flabby white I was used to.

Representative Hagadorn stopped me in the circular hall that rings the Senate chamber. "Is everything OK?" he asked.

"I'm fine," I said grinning, not able to register the concern in his tone. "Why do you ask?"

The representative's eyes darted downward from my face, his brown goatee pointing.

"Your physique," he said, "has changed."

Because it was my nature or maybe because I chose to ignore their gazes, I had, for eight years, believed my colleagues didn't notice my breasts.

Yes, now I had no breasts. With my hair as short as it mostly had been since college, I was smooth and muscular from early morning kick boxing, water aerobics, and running. In my zigzag through gender, I was happiest mixing skirts and military shoes, layered black shirts, ranch coats, and jeans. The more delicate or feminine my dress and heels were, the more this felt like I was doing drag.

When I wore a dress to a queer bar, drag queens sometimes admired my cleavage, or maybe my stature, broad shoulders, narrow waist, and queen-sized feet.

Sometimes they called after me, "Hey, Gorgeous."

I'd get a kiss on the cheek, feel the muscles of their arms or the press of the stiff foam projectiles on their chests.

On this particular night, the bar blazed. Bandages under my white tank top and blue checked shirt seemed to dissolve. I lifted myself over the discomfort, over the pain detectors in my mind.

Lights shifted color, blinking across the span of tall Formica tables and bodies on the dance floor. I looked down and flexed inside the smoothness of my chest. Finally, I was rid of those two artifacts, those lumbering signposts for a gender I'd only ever half committed to.

The pearl snaps on my shirt pressed on my flesh. I stepped to cross the crowded floor, headed for another tonic water. I felt warmth, a body behind me, the brush of someone dancing. I spun to find a gay man I'd known for years.

He swung his hand around and pinched my ass. "Cute," he shouted back over his shoulder turning away.

Gay men in their flirting were hands-on. Other men with their own flat chests brushed past. On all sides, dancing couples blurred. My mind sparked. I thought I'd arrived. The moment exquisite, my body buzzed. I felt a happy blurring of the lines of sexuality and gender that fit me.

I'd never been much of one for visual attraction. I was more tactile. It seemed from memory I'd not exactly found men unattractive. I'd simply never been able to function in relationships with them. And I'd never met straight men's expectations of me, a person they very much saw as a woman.

I'd soon turn forty-eight. The eleven years with Carol were a testament to how much happier I was with someone I shared a gender with. Carol and I agreed how lucky we were, how we wanted to grow old together. Though I'd once wanted children, the desire had faded into the peace of being with Carol. I worried, too, about my incapacities. Inside the idea of children, I still saw ducklings floating.

To succeed in the Senate, I'd spent six years struggling to be sexless and yet just feminine enough, just neutral enough not to visually remind people I was queer. I needed their minds to focus on my words and the harm we faced, not on bodies in bedrooms.

It was absurd for me to expect that was possible. Still, the simultaneous invisibility and attention-getting was exhausting. I pressed at using other legislators, young activists, parents, couples, and trans friends as conduits for messages. Whether that was succeeding, I still didn't know.

At home, Carol often recoiled from me, from the emotional unpredictably as I showed up from the Capitol each night. It was impossible to know what might trigger me to frantic telephone calls, running to my computer, cursing, or crying on the bed in our room.

Many days, Carol knew better than I did what happened in the Capitol because it was possible to watch the floor sessions—our votes and debate—through a video feed online. I always smiled after getting texts with the answer to a question Shirley or some seatmate or opponent had asked or after seeing a little text bubble telling me "Good job, babe" when I battled for or against a bill.

When we were apart, the two of us texted all day. Our lives were that entwined, that beautiful.

But the house had to be lonely and the job of being my spouse more than one of patience. I wasn't the one who did laundry or dishes. We cooked together on weekends when I wasn't at legislative outings, but my absence in everything to do with keeping a house or maintaining finances, bills, mortgage, and care for aging cats and our new puppy, Kaza, fell entirely to Carol.

And I hardly noticed. The one task I'd promised to do, cleaning the toilet and shower, meant I would let colonies of orange algae begin to grow in the corners of the shower stall. For a time, the toilet bowl, too, would take on organic hues.

When Carol got frustrated and took on a task that was mine, we'd argue. I'd feel I had no chance to do a job I'd offered to do and was being shamed. I grew angry, believing I deserved more time, insisting that Carol was playing martyr.

At the same time, inside me, daily in the Capitol, my skin was expected to contain what had become a feverish rumble of voices and stories. Since the day I'd been elected, I'd become a repository of them.

If there was queer tragedy, people came to me—from the street, in pages of handwritten letters, at all hours through my cell phone. Rural residents, professionals, transgender prisoners, parents, and those who'd lost some essential part of life—whether it was a job, a rental house, or a sense of belonging or purpose—somehow they found me. And I let them because what other part of state government could they call? I posted my cell phone number publicly on my website, on my literature.

"Is this Senator LeFavour?"

I'd scramble for paper.

Some stories I couldn't share because doing so could cost someone their job, make a target of them.

If Republican leadership was going to keep killing our bill, drowning it quietly in the statehouse toilets, I had to stand up and keep walking, find new ways to bring queer voices into the Capitol.

16

ADD THE WORDS

2011–2012

Idaho State Capitol, Boise

My boot heels clicked the marble floor of the Senate's underground committee wing. In one hand I held a stack of sticky notes, each with a written message to Chairman McKenzie from a different person. I needed to hurry.

Stuck to my finger, one little note read: "Senator McKenzie, It's time for your committee to hear some new voices and the reality they tell. Please schedule a hearing on S1033." I pasted the message to the committee room door.

Senate Bill 1033 was our latest nondiscrimination bill. At the start of the session, Edgar and I tried a seldom-used back door for getting our language into bill form. We filed our draft with the Senate secretary as a "personal bill," a bill that could escape a pro tem's culling process. Our draft was given a bill number, listed on the website, and printed by Legislative Services for reporters and the public to read.

The problem was that the bill was doomed. The whole backdoor process brought on a procedural curse. With few exceptions, personal bills like these died quiet deaths, never given public hearings and never debated on camera for public TV's legislative feed. At least, though, we now had a bill and a bill number. Public pressure was mounting. If we could force a public hearing, I felt sure SB1033 could be passed into law.

Edgar, elected as the new leader of Senate Democrats, had agreed to be our sponsor. With his name on it, SB1033 was now sitting in Senator

McKenzie's State Affairs Committee where it might stay until the end-of-session gavel fell.

Trans leader Emilie Jackson-Edney, soft-spoken and supremely sensitive to following the rules, had met with lawmakers for nearly a decade and was done coloring inside the lines. She wasn't alone. Mistie, several older lesbians, faith leaders, gay men, and students had plotted with Carol and me. They'd be the face of the bill and would push the Senate in dignified ways to earn public sympathy. They'd be very hard to ignore.

I knew better than to think it was Senator McKenzie's decision whether a bill was heard. We'd begun addressing our the notes to him because I needed him to push back, needed him to hate the attention and argue with Republican leadership for a hearing.

I hoped to fade into the background of the Senate, let Senator Davis and Republican leadership feel the press of bodies other than my own. Every day, Carol, Emilie, a student, or another volunteer would slip into the Capitol underground beneath the skylights. They'd wait for the committee hallway to empty and then quickly stick a handful of notes to Chairman McKenzie's door.

That day, my Senate colleagues were at lunch. With the building feeling vacant, I'd snuck away from my desk hoping to deliver the day's batch of notes to the glass of the committee room door. Charlie, the tall, sweet-faced security guard, saw me. He stood up from his desk and started slowly down the hall. It was his job to stop me—to stop all of us—to peel notes from the glass and make the words go away.

One eye on Charlie, I heard another set of footsteps from somewhere. I turned to see Senator Davis walking toward me from the other end of the corridor. What we did violated Senate rules. We didn't care. Our, notes flowed every day. People dropped them off or came to my office, borrowed pens, and wrote them.

I stuck another three-inch square to the glass. Each was handwritten from a different person. The strategy wasn't winning me friends in Senate leadership on either side of the aisle. We'd sent out press releases about our campaign and our bill. This created tension, good tension.

Fumbling with my phone, I tried to get photos of McKenzie's door covered with the sticky notes, hurrying before Charlie could step in and take them away. Senator Davis hung at the edge of my vision, completing his casual amble down the hall. The senator was the enforcer of rules He had so much power and it was a risk making him mad.

But as he neared, Senator Davis smiled. He said, "Charlie, let her do her job." He gestured to me and the messages stuck to the glass panes in the doors. "Let her finish taking her photographs. Then you can take them down."

Outside Senator McKenzie's committee, I eyed the back of Senator Davis's suit as he vanished down the hall.

Standing next to me in his white uniform, Charlie looked down at me and grinned.

I grinned back.

This session again, my Senate sponsors were gagged.

Senator Brent Hill, a supremely moral, white-haired, accountant had become president pro tempore of the Senate. A decade earlier, when first elected, Hill told me he thought firing someone for being gay was wrong. Now he was our most formidable opponent. He seemed tasked with the job of making sure we disappeared.

From the opening of that 2011 session, before we tried coming in through the Senate's back door, Pro Tem Hill made clear there'd be no hearing on any bill to include LGBTQ rights in the law. His committees would take no testimony. Curt, as appointed chairman, was expected to hold our bill in his drawer. A pro tem has the power to give and the power to take away.

For months, we posted sticky notes with handwritten messages and stories on the glass panes of two doors. They stayed until Charlie took them down. When he did, we posted more.

In the second week of March, a carefully neutered bill I wrote to prevent bullying in schools passed the Senate with only three no votes. This bill crossed to the House, where I got it passed out of the House Education Committee. The previous year it had been held there by Education Chair Representative Bob Nonini. This time it escaped but hung for weeks on the House calendar, waiting for a final vote of passage from the whole House so it could become law. But it never got this vote. So there my anti-bullying bill died once again.

And, at the same time, the colored squares of paper kept flowing into the Senate, asking for an end to discrimination and passage of SB1033.

They told stories of isolation and suicide. In my mind, inside every tragedy, lay my failure. This failure became an ache I couldn't stand.

In the hours I was not debating bills in committee or voting on the Senate floor, I lobbied my colleagues. I tried, through Senate procedure, to pull SB1033 from McKenzie's committee to the Senate floor. I worked to force a public debate on the bill's contents. I organized in the community. I tried to negotiate.

The session ended that year and my life trailed behind me like a string of failed motions, failed legislative maneuvers witnessed by statehouse cameras, empty television screens, a cluster of people in the gallery, a Facebook audience of likers, or no one at all.

While some in the queer community gave up, viewing the series of failures as typical of our legislature, I didn't. Mistie didn't. Carol didn't—nor did Emilie Jackson-Edney. Emilie had been misgendered, harassed, and disrespected in the Capitol and, at times, in the community, as she transitioned, retired as an engineer, and worked collecting stories for us. She didn't give up. She spoke to the media and to college classes, laboring to educate the public. She cochaired a new LGBTQ rights organization and just turned the heat up, one notch higher.

As the 2012 session neared, Idaho's Department of Administration issued a rule. Attaching anything, temporary or permanent, to any surface inside the Capitol would be an offense worthy of arrest. A person could even be barred from the Capitol for a year. The media coverage we were getting bothered them. Someone was struggling to shut us down.

The move was good for us. I figured, let them try to arrest or ban one of us for using a sticky note and see how that flew with the media and people of the state.

In August 2011, before the 2012 session began, Mistie freed up time and I trained her as our new spokesperson. She was quick and good at storytelling. She also innately understood the sound bite, knew the tenets of the LDS faith, and was strong, not just with the media but with the Speaker and especially our new and unmovable Senate president pro tem.

"In the LDS faith, being gay rests on a par with adultery and taking the Lord's name in vain," she said. Yet, no one seemed to be asking for laws to turn away adulterers or those spewing expletives. Why did the church need to protect those who refused to serve us? Were they now part of a broader Christian Nationalist movement, or did they have reasons we didn't understand?

In October we all agreed our name—The Safe Schools, Fair Employment Working Group—was long and awkward and we rebranded ourselves simply as Add the Words, Idaho.

I spent late nights setting up a Facebook page, recreating our website and adding links for emailing lawmakers, forms for filling out sticky notes, and a map to let the public track our progress getting messages from every Idaho town. This time we wouldn't politely confine our notes to the Capitol's basement and McKenzie's committee room doors. We'd post them everywhere.

For Halloween, we carved pumpkins with letters that spelled out "Add the Words, Idaho." After dark, we gathered on one side of the bone-chilling Capitol steps and I took one of my favorite photos from those months of work. The carved letters in the lit pumpkins glowed, and Mistie sat with her partner and their four children. Other leaders, Hannah and Finn, held their son. Carol, Emilie Jackson-Edney, my ex Drew, and two other trans men stared into the camera; straight allied leaders Cindy and Chryssa sat in the middle. The steps rose in orange lamplight and the faces shone just slightly in the darkness.

This moment, before the session began, was a moment from a life I would soon leave, from power I'd shred, a part of myself I'd lose.

I stayed out of the photos, which we made public or sent to legislators. My colleagues were tired of my pressing. If we were to press hard—if we were to make constituents and the media ask lawmakers questions, make them uncomfortable—I needed queer, allied, even Republican voices and stories that they couldn't possibly dismiss.

And, too, I was keeping some of my powder dry.

December arrived, cold and bare in Boise. Ice fog settled.

"How many should I get?" I yelled to Carol.

I was trying to order DVDs of the movie *Brokeback Mountain*. I decided on eighty copies.

I always sent holiday cards, thumbing through my address book and the notes in my legislative directory. Most of the lobbyists and lots of lawmakers did. Our cards usually featured a family photo of the two of us, the cat and the dog, at night, with a lit peace sign in the background. We would wish my colleagues "Happy Solstice. A Merry New Year."

Religion was the one topic Carol had reminded me not to talk about, ever, since that first day I climbed the steps to work under the Capitol dome. I'd come to dread that I might say the wrong thing to someone who believed their religion was the one true religion, defining the one true God.

I know faith can give moral guidance, meaning, and hope to those who feel lost or unsure of their purpose in the world. I follow in my family's religious tradition. I am not religious but am guided by compassion and by a love and faith in humanity and nature. To me, the mountains and their wild come as close as anything to god.

Still, I served in a place where I was expected to pray publicly every day. Representative Cherie Buckner-Webb's husband, Hank, was our Senate pastor that year. Hank's Jesus was a fairly gentle one. Cherie was a jazz vocalist in addition to being a well-loved leader. Her connections in the community were deeper than mine. I'd worked to help elect her because I was sure her unwavering conviction and powerful speeches would make the Capitol a better place for all of us. I wasn't wrong.

Cherie came from a family of strong Black leaders who'd braved Idaho through cross burnings and the slow dawning of the civil rights movement. She quoted her mom to me on occasion, especially when I was in some kind of trouble for taking sides in primary elections or applying some sort of unconventional pressure to the Senate or House. "You go, girl," she'd say to me. "As my mama said, 'Disturb the peace. Disturb. The. Peace.'" She'd shake her head and smile.

That December, I didn't send DVDs of *Brokeback Mountain* to everyone. I skipped those I thought it would offend. Offending them wouldn't sway them. Also, I skipped the Democrats because they no longer needed persuading. They were on board and some were deeply involved. With each DVD, I tucked in a carefully folded, personalized note about the film. The closing read, "Watching to the end you will know this is a sadly common Idaho story. We all know young people we hope will never face such sorrow and older people we hope will not die like this alone."

Most members of the Church of Jesus Christ of Latter-day Saints don't watch R-rated movies. As Mistie had pointed out, the church considers adultery, homosexuality, and taking the Lord's name in vain as equally sinful. *Brokeback Mountain* featured all of them, on repeat, in rapid succession, so I included a strip of paper in each envelope, listing the timestamps of the few scenes where sex, nudity, or serious swearing occurred. The only sex scene between Jack and Ennis takes place in the dark of a small tent and the sex is more suggested than seen. The unavoidable sex is between Ennis and his wife.

In the wake of this gift giving, I had weeks of intense conversations with my colleagues. Clearly far more of them had gay children than I'd imagined.

On the Senate floor, tall, soft-eyed Republican Senator Jeff Siddoway held out his copy of the DVD to me. A sheep rancher with large hands, he had guts and gave impassioned speeches about ranging with his herds and how a way of life he loves is vanishing. When not in the Senate chamber, Siddoway wore a gigantic cowboy hat.

The two of us stood in the oddly hushed aisle between our two formal desks. Taking the boxed disc from his hands, I could see the clear plastic seal on the DVD was unbroken.

He looked me in the eye and said, "I raised my children to respect people regardless of their race, religion, or sexual orientation." He didn't even pause on the term "sexual orientation." It was so rare in those chambers that anyone said those words.

I smiled and said, "Jeff, if all parents would raise their kids as you have, we wouldn't need antidiscrimination laws."

Bob Nonini, however, was far less kind. He was quoted in a newspaper saying how offensive it was to him and his wife, Cathyanne, both deeply religious Catholics, to receive such a video as a Christmas gift.

Years later after the pandemic, Cathyanne, in the process of moving to Massachusetts to escape Idaho's extremism, would send me a Facebook message to apologize. Bob, too, after he'd gone through chemotherapy, would later tell me that what mattered to him had changed.

I look back at the place and I think how the power to destroy lives is weak compared to the power to improve them. It is easy to comply with the force of greed. Greed always presses, as does prejudice. What's hard is working against those with material power for the sake of those without it. We gain illusory power the day we are sworn in and given a title. The kind of power we choose makes all the difference.

In 2012 one newspaper roasted me in the "Cheers and Jeers" column. Sending an R-rated movie to Mormon and Christian lawmakers, especially a movie where someone drops the f-bomb in the first five minutes of the film, was seen as a prank done in very poor taste.

In my defense, I wish I could have done it sooner. I'd long been searching for ways to talk beyond policy, to evoke sympathy and give others an understanding of the violence, love, and pain of closeted people in rural places. I could have never sparked the conversations I had that year without *Brokeback Mountain*.

Even Senator Denton Darrington—imposing LDS chairman of the Judiciary Committee and opponent of my sentencing reform bills—told me he'd seen the movie before but was getting his daughter to set up his DVD player so he could watch it again.

Senator Darrington I called friend by then. He was coming around on the use of mental health and substance abuse treatment in place of prison time, but he, the longest serving member and the Senate's master of rules, would announce he was retiring as would Senator Malepeai and a long list of others. By January, when the 2012 session started, Joe Stegner was already gone.

That year, we all had a moment where the votes still hung in the balance. After watching those around me slowly begin to grasp the pain, after hearing them whisper the names of the queer people in their families and acknowledge the forces leveraged against us, there was a chance they'd be brave.

But it felt like it might be a final moment, an opening that would close, leaving us at the mercy of leaders who had crowbars and pliers hanging on their walls, those who had a higher tolerance for inflicting pain.

Boise was becoming more urban and had transformed slowly to a place with gay bars, queer-owned coffee shops, Pride celebrations, lesbian couples, singles, and gay men who'd come home to raise their kids. Counterprotesters no longer showed up at our events with banners reading "The Only Good Queer Is a Dead Queer," as they had in 1996. A beautifully queer ballet company, the Trey McIntyre Project, had based itself in Boise, traveling the world and staging pop-up street theater downtown that was unapologetically diverse and far from straight or White.

As the 2012 session started, in separate meetings with Mistie and me, Senate President Pro Tem Hill told us flatly again that the Human Rights Act proposal would not be heard.

For months, we'd prepared for this. On January 10, the second day of the session, I sat at my desk on the velvet-shrouded Senate floor, struggling to seem casual. Behind me in the entry, that same place where Ollie and I had sat with Senator Davis twelve years earlier, Mistie held a phone camera, recording daring young Cody Haefer, his classic grin fixed, shakily placing sticky notes on the double glass doors in front of the Senate doorkeepers desk.

Mistie and Cody were not in the basement. They were in the foyer to the Senate Chambers. Sweet Charlie was not going to be the one to interrupt them. The Senate's own doorkeeper would.

Pro Tem Hill stood on the central dais in front of me. He led us all through the pledge and the prayer. From where he stood, he could see where Cody stood poised with sticky notes in his hands. In Mistie's shaky video, a state police officer approaches, explaining that her group would be arrested if they posted the notes again.

I hated that I had to be inside in my comfortable seat. If the laws of the state had let me be arrested with them, I would have been. I knew arrests would shine light on how long we'd waited. It would let Mistie talk into cameras about the harm and the Senate's refusal to allow even a hearing on our bill.

The next day, the two came back with more sticky notes, but the police didn't come. Pro Tem Hill—or more likely Senator Davis, as the Republican Party's leader and strategist—seemed to hope to ignore us. They understood that arrests would draw attention to the Senate—far more attention than overlooking the rules they'd written to keep our sticky notes from intruding on their peace.

So, in the weeks that followed, instead of limiting our notes to the Senate Chambers, we took photos of them on glass doors all over the inside of the Capitol. On January 28, for the second year in a row, we held a weekend of rallies and vigils in small towns and cities. This time, thousands gathered, half of them wading into the Capitol with their own notes asking lawmakers to "Add the Words."

By then, every lawmaker knew what "Add the Words" meant. They'd seen the hundreds of Facebook posts, the news stories. They knew it meant expanding our state Human Rights Act to let our Human Rights Commission accept complaints of discrimination—not just on the basis of race, sex, religion, age, and disability but on the basis of four new words, "sexual orientation" and "gender identity" as well.

February began, and in spite of Pro Tem Hill's clear message in January that there'd be no public hearing, no bill to "Add the Words," Chairman McKenzie scheduled not a hearing but a first vote of introduction on that year's proposal.

On the draft I'd listed Senator Edgar Malepeai as the only sponsor.

The time for a doomed "personal bill" had passed. We needed the Senate to vote.

The night before the vote to print our draft, Edgar and I walked a block down Eighth Street from the Capitol to strategize. Unless the committee asked questions, no one but Edgar would be allowed to speak.

"Write it out for me," Edgar said. "Tell me what you want me to say."

In the dark bar, I took a sip of my wine. "I'll do that and I'll send something extra to use only if it all goes to hell."

That night I texted him a string of points, parts of a speech.

"Hell, yeah," Representative Cherie Buckner-Webb said when I asked her to add her name as a cosponsor. Cherie was still in her first term. She was not someone who needed great guidance speaking for queer people. She had always asked questions and understood it all, even the subtleties.

Senator Tim Corder, kind and brave as before, agreed to put his name back on the sponsor list. I could see the defiance mixed with worry in his eyes. In the next election, this favor to me, to our queer community, this bow to friendship and to justice, would cost him his election and seat in the Senate.

Edgar and I stood by the legislative stage of the Senate's Lincoln Auditorium, a three-hundred-seat room, guarded by a metal bust of quietly queer and emancipating President Abe. The gavel hadn't fallen yet so the room was loud, every seat filled, the walls lined with others standing, all pressing for the committee to allow us to testify.

In a green two-piece skirt and suit jacket, hair short and carefully gelled, I fidgeted. "I think the chairman will vote with us," I told Edgar, referring to Senator McKenzie.

Standing next to me, Edgar was somber. We needed three Republican yes votes. My optimism is boundless.

"I spoke with the chairman," he said quietly, grabbing my shoulder and gently giving it a squeeze. "Not good."

I looked up at him and realized I was shaking. This was all I had. There was no other path for changing the law.

I took a front seat in the audience with Carol. Scattered through the room were people we'd prepared in case the vote went badly. Like me, they were hopeful. People do not last long in resistance and organizing if they can't find reason for hope, cannot see some path forward.

Edgar rose to the podium knowing we were all about to fall.

In his dark suit, white shirt, and tie, his voice was deep. He said, "This legislation is very simple. It just adds the terms 'sexual orientation' and 'gender identity' to Idaho's Human Rights Act so the commission can investigate, mediate, and make findings in cases of alleged discrimination."

He asked for the Senate's determination to do what was right, began reading from what I'd written, the part he was supposed to use if things went terribly wrong.

> It would be profoundly disrespectful not to afford those tens of thousands of families affected by this legislation the decency of printing the bill. We owe to those who know and love their gay family members and friends to take this issue seriously and allow them to speak about the harm they see being done each day in Idaho without the voice of the state finally saying that discrimination is wrong.

He paused, looking down, clearing his throat, surely feeling the weight of the force he pushed against.

But the committee just sat. Not a single senator asked a question.

Chairman McKenzie asked the senators to vote.

No one remembered to ask for a roll call so what we heard was just a voice vote, an uncounted little chorus of ayes and then louder nays. I tried to pick the sound of Senator Davis's voice from the chorus but couldn't.

Around me in the auditorium, hundreds of gay people, trans friends and their friends, parents, business owners, students, staff, and interns leaned forward toward the committee, waiting.

Pale-faced, his chairman's gavel in his hand, McKenzie looked out across the auditorium and down again. He said, "The nays have it. The motion fails."

At that moment a window closed. I'd expected more, some debate, some reason, some justification, some words to say why we were being turned away, left to cower in jobs and apartments, in shops and schools—for how long I couldn't know.

As much as hope is a thing of my blood, we had all discussed beforehand what we'd do if the committee voted no. I stood from my seat, didn't wait for the gavel to adjourn the committee or for them to rise. Striding to the front of the room, I pulled a sticky note from my pocket. Carol, Mistie, Emilie, and the rest of the room followed me. The response felt punny, but it was better than sitting there, accepting what had just been done.

Tears pooling in my eyes, I swallowed, stuck my note to the long dais that my colleagues sat behind. In his tan suit, moving to leave by the back hall, the Senate's youngest senator, John McGee, looked ashamed. Bart Davis was stern on the outside; underneath, I don't know.

More than fifty of us still in the auditorium started flowing into the skylit hall. That day, in front of McKenzie's committee room, we put in motion a part of our Add the Words movement, a gesture that would grow and multiply like the sticky notes had.

In tears, Emilie, tall and furious, then Mistie, young Cody, and twenty others pulled off coats and sweaters, uncovering black shirts that read "Add the Words, Idaho." Together they stood along the underground hall where the light blazed from above and the marble gleamed. Each one held one hand up, palm flat to cover their own mouth.

Seeing that gesture—all those hands held over mouths, repeated over and over down the hallway into the distance—made me feel as if an arrow had been sent into the heart of the Senate's silence, into the invisibility they wanted from us.

It was an answer, a calling out of the hushing I'd felt since I first arrived there as a thirty-four-year-old, wandering under the gray-blue dome with its painted stars, sitting with Senator Davis and Ollie, thinking I could change minds.

PART 3

FORGIVENESS

17
FLATTERY

2012, MARCH

Boise, Idaho

Alone in the Capitol, seated at my computer in my basement office, body wrapped in the speckled light of the Women's Night disco ball, I had to decide if I would stay or go.

What we'd been doing still wasn't enough.

"I need to leave so I can do more than sit here while we slip backward," I said to Mistie and others.

We had pressed at the door of civil disobedience. Republican leadership had resisted arresting any of us. They hesitated to take that step. House and Senate leaders knew arrests in the Capitol would not look good. It would bring questions down on them, questions they didn't want to answer.

The constituents of my district said they wanted me to stay. I could do that, keep the title and the honor of serving them. I could remain a well-behaved paragon of self-restraint and debate forever against the losses. I could swallow into myself every bit of pain the building was sending outward and turn it into fuel to build something stronger.

I feared that my leaving would signal failure. At the same time, I didn't believe I could stand to stay. I didn't think I could sit there another year crying uselessly in the budget committee or listening to Senator Davis say, "Next year."

I couldn't gather Republican sponsors for a bill that would put targets on their chests and hurt their chances of being reelected. I couldn't *again* convince my community a bill would be heard—if we only pushed hard enough, if we only posted enough sticky notes, sent enough email, organized big enough rallies, and waited patiently for the leaders of the Senate to hear us.

I didn't believe it anymore, didn't believe Senator Davis's promises. I had no space left for more pain. I couldn't promise to my own queer community that if we continued to do things the same way, we'd make progress, get a hearing and an up-or-down vote.

But leaving meant giving up a seat in the only lawmaking body of our state. It meant leaving government, existing again outside it, without access and membership to that club. I'd spent decades patiently trying every strategy. I'd brought thousands in from the outside. I'd earned powerful cosponsors. Still, with each step forward, forces from outside seemed to grow more entwined with the force of religion inside the pro tem's office.

Both our state and the US Constitution were supposed to protect all of us from having to live under other people's religions. Our state founders, like Lincoln, argued for a government of, by, and for the people. Inside political parties and their efforts to battle for power, all that ink was growing faint, obscured by the pain of crowbars and pliers. I needed conscience to matter.

I sent out a press release announcing my departure.

Under the dome, I stood in my formal coat and senator's badge. In the heat of the flood lights, I answered questions. My reflection pooled in cameramen's eyes.

Later, at the local public radio station, I sat with the female anchor. Soberly, she asked, "How do you want to be remembered?"

It was as if I was being asked to comment on my own passing. I wasn't sure what to say.

There was no retirement party. No roast. Nothing to celebrate.

I had failed also at the most significant and powerful relationship of my life. I'd failed at being Carol's partner, lover, person, the one who'd wake up, roll over, stare into those eyes, make a comment related to nothing, wait for the wit, the honesty, until we both laughed.

Months earlier, we'd stopped laughing.

I had packed a sleeping bag and was sleeping in odd places. I ran from fights of my own making. What was left of me was thin and flighty.

Some in the community were angry. I was terrified they'd believe I was giving up. What I struggled to explain was my feeling that a person cannot organize civil disobedience from a place of safety—removed from the risk of being handcuffed and arrested—alongside those they are urging to take that risk.

The TV camera lights went dark, the Capitol heavy and cold. I packed boxes. It was time to give up my lone voice, time to work so I could join the many. I had to figure out how to return in a way lawmakers could not step around, could not look away from, could not restrain themselves from arresting. I needed us to come back in a way they couldn't ignore.

It was flattery that made me run for Congress.

That year, I ran the long hall of the Capitol's first floor, rushing to make the filing deadline, running to submit my petition to the secretary of state before the doors closed and the 2012 campaign season was on.

Years earlier, I'd weighed out a run for Larry Craig's open US Senate seat. It might have been poetic. The polling said my name recognition was positive and strong but the race wasn't winnable—for any Democrat.

Six years probably hadn't changed much, but the loveliness of flattery made me tell myself I had something to prove, that my years of talking on issues into cameras translated into trust, that the state's huge block of unaffiliated libertarian independents and Mormon women would flow my way in the privacy of the voting booth.

My opponent in the second of Idaho's two congressional districts was Congressman Mike Simpson, a powerful long-serving moderate who'd voted against the Lilly Ledbetter Fair Pay Act and balanced his moderate votes and support for designated wilderness with rhetoric and decisions that were far from moderate. He pandered to our state's new closed primary election laws that built walls around the Republican Party's ability to install extremists and control the outcome of elections.

I knew campaigns. I would not have run if, in my own mind, I didn't have a path to win. I hired the best staff I knew, our media director from No On One, along with Rialin Flores, one of our most wise and hardworking young organizers from Add the Words. I found a scheduler who was a Spanish speaker and had worked for the census. She understood me and made me laugh.

Still, no Democrat had won a statewide election in my half of the state since our superintendent of schools nine years earlier. National forces had designated us a political wasteland, a red state to be left to itself, tilting ever more steeply toward industrial and restrictive religious control, festering in the center of our vaguely united states. The seat I was running for hadn't been held by a Democrat for twenty years. I didn't want to waste anyone's money or time, but I thought, if all went the way I hoped it would, I could win.

On paper, I was a good candidate. In the flesh, I was a disaster.

That summer, Boise's rooftop tiki bar served strong, sweet drinks in ceramic cups shaped like Polynesian Gods with oversized heads. I sat on a stool drinking with Meg.

"Did you have sex with him, yet?" she asked.

I looked up from the nautilus shells frozen into the aqua-colored concrete bar. Meg had grown statuesque since high school. She was tall, half an inch taller than I was, also graying. Looking at her, I realized she had the body I once wanted, lithe and small-breasted. Perhaps I removed my breasts to make it my own.

The accident was that my new shape made me remember the boys whose bodies I once envied and the gay men I now half wished I could be. If I were a gay man, the flame I was carrying might really want me. I knew he would. I didn't want to be a man, but at times I wanted male parts, male on male sex. But sex was a distant confusion to me by then.

I looked into the sky above the gay bar two blocks away and I saw myself watching: Bic Lighter circles the dance floor in the strobe lights and pounding music. I watch him pass, imagine him dragging fingertips over men's bare chests and half-clothed crotches.

"He kissed me in an alley," I said to Meg. My eyes were puffy from leaking my disappointment into the ripstop nylon of my sleeping bag. I had left Carol. For months, my sleeping arrangements had been questionable. Of particular note were the nights I'd slept under my campaign office desk and in the dry grass of the foothills. Months later, I'd spend much of late fall squatting in a large house on a cul-de-sac, one of several places I'd sleep, largely unauthorized.

Meg looked at me quizzically.

I whispered, "I was leaving town. He wanted to say goodbye. We stood in a doorway. It was kinda beautiful." I sipped my drink. "But that was a week ago. Now he won't answer my texts."

I had no idea how pitiful I was.

Meg gave me a hug. She was married and had a daughter a bit younger than my niece and nephew. These were the very niece and nephew I had borrowed from Cree twice a year. Soon I'd borrow thousands of dollars to take them to Europe so we could live for a bit in a world of late-night train stations, graffiti art, gondolas, cafes, and monuments to centuries of resistance.

Meg eyed me. During my senior year, she saved me from a lifetime of thinking no one would ever understand me. With her daughter Mira and a cardboard sign, she had appeared at political rallies, had talked to voters in campaign phone banks, had paused in hiking to spend hours obsessively pulling weeds with me, always saying, "Just one more."

Though she and I never ran off into the mountains or a city to have babies and be single parents together, we'd stayed close all those decades since high school. My brain police are good. I do not think about sex with people who wouldn't welcome the idea.

By some twisted hormonal fate, Meg and I both numbered among the women for whom perimenopause caused absurd surges of mind-numbing sexual attraction to men we would have been better off not attracted to.

There at the bar, between the bamboo-filled planters, under the palm thatched roof, I saw Meg had colored her hair a sort of orange-bronze. I myself was wearing some sort of low-cut top that revealed a slice of my brown, toned abs and a sea of the wrinkled skin over my well-pumped pectoral muscles. These were standing in for my lack of actual cleavage.

We were eleven days apart in age and neither of us was aging gracefully. Like two other friends my age, Meg daydreamed about male co-workers, fed younger crushes, and lived for innuendo and flirtation but had stayed completely faithful to her husband in a way I was not to Carol. I had to touch. I had to kiss. I was that pitiful.

Meg raised her eyebrows, shook her head and alluded to the torture inflicted by one man she worked with. "Fucking flirting," she sighed. She sat down and we sipped from the ceramic heads. Frustration burned a pattern at the corners of her eyes.

From my stool, I gave her a sideways hug.

I had left Carol and had begun to careen through the wide unknown of midlife. I could have bought a red sports car or gone home by then, but I did not. I was Meg's trial balloon and, so far, I was sending back signals indicating "code red." I had run off to be free from domestic routine, to embrace the chaos that organizing brings, and to have more sex.

Well over half a year later, I still had not had sex.

Meg and I would be fifty soon. We—two thrill-seeking outdoorsy humans born in the summer of love—would not go quietly into the next decade. Our fiftieth birthdays were looming but there would be no party. We would refuse to celebrate.

Weeks later, I sat stiff in a chair in an office downtown, two blocks from the Capitol. Former Democratic governor Cecil Andrus leaned back, and let his white hair rest against his chair. From the walls of his fourth-floor office, iconic images of him stared out. The governor with a hunting rifle. The governor, turned US secretary of the interior, standing midstream, a fly rod in flight over a wild river.

People who knew him called him Cees. Somewhere I had a little series of endorsement photos of me taken with him when I was newly elected. Democrats were supposed to use them on their literature and websites.

In mine, the governor's expression was uncomfortable, not quite warm.

From his seat, he leveled his stare at me. Answering my question, he said, "No, I won't."

I was doing what every other Idaho Democrat, every real-estate agent, rancher, professor, and railroad man had done in running for higher office since the 1980s. I was asking for his endorsement.

His answer was no. It seemed I was not worthy.

This governor had been pictured and named on the campaign literature of unsuccessful candidate after unsuccessful candidate, running for exactly the same seat I was running for. Most had less experience than I did. I was a sitting senator. I had no scandal associated with my name. My work for the Democratic Party was stellar. The only difference was I was gay.

His face hung. The room got cold. I wished he was joking but he went on. "You won't get thirty percent of the vote."

Of all people, I thought.

"I bet you a beer I will," I said, straining to lighten the mood, to give him an out. Maybe though, I was too practiced at political disappointment. By running, I was doing the party a favor. They struggled to recruit people willing to spend the time and brutal effort to run against the popular Republican moderate I was running against.

The governor was deadpan now. "You should have asked me before you decided to run."

I was too angry to cry. All the way the short block and half back to my campaign office, the office where good human beings would spend nine months pouring their love out into phone calls, backyard events, long nights of data entry, fundraising, door knocking, and still more phone calling—all the way back to that office—I was too pissed to even contemplate weeping.

Not even 30 percent? The Democrat who'd run two years earlier had earned 24 percent. Four years earlier, the real-estate agent he'd endorsed had earned 29 percent. I was running in a presidential year, alongside Barack Obama, a man I admired, had met, and had been asked to represent in debates for the media in his first campaign. I had skills and relationships but what the governor knew, which I hadn't considered, was that no member of the party had gotten more than 30 percent of the vote in a presidential election year—not since Mormon Democrat US representative Richard Stallings held the seat in 1993.

On Election Day in November 2012, after all the votes had been counted and my exhausted campaign staff had taken a bow and gone home, I sat alone in a hotel room in a tangle of sheets on the floor, and finally, I cried.

I cried for gratitude and for ingratitude. I cried for all that others had done for me, for guilt over all the waste of my running.

I had truly believed we could win.

I feared leaving the Senate had been wrong. Someone had to speak for the losing side.

My formal power was gone. What I had left felt puny, solitary, fragile.

My campaign staff—who'd put up with my stress, my loneliness, my hormones, and the ill-focused, distractible creature that was me—would soon scatter to the wind, celebrated for the tens of thousands of voters they'd ID'd, the hundreds of thousands of dollars they'd helped me raise. They'd go on to direct political action committees, profitable consulting firms, funding projects, and wings of the party, trying to hold the line as our red state attracted more White Nationalists and slid slowly deeper into the extreme.

That night, when the general election count was done, I got 34.8 percent of the vote, 110,847 votes. That was more votes in the eastern congressional district than any Democrat had earned up to that point in history. The boy with the Super Bowl ring—the Democrat running beside me in the state's first congressional district, a candidate Governor Andrus did endorse—got just 30 percent.

My 35 percent was just enough to set to rest the nagging question of whether Idahoans would actually vote for a gay person.

Governor Andrus, may he rest in peace, still owes me a beer.

18
BREAKING THE LAW

2012–2014

Boise, Idaho

In a house almost bare of furniture, deep in a fancy subdivision, I lay on a big bed staring at the ceiling. My phone dinged again. Carol.

I had careened earthward, falling from the perfect domestic routine of a life with Carol in exactly the way a person does when they are in denial. I'd dismembered our home and our twelve years of nights curled together, our dog walking, splitting wood, gardening, cooking, and backpacking in the wild. I told myself that I was willing to be alone.

Carol's text was two words: "Come back."

I typed two letters: "No."

The owners of the house on the cul-de-sac were absent. One was in a Buddhist ashram in India. His wife had left him, packed the furniture and moved to DC. He did not know this yet. Not exactly. She had, over his objections, told me to stay in the house. It was sitting empty and unused and I had no place to stay.

I no longer had to spend scattered nights in grassy hollows in the foothills or under my campaign desk.

Still, I hoped I'd end up with the gay man who'd promised he'd run away with me. That hadn't happened. Probably would never happen.

I felt this odd mix of masculinity and femininity surging in me. I was strangely free. Maybe I'd have children.

I was squatting in someone's house and had taken leave of all gravity that ties a person to propriety. Carol's therapist said I was mentally ill.

Carol argued it was not unlike me to sleep in the wild. That was true. But this was not the wild.

My therapist, however, said I was sane, that I should be who I was.

My phone dinged again.

"Sometimes I hate you," Carol wrote.

"You should. I deserve it."

"Come back," the screen said.

"No," I typed again.

And, in the bell-like text sounds of my phone, Carol was an almost constant presence, the voice of someone whose world has folded in on itself, whose mind has pulled the kitchen knife from the drawer, the poison plants from the yard and was preparing to invite death in to sit in that blue bedroom in the night. And still I did not go back.

"No." I typed into my phone. "No."

I was aging and my relationship to my body and to gender was changing whether I wanted it to or not. Already I had wasted a lot of life trying not to violate gender norms.

Standing in the pharmacy line I could feel the press of a culture that would sell me razors or shame me with stares when I let my leg hair grow. The extremes of the gender binary and the insecurities that are created by them fuel industries that promise us perfection and desirability of one kind or the other, if we will only buy this product or procedure and comply.

I watched Emilie, Nikki, and other transgender friends face pressure for their bodies to conform or "pass" after surgery. The idea that some tidy extreme of the binary equates to desirability felt soul killing. I know trans men who grow beards, sport ripped chests, body hair, and abs, and yet, because of the risks and imperfections of the surgeries, still choose to have vaginas. Vast continents of ground exist between the binaries. Gender-nonconforming people, like Carol, often straddle borderlines, while others, like me, zigzag between them.

Even within sexuality, gay and straight are offered up as a binary, an either/or. Yet all manner of history shows people float in their attractions, majorities of people are not exclusively straight or gay. Bodies, body parts, brains, hormones, sex, and genetics are not binary. And because none of these is simple, sexual orientation becomes complicated, stretching up and down, back in time and forward, sideways into dimensions we often don't notice as we walk a room or let fantasy play out in our subconscious.

Binaries are comfortable. They're easier to understand than Venn diagrams.

"It's about *who* you love, Dad."

My identity is elusive, so are my attractions. I could blame my openness to the flirtation of gay men, my intense physical reaction to being touched by them. I could blame it on hormones, on the last gasp of aging ovaries contemplating their own mortality. But I won't.

Looking back, I could blame my sudden interest in sex after ages of tepid initiative on my loneliness, on the pain of trying to be so perfectly sexless in the Capitol for too many years. But that's hardly an excuse.

I could chalk up my unfaithfulness to love or simply to gullibility. I could pin my recklessness on the indulgence that comes after too many years of self-loathing. In truth though, the self-loathing came after.

I could blame Carol, which at my lowest point I did. I picked fights with Carol. I resented the patience and endurance Carol fed to make it possible to live with me, to love me. As absent and preoccupied as I was, I didn't want to be endured. I wanted to be fabulous.

But I wasn't fabulous.

For a whole year I stepped back and let others try their strategy in the House and Senate. I brought my small bag of clothes and took care of a friend's cat, stayed in their polished three-bedroom house while they traveled. When my teaching income wasn't enough to afford rent, I bought a motor home and parked it in yards and on side streets, later in a goat pasture, a place with real goats and ponies.

Then I began whispering to people in cafes and at the Balcony Club, where big speakers thudded and the smoke curled out of machines, fog simulated in the flashing light.

"I think we need to do civil disobedience, maybe block doors," I said.

"Maybe," I'd hear.

But people had jobs they'd lose if they got arrested. They knew getting hired almost anywhere afterward would be harder.

Mistie was still cochair of our political action committee, Add the Words. She had young kids at home. Her custody situation made her vulnerable. Having come out as gay had been hard enough in court.

In my tank top and a small skirt, I wove through the bar crowd at the Balcony Club in the dim light. I was thin, thinner than I'd ever been. I'd never been a small person but now I bicycled everywhere. My bathroom access and showering was courtesy of a YMCA membership. The money in my bank account let me buy day-old muffins, peanut butter, and crackers.

The bar manager had given me a pass so I didn't have to pay cover. I ordered plain grapefruit juice or tonic and, almost always, people bought me drinks.

One of our Add the Words leaders, Cody Hafer, stood in the crowd, near the door, cocktail in hand, grinning as he always did, even though we were talking about the Senate. Cody had been the first to disobey the statehouse order and risk arrest for posting a sticky note on the chamber doors.

"Another rally won't do anything," I said.

"No. They're good at ignoring us." He smiled, leaning in, through the noise.

"We have to force them to arrest us. It will give them a choice, pass the bill or take a bunch of us to jail."

Cody's glee reflected the mischief of the idea. "That's pretty much all that will work."

"Will you do it with me? If we organize a group of us?"

His eyes met mine. "Fuck, yes," he said.

On the day the Supreme Court struck down the federal Defense of Marriage Act and same-sex couples in Idaho were free to marry, I danced in the streets with Mike, the gay anthropology major and muscle man who answered all my questions about male bodies and sex, the one who walked late nights through neighborhoods with me and took me along to his Buddhist practice. He was the one who helped keep my mind off how un-fabulous I was.

While the rest of the nation celebrated full legal equality, in Idaho, our celebrations were beautiful but tinged with frustration.

I danced with Mike and thought about Carol, thought about how far from love, how far from being coupled I was. I joined the celebration of the five lesbian couples who'd won their court case for us all, women who'd decorated the hall with Carol and me for the women's dances, sat at our Thanksgiving table, and stood beside me for decades, pressing the Senate for change. Some would have children and grandchildren. Some would divorce. But on that day, the feeling that the world was moving toward love and justice was inescapable.

Marriage was oddly abstract to me then, like a narrow corridor that my body and mind couldn't fit through.

Except in a few cities, red-state queers could still be fired if we put a wedding notice in our small-town paper. We could marry, but no one was obligated to sell us salad greens, fix our car, or sell us gasoline if they didn't like how we didn't fit their beliefs about women and men.

Married queers still had daily lives to live, bias and cruelty to navigate. My whole being was stuck on that thought. The nation had nudged us forward, but we all still lived in one of many states that had gone to court to fight against our right to legal recognition, a state that had spent eight years successfully avoiding any legal statement that discrimination against us was wrong.

After the dancing, the flowers, and the rice, we all had to go home, go back to work. I had to focus on ensuring that those living outside cities had a right to a livelihood and could shop at their small town's only hardware store. So, for a year, I kept whispering in barrooms and meeting halls. A plan was growing in my mind, a way we could do something the Senate could not ignore.

Beware those who suffer, those who feel they have little left to lose.

That winter, sunlight shone through big windows onto the dance floor and carpet of the Balcony Club. People pulled off coats and filled out forms, offering legal details so I could ready our volunteer attorneys.

Our midday meeting was secret. Tall, media-savvy James Tidmarsh was one of our best strategists. He had sent hundreds of texts in code to our list. Gathered just three blocks from the Capitol, we felt vaguely exposed. For months, we'd been training small groups in the bar and in nearby Alia's bagel shop, and it was possible some inside Republican leadership noticed. In recruiting for the trainings, I'd talked of civil disobedience to hundreds of people. The Senate almost had to know.

Half the people we trained were grandparents, clergy, retired hippies, members of the synagogue, people who'd never set foot in a gay bar. The other half were activists—under-employed or self-employed queers who either chose to risk their jobs or were insulated from being fired by supportive employers. Some just flat-out didn't give a shit; they were in.

Because my recruiting had been broad and blatant, we took precautions in case the Senate or state police had grown curious, in case they had access to our secret Facebook group or tried to intercept texts from my phone. Using code became habit. The word "music" in our conversations stood in for everything to do with arrests and civil disobedience.

When the time came, James would send a message to our list and trainees, something like "Those willing to do music, please arrive at six a.m. Bring photo ID and medications. Leave personal items, jewelry and other valuables at home."

We reasoned that even if the Senate found out what we'd been training to do, keeping them from knowing *when* and *where* was what mattered most.

To every group of trainees I said, "We will have to be perfect."

Clergy members sat beside activists like Emilie Jackson-Edney, swaggering Evie, and others on barstools as I told them what happened in 1990, when protesters from the university threw Monopoly money over the marble balcony from the House gallery, trying to get the House to pass the minimum-wage law to protect farmworkers. Lawmakers acted like they'd been hurt by the falling paper. To the media, they described the incident as an attack, treated it as an assault.

Inside the Balcony Club, people crossed the sticky carpet to pile their things upstairs by the DJ booth. In groups on the wooden dance floor we started a role play with me pretending to be Senator Davis, yelling like a state police officer and then the Senate's pissed-off sergeant at arms, a woman named Sarah Jane.

The sound of Lee Taylor's wheelchair was a high-pitched, mechanical whine. She materialized near my elbow, her Navy cap and breakfast sliding off her lap. Her ageless eighty-year-old face grinned up at me as she pulled her black-and-white protest shirt down, layering it over her dress shirt and bolo tie. The idea of going into the Capitol and blocking a door was personal for Lee, personal for most of us. We all knew someone dead, someone who'd met that wall in state law. We knew someone who lived with the fear that comes from pretending you're not queer so people won't exact pain by scratching a slur deep into your skin or the paint of your car.

When we sounded angry, I reminded myself that this was because that's where we'd arrived. People terrorized, long denied safety, or the ability to earn a living and sleep in a place out of the cold end up desperate. Desperate people can be radicalized, turned defensive, made unwilling to sit still and wait for the next tragedy, the next beating to fall on someone they love.

To the room of our trainees, I said, "One angry look captured by a reporter's camera, one wrong word caught on tape, one touch to an officer, and we will be painted as aggressors. So, we'll be silent, peaceful, respectful. We'll give them nothing to use to call themselves victims."

Next to me, five-foot-tall Judy Cross nodded. She'd once been a southern preacher's wife. At the height of her activism in the civil rights movement, her house had been firebombed.

In my own mind, I remembered billy clubs falling, blood flowing from skulls onto sidewalks in San Francisco.

"We need to prepare for anger, even violence," I said.

We would be mostly White people in a Capitol building filled with cameras. Violence against us by the police was unlikely. But we'd trained our own legal observers just in case. They'd go everywhere in the statehouse we went. Using their phones to record video, they'd be our witnesses to any provocation, violence, or cruelty by the police, legislators, bystanders, or staff.

In an hour of role-plays, Judy, our trainers, and I acted out arrests, yelled slurs, pulled on trainees, screamed in the midst of our mock demonstration. We tested each person's calm, their readiness for worst-case scenarios.

We prepared for the Senate to refuse to arrest us. We made sure there was no way they could make us quietly go away.

We learned to turn our bodies into a human wall.

We practiced communication behind our hands, whispering "I need a break" to mean the pressure is getting to me, my bladder is full, I'll be right back.

Or, "Do you need a break?" to mean: Are you OK? Something seems wrong. Are you tired? Are you hungry? Do your feet hurt? Do you need to sit down?

Or, "*You* need a break" to mean the pressure is getting to you, calm down, let's go to the bathroom where you can cry, vent, or decompress for a bit. Let's go.

Our answers were all supposed to be nods, followed by a disconnection from the line, our own untangling from the wall we formed when we interlocked ourselves. With each absence, the line would close quietly behind us. By rote, one loose arm would find another, until we were solid, silent, impenetrable again.

The risks of civil disobedience were great. We might alienate not only members of the Senate but the sympathetic public as well. While almost three hundred of us were trained and ready to go, I wanted in every way to avoid doing what we were about to do.

The 2014 session began. President Pro Tem Hill said once again, without apology, there'd be no hearing on a bill to add the words.

I met with newly elected Speaker Bedke, hoping to pave a path forward without arrests. In what seemed like a stroke of fortune, Scott Bedke, the man I'd sat with to explain gay sex and Larry Craig, now was the highest Republican leader on the other side of the Capitol, Speaker of the House.

Time had not been kind. His position on adding the words "sexual orientation" and "gender identity" had changed. All Speakers are elected by the members of the House. He was Mormon, and now a majority of the seventy-members of the House were also Mormon. Over the years, he'd gone from shopping the bill around and considering sponsoring it to something less.

After waiting with his secretary, I sat across a wide desk from him, showing him the latest draft of our bill to add the words. Behind his wire-rimmed glasses, his blue eyes scanned the pages.

"Will you sponsor?" I asked, leaning forward. Asking him again what I'd asked years earlier. "With your leadership, members will follow. They'll vote yes."

The Speaker eyed me, smiling. "I'll be your thirty-sixth vote," he said, meaning something like, "After you've pulled a miracle out of your ass, I'll break a tie for you."

My alarm went off in the dark. Even my phone listed the event in code. The words on the rectangular screen just read "Music."

I dressed in the thin frozen box that was both my bedroom and kitchen. Black jacket, formal dress, black tights. I stepped out into the snow, locked the door behind me, and drove my little car past the horses and goats, down ice-covered empty streets, toward the state Capitol dome glowing in its own light.

In the midwinter dawn that morning, at the edge of the Idaho desert, well-dressed shadows stepped from dark neighborhoods, black-clad, in pairs or alone. Snow fell gently. A block from the Capitol, we gathered on a cold sidewalk, shuffling into the basement of the Huntley law office.

In a windowless room, dozens of us stripped off coats, stowing them with keys, jewelry, and valuables. Videographers hefted battery packs, tripods. We'd carry only essential medications, IDs, social security numbers.

Back out in the cold, it was 7:42 a.m. and still dark. I stood with Judy Cross and Matthew Montoya, a young gay man, professional looking with shoulder-length black hair. Matthew set out down the sidewalk, leading half of our people to the Capitol where they'd pose as a tour group. Though it would soon change, the Capitol then was always open. It was supposed to be the people's house and, at that hour, was typically empty, few staff, no senators. I hoped they'd walk in, climb stairs, and make it all the way to the Senate's heart.

Judy left a short time later for the Capitol, leading twenty people of her own, activists like Evie and James, those most recognizable to senators and security staff.

The two groups made their way separately through the snow. Matthew wound through the Senate wings, up the wide marble stairs to the fourth floor. Judy waited, taking her group quickly up the elevators to the top, directly into the Senate gallery.

In just three hours, senators would be streaming in from basement committee rooms to debate and vote on bills.

Alone in the snow and lamplight, I watched each group round a corner out of view. Their sound grew muffled as light began to tinge the space high up, beyond the Capitol dome. I stayed out of sight, walked in a wide circle around to the streets on the far side of the building. Checking my watch, I headed back toward the trees that tower out of the park at the Capitol's feet.

At about that time, Emilie Jackson-Edney and eighty-year-old Navy veteran Madelyn Lee Taylor made their way to the third floor, hoping to reach the Senate chamber. Lee rode her electric scooter. Emilie's leg was broken. Neither could climb stairs. They needed to get past Al, the Senate doorkeeper.

Forty of our group waited above in the gallery.

By this time, Al was reading a newspaper at his desk, the Senate chamber behind him. Navy cap on her head, Lee Taylor rolled up and told him she and Emi had an appointment with the Senate Democrats.

A floor above, in the gallery, Matthew, in his tie, and Rabbi Fink, wearing his yarmulke, rose from the gallery seats, quietly joined by Reverend Debbie Graham and Pastor Schlegel in their collars. Together with grandparents and conservative-looking high school students, the tour group moved toward an odd spiral staircase to be used only by senators and staff.

Outside a set of doors fitted with glass, Al's back was turned when the groups descended the stairway. With barely a word, they arranged themselves into three silent formations in front of the three entrances to the Senate floor.

I crossed Capitol Park quickly, walking in through the far end of the building. The sound of my heels clicking on the marble floors was sickeningly familiar.

Outside the Senate Chambers, Al met me with a nod. "Senator," he said.

I sipped from a hastily brewed cup of tea, nodded back as I had, day after day for all the years I'd spent serving in that place.

Behind Al, our videographers set up equipment, quietly stashing camera bags and bottled water between rows of senators' desks.

It was 8 a.m. I grinned at Judy and Lee Taylor, seeing Rabbi Fink and the other twenty gathered quietly at the closed glass doors behind Al. Following the curved hall, I passed the photographs of the White male senators. On the back side of the chamber, I helped first one group then another set themselves up to block the Senate's two rear doors.

At all three doors, each person took a printed black tank top and pulled it over their heads. I kept my own shirt tucked under my coat as I helped adjust the position of each row of bodies, the spacing between shoulders. Each person locked one arm through the elbow of the person beside them. They raised their free hand to cover their own mouth. The gesture was the one we'd used two years earlier, after the vote to reject

Edgar's bill. It was a gesture of silencing. It represented how the Senate had never let us speak and how they refused to say a word about the harm.

Senate sergeant at arms Sarah Jane McDonald was first to arrive. Red-haired staff enforcer of Senate rules, she rounded the Senate corridor to see in front of her a perfectly layered wall of bodies, solid, formally dressed, and completely silent.

Her eyes narrowed. "You need to move," she said.

No one moved.

She turned to me.

Holding my stack of statements for the Senate and law enforcement, I eyed our walls of protesters. Deep in myself, I wished I could smile.

Sarah Jane vanished into her nearby office.

Early arriving senators gathered in the hall, whispering. At all three doors, one message blared in white letters on each protester's chest: "Add the 4 Words, Idaho. Finally say that cruelty to gay and transgender people is wrong."

When Brent Hill, Bart Davis, and other Senate Republican leaders arrived in the Capitol, the bustle and whispered conversation quickly shut itself behind Sarah Jane's door. Videographers watched. They followed as I moved from one group to the next. Whispers repeated, ricocheting along the corridor until one voice became many. The building was still quiet. Too quiet.

In stiff-rimmed trooper hats and black uniforms, two state police officers appeared. They warned us to move. No one did. No one whispered. Not one hand dropped from its place over a mouth.

"If you don't move, you will be arrested."

My legs shook. The officers left. We'd rehearsed these words in the role-plays.

Even if no media came, I believed they'd hear of the arrests. Brent Hill and the others would have to answer.

Time ticked. The police didn't return.

I stepped away from the line, removing my printed tank top. Filling time, I posted photos on Facebook and Twitter. I tagged friends, Republican chairmen, members, leaders. We'd be visible, the message on our shirts clear, obvious to senators' gay children, to farmers, parents, Catholic leaders, Mormon bishops.

An hour passed. Fatigue visited. For those in the lines, small muscles began to wear. It grew harder to stay motionless, to keep one hand raised. So, the groups switched, in unison, left hand to right, right hand to left over the mouth. Some leaned against each other.

I worried that Hill and Davis had decided that they could wait us out or had something else planned. The presence of media would make us safer, help create pressure we needed the Senate to feel.

Detached from the line, I walked between the groups. Rather than nodding, I mostly ignored the senators and staff who gathered at the sides, glaring or staring puzzled at my face. Maybe they worried this would come to violence. I hoped they knew me better than that. I passed out the papers, our "ransom note," explaining our intent.

Still, no media had come with the exception of a blogger and reporter from a North Idaho paper, Betsy Russell. She had watched for years as I gathered cosponsors and over and over was refused a hearing on the bill to "Add the Words." Betsy flipped open her notebook and asked me what we planned. I handed her the press release and one of the papers. After all she'd seen, she smiled a bit reading our gentle ransom note. Part of it read, "We have tried every avenue to get the legislature to hear our stories and see the harm being done to good people's lives. We feel this demonstration is our only remaining avenue to ensure they hear us and finally, after 8 years, stand up and say that cruelty to gay & transgender people is wrong."

We had trained to be silent so the job of those in the lines was to stand, to defy the unwelcome, take the taunting of zealots, to endure the police warnings that we were breaking the law. Our task was to be thirsty or sore, knotted, hungry, sad, or frightened, to stand until the click of handcuffs and the words "You are under arrest" freed us to be simply prisoners, simply people who had broken the law.

Standing in the lines, we were electric when we were connected. Knit one to the next, shoulder to shoulder and intertwined, we were wordless, unmovable, a single complex of flesh at the Senate's doors. The longing in each of us, the calm, and the sorrow leaked out through the tension of our muscles, the heat of our palms on another person's arm.

Before we stood together, we were individual beings to be acted upon, beings with skin stretched bare in the cold where sharp things flash. In the line, we would be a metaphor for the cause of friends' deaths, our lovers' shame, for a million kinds of loss and violence we had each witnessed or faced.

The state police came again with warnings, then retreated to Sarah Jane's office with Senator Davis.

I hauled heavy wooden pages' chairs from the chambers for those whose knees or feet were giving out. The rows of five to ten people continued switching which hand they held over their mouths. As they stood fixed in formation, on the polished stone outside the three Senate doorways, time slowed.

An hour and half passed. By 9:30 a.m. our uniformity was breaking down. Stepping in and out of line, I helped adjust the positions of hands and the spacing of shoulders.

The media began to arrive then. I felt relief as TV reporters set up tripods and lights and started filming. We'd trained for cameras. Each stood, staring carefully upward and away, avoiding meeting the gaze of the lenses so no image met a single set of eyes.

Tape recorders and cameras began to broadcast to a world beyond the Capitol, a world of people in living rooms and offices, maybe even a world beyond the state's borders.

It was time to be perfect. If we showed ego or stood in mockery, supporters who believed civil disobedience would only do harm to our cause might be right. If we projected anger or hate, lawmakers could say they were justified in silencing us, justified in never changing the law.

By 10:25 a.m. lobbyists were sent away. Pages who normally streamed into the Senate entry in early morning were herded to the fourth floor, maybe in hopes they wouldn't see our protest. Senate Pro Tem Hill emerged from the war room in Sarah Jane's office and walked to the edge of our formation at the Senate's double front doors.

With this, I took my black tank top from under my coat and pulled it over my head once again so it covered my black jacket and African-print dress. I stepped into formation, raising my hand to cover my mouth. I reached out gently slipping my arm around the elbow of Nikki, a soft, blond transgender woman, an old friend who stood tall at one end of a line.

Lights heated the air. The pro tem's hair shone almost iridescent white.

"These are the people's chambers," Hill said. Cameras eyed him. Microphones strained toward him. "You're keeping us from the people's business." Indignant, his voice turned matter-of-fact. "If you remain, you will be arrested. You will have a criminal record."

The pro tem's tone changed again. To the few assembled near him he said, almost casually, "Now if you'll just move for a second, I need to get to my desk." Someone in the middle moved and Hill stepped toward Judy and the opening. He pushed then grabbed her shoulder and I suspect that what he did was calculated, intended to test whether we could be moved—forced or enticed into stepping aside to let senators in without the attention that came with arrests.

Hill leaned into Judy, trying to wrench her to the side. She held tight to Lee Taylor and the other smaller women, standing hand over mouth on either side. I hoped they'd hold.

We'd practiced being pulled and pushed. Police use many tactics to disperse protesters. Holding one hand over our mouths was symbolic, but linking arms was strategic. It helped us form that unbreakable wall.

Hill raised his voice. He was not accustomed to obstacles he couldn't melt with a rule, a law, or piece of doctrine. He pried at Judy. He said again, "I just need to get to my desk."

From where I stood, knit arm in arm with Nikki, I could see his face redden in the camera lights. His fake casual demeanor melted. Judy squirmed in pain and Hill let go, retreated, leaving the hallway to the news media and the forty-four of us blocking the doors of his chamber, his white castle in his private Idaho.

The chief of the state police came out of Sarah Jane's office and gently stood before us with his final warning.

Ty Carson, dressed in a suit and tie, answered the media's questions. Gruff, layered over gentle, Ty passed as a man in his technology job. But Ty's daughter Denae, who stood in the back row in front of the Senate doors with hand over mouth, still called Ty "Mom." After decades of often violent reactions from outraged people believing Ty was in the wrong bathroom, he grew careful. In traveling for work across Southern Idaho, he mapped out the gender-neutral restrooms so he could pee in relative safety—every working day, year after year.

There in the lights, reporters pressed at Ty and at me. *How long have you been planning this? When will you move? Won't protest like this do more harm than good?* Ty answered, not practiced but genuine. I answered, turning focus back to the Senate, talking about the harm being done absent changes in the law.

Time slowed. The 11 a.m. hour, when the Senate was supposed to convene, came and more state police officers gathered in the hall. Our time was up and had passed. Officers stood and asked if we were willing to leave. When we wouldn't answer, they came to warn us again, those same officers who, over the years, had been kind when I got death threats. These were the same badged, black-clad men and women who'd nodded in the hallways and intervened when we began posting sticky notes on windows and doors.

"You will be arrested," they said.

Judy, Rabbi Fink, and all those in the front braced, stiffening the muscles linking their arms. One officer, then another stepped forward placing hands on arms and shoulders. To Judy and Ty and the others they said more firmly, "You have to move."

In my mind, I saw that the Senate still hoped to avoid arresting us. They didn't want the world looking at gay and transgender people petitioning to be heard.

From the hall, more officers came. The troopers pushed forward, pulling on people, gently trying to move them toward the door. My chest tightened, waiting to hear the words we'd all trained to say when an officer touched us.

I heard the words then. "Am I under arrest?" someone asked.

An officer answered, "Yes, you're under arrest."

It had begun.

I breathed then.

In fours and fives, Judy and the others were led out, uncuffed, hand over mouth, past Al. One officer walked in front and another behind. Each arrestee was humble, silent, peaceful, respectful. Perfect. Beautiful.

I clung to Nikki until she was arrested.

Group after group was escorted past the bank of TV cameras to somewhere I couldn't see.

A crowd milled, watching. Parents brought kids. Al joked, recounting for a group of lobbyists and journalists the story of Judy and Matthew's early morning descent down the private legislator-only stairs from the fourth floor to the Senate chamber behind him.

"They bamboozled me," he said, shaking his head.

The state police came back, again arresting those on either side. I melted back into the line behind me. Arms unhooked, attached themselves on either side of me, seamlessly. We were down to only one thin string of people securing the Senate's front doors.

Those at the back doors came then. Matthew and then Emilie led their ten demonstrators over the carpet, across the well of the Senate, between the rows of big leather chairs. They stood behind our thin line, filled in the vacant spaces where those who'd been arrested had stood.

Three times our numbers dwindled. Each time I was left blocking the doors.

The last person left standing next to me was a gay man my age. Rick stood with his arm looped awkwardly through mine. We didn't speak but tried to keep our eyes raised to avoid staring into the bank of cameras. We waited for the state police to come and say we were under arrest.

Behind us, senators came in through the now clear rear doors to take their seats on the Senate floor. Using the legislators-only elevator, most came all the way up from the basement, completely unseen by the media or public. Not a question did they have to answer about the bill or protests.

Senator Davis appeared in the hall in front of me. The Senate was convening. He had a job to do on the floor. Eyes alive, he walked toward me, avoiding the small wall that Rick's and my body still made. As he brushed past me on his way to his big seat, he reached out and gently pressed his hand to mine. Tears welled somewhere behind my eyes.

The gentle tap and squeeze felt reassuring. It was, I thought, perhaps the last reassuring gesture the senator would ever give me. From there, a movement that would lead to many protests and almost two hundred arrests would divide us. But, at this moment, Senator Davis's gesture was kind.

Immediately after it, state troopers stepped forward and arrested Rick. His arm slipped from mine and he was gone. Troopers retreated. I was left alone.

At first I'd thought I'd been left last so I could witness the arrests of all those I'd brought to the statehouse. I thought it a kindness, meant to allow me my role. Minutes passed and I still stood in the TV lights. Did they want me to walk away? Did they hope not to arrest me because of the attention that would bring? I needed them to just take me because, like the others, I had to stand there until they did.

I tried not to cry. In all the photographs my brow is furrowed. We'd never prepared for anyone to be left behind. We'd never prepared for me to be left behind.

Sarah Jane stepped up to me, close in her stiff suit jacket. In my face she spoke firmly, almost angrily and like I might not hear.

"In. Or. Out!"

It was less of a question than a command. As a former senator, I vaguely realized I had a right under Senate rules to be inside the chamber behind me. But I was blocking the doorway and standing on the threshold. I had no intent of being inside. I wanted to go. I wanted to be with Ty, Judy, James, and everyone I'd spent months training and preparing with.

We'd heard rumors that a prison bus was parked in front of the Capitol. With my hand still over my mouth, I had the check for bail in my pocket. I didn't know how everyone would pay bail without me. I'd promised them. I had to take care of them.

Ada County jail buses hold forty-three people. There were forty-four of us. Maybe they had no room for me. Maybe leaving me was some strategy of Senator Hill's. Regardless, it was creating its own spectacle. The media was watching. I was the only one left for them to film. As alone as I felt standing there, I was far from alone.

Senator Hill returned. He told reporters, "You have to clear the area now. Senate is convening." Some had floor privileges and argued they had a right to stay. TV cameras were escorted out, past Al, to the entry. Some stations moved and filmed through the glass from the public waiting room. Some climbed to the gallery and filmed from above.

Our legal observers were pushed out, the glass doors behind them shut.

Sarah Jane raised her voice. Again she barked, "In. Or. Out!" using her foot to lift the stoppers on the glass doors on either side of me. Pushing, she tried to close the doors against my body. I spread my feet to stop each one so I could stand on the threshold, still outside the chamber.

Each day, the Senate *had* to convene so, behind me, a red-vested young page rose to the dais and began the daily Pledge of Allegiance. One hand still over my mouth, I put my free hand on my heart. After the pledge, the Senate chaplain rose and began the prayer. I'd spent eight years in the Idaho legislature expected every day to pray in the name of other people's gods. But I could not. All those years I stood silent and reverent, fingertips on my desk, but I did not pray.

Shaking, I stood there, my back to the Senate and to those whose minds I was there to change. I wanted them to see my face, the hand over my mouth. I wanted them to have to look at me if they were going to leave me there on that threshold.

I turned around—my feet still lodged in the doorway, holding both doors partially open. I faced President Hill and the Senate where for four years I'd failed with what seemed like more grace than I now had.

The gavel fell and Pro Tem Hill convened the day's session. The secretary started running bills. Her voice rolled monotonously through numbers and titles. They moved through orders of business to motions and resolutions. To my left, behind one of the big desks, Senator Davis stood up, speaking into his microphone. He made a motion, one I didn't fully hear. To my right, Michelle Stennett, the Senate's new Democratic leader, said, "I second the motion."

There was no debate. No discussion of why I was standing in the doorway. No discussion of the thousands of people waiting for a chance to live and work in peace and safety, waiting to tell their stories in a formal hearing.

The motion passed without a single no vote. I was only vaguely aware it even concerned me. I know now that the Senate believed they could not arrest me because, as a former senator, I had a right to stand where I stood. I was not trespassing. Clearly, I was blocking doors though, violating other laws.

Senator Davis knew me. I think he understood that if he didn't move to allow me to be arrested, I would have stood in that doorway all day and then all night. I would have stood until I couldn't stand any more.

In a blur, finally, from behind me, state troopers pulled the doors open. I felt a hand on my arm.

A polite voice said, "Ma'am, come with me."

"Am I under arrest?" I asked.

"Yes, ma'am. You're under arrest."

19

GOAT PASTURE

2014, FEBRUARY

Boise, Idaho

On tall posts, yard lights shine, reflecting off snow. I squint, frost on my lashes. Bodies blur in the ice fog, hooves scrape gravel and straw. Two yellow eyes fix on my face.

I step from the path, try to go around, but they follow.

Lifting my mind from the two pairs of horns and yellow eyes, I move toward the trees, toward the wire panels that protect my yard.

Once inside my motor home, I switch on the lamp. Tiny squares of light pierce the ceiling and cabinets. I smile, a small smile. I've upended a life lived in houses, brought paintings and books, folders of paper for teaching, and for making and breaking laws.

I remember Carol's voice, "Lawmaker; lawbreaker," eyebrows raised, a tight curve at the corner of that mouth. Carol.

In an elevator, Speaker Bedke told me he'd see what he could do. But then someone leaked this to a reporter and the Speaker had to recant. We have blocked more doors in the Senate but we are back where we started a month earlier, or worse because I have no exit plan. My exit plan is a public hearing, passage of the law.

That's not an exit plan. I see that now.

In memory, I feel the cold, heavy steel, the scratch-echo of voices from outside the jail cell where I waited hours earlier with the others. Another protest. More arrests. Not tidy, not perfect because I planned badly, led people astray who counted on me.

I've made mistakes. I've had help sometimes. Someone has been sharing our group's private messages with gossip columnists, a reporter, and those who never thought our arrests were wise.

I need them to suffer, Bart Davis and the other senators. I do. I know it's wrong, but they have to suffer enough that they need us to stop, need to hear us. They need to stop stalling and add the words to put us in the law.

Nothing will change until it's too hard for them to ignore us and easier to do what we've spent sixteen years begging them to do.

My head fills with words, with shame, with all the loss I've caused.

I've suspended my life because I left something undone. Something raw is wrong with the world and I can't let myself rest until I fix it. I'm exhausted but when I sit still, the ghosts I face are kids I fear will take their lives, or those who already have.

It's unlikely I can hold a job now. I don't follow rules or instructions well. I teach English, barely. There are well-paid jobs I'm qualified for, but I'd likely be fired or suspended by my employers with each new arrest, each new charge.

I don't even try to come up with money for rent. I live in a goat pasture instead.

The arrests have cost others their jobs, young people—Sheena and Elliot, Paddy, maybe Deja. Others. I worry all their pain is for nothing.

In trying to make lives better, I've made them worse.

Maybe I've broken our chances of passing the bill forever. Maybe I've angered conservatives, past the point of disgust, into hate. Maybe the child who died in Pocatello would be alive if I'd just stayed in the Senate, continued to serve my time.

I worry my own neon freakishness, my misshapen queerness has become a liability for everyone. I worry I destroyed Carol's life for nothing.

When the ambulance comes, it's at my calling. Paramedics and police cross the pasture to my camper. Meg is with them. I've texted her to call them, told her not to call Carol.

I'd hoped by the time they came, I'd be gone.

Instead, they're here because I've become uncertain. Even if I want out of the world, out from under the weight of all the mess I've made, I worry how my own death might lead to others; how nothing is fixed with death. It's only made more broken.

The brave part will be staying.

But I've missed a protest in the passage of hours, crying alone in my sleeping bag, outside, under my picnic table, with a knife. I do not feel brave, but I crawl out from under the table anyway. It is a table that fed Hunter S. Thompson and the people my parents loved in Woody Creek, a table that sat on the deck at my mom's elbow as she met missionaries with her shotgun.

I dress, dry my face, make my way to the Capitol where Ollie, Ty, James, Joe, and the others have already scripted and lead a protest. Left to make the decisions, they chose not blocked doors and arrests but to read their testimony and stories from their lives into the air of the rotunda. With the House and Senate making law on both sides of them, a documentary film camera as their witness, they spoke aloud, together, to no one, testified to the underside of the dome and the painted stars.

Handcuffs are cold and heavy. They pinch.

Seven times that winter, I would wear handcuffs or zip ties; I'd ride prison buses, and hear the words "You're under arrest."

Standing in the lines is the opposite of isolation. It is belonging. It is an act of living, of giving for others.

I would trust those in the line with my life.

Many in the group that stood outside the Senate Chambers once tried to take their own lives. Many were ready to risk anything to make the pain stop. Red-haired Joe Kibbe once lived in a refrigerator box in an alley. Matthew, as a teen, was forced from his home into the street.

We worked to keep the media's pressure focused on the Senate. It was the only leverage we had.

At the end of February, a hundred of us came out of an alley, walking toward the building for a peaceful demonstration—again, not arrests, just a hope we could wind through the Capitol, hand over mouth, dressed in black, one of us behind the other, in a long, somber line.

On that day, someone heard senators call out from the windows, "They're coming. They're coming," as if we carried pitchforks and stones.

Jail has a smell. Maybe it's the cleaning products or the cement or the fact that the holding cells are underground, under the courthouse. People go about walking along sidewalks, eating ice cream, and feeding their parking meters, and under their feet, a city of people wait in chains and zip ties.

We're not desperate here, where by nature people are desperate. We were desperate before, when nothing we did made the flow of tragedy slow to a drip. Each of us who's come here has accepted a life under the banners "prior arrests," "misdemeanant," and "criminal record."

Around us, the lives of other arrestees unravel. For those who can't pay, it will be the beginning of the hard part. But our bail is prearranged and donated. We have more volunteer attorneys than Skinner and Skinner Law can manage.

Bail agents wait for our call, unpacking sheafs of paperwork and pens. They laugh, share our snacks, from the wee hours until late in the morning. People bring brownies, cold cuts, vegetable trays, and fruit for us. The waiting room fills with family and friends, with people who read about us online, people who cheer when one of us climbs the ramp up from holding into the brick jailhouse lobby.

Meg sends money for the others. Dad, too.

We've decided only more pressure will free us. Mistakes or no mistakes, everything is better than silence.

20
THE CLOSET

2014, MARCH 18

Idaho State Capitol, Boise

The formal lounge behind the Senate chamber is normally empty. It's like a movie set staged with uncomfortable historic furniture and two push-button gas fireplaces, one for Republicans, one for Democrats. One day each year, the room fills with food. Staff come along with current—and occasionally former—senators. They are, as always, attended by red-vested high school pages. The senators, on that day, have a party there. The rest of the year the place sits empty.

It was safe for me to count on the place being empty.

It was the late winter of 2014, after months of arrests in the Capitol, after the snow had melted, the geese had begun nesting again, and lawnmowers roared on Capitol lawns. I walked into this room, the Senate lounge. By this time, we'd entered the building again and again and had been arrested and charged with trespassing for standing silently in doorways or staying past closing time. Repeatedly, we'd stood on the inlaid marble star, four stories below the painted Capitol dome, and we refused to leave.

Thousands of photos filled the Capitol and my feed online, photos of people standing, one hand over their mouths, faces somber. Singer-songwriter Carole King posted a photo of herself in a blue jacket, eyes sad, hand over her mouth with the hashtag "addthewords."

We'd attempted but failed to again block the doors of the Senate. We'd blocked the doors of the governor's office, and in one day, fifty of us had walked in early and closed down the entire underground wing holding all the committee rooms of the Senate.

I had been arrested six times by then. By the end of that spring day when I walked into the empty Senate sitting room, the legislature would make clear that it was done. It was leaving us and our issue unaddressed. By the end of that day, I would be arrested one more time.

I walked into the Capitol just after the doors opened at 6 a.m. I was prepared for a long stay. In my little leather backpack were a grapefruit, a spinach pastry, a water bottle filled with tea, and an Altoids tin filled with bits of metal, magnets, a length of electrical tape, sticky tack, and paper clips. I hoped these would help me disable the lock and sensors on the automatic door to the back stairway behind the Senate floor. I had no idea precisely how the sensors on a security door work, but hoped that wouldn't matter.

We planned for me to spend the night in the building. Early the following morning, I'd disable the door, run down the stairs, open a little-used basement entrance, and thirty or more of us would climb the stairway to protest at the epicenter of the Senate, finally again on the Senate floor.

It seemed like a reasonable plan at the time.

The real problem was that the whole thing required me to hide inside security, in that closet behind the Senate chamber for an entire day and night.

"What if I'm caught?"

"You'll be fine."

"No. I think it'll look bad. They're pissed at me. I'm a huge pain in their ass."

James Tidmarsh, wise strategist, gave one of his powerful, angular smiles, "It's a closet. It's perfect."

"It's not perfect."

"You're a gay person. It's a closet. The media will totally get it. You'll be fine." James grinned and grinned and wouldn't stop. Now in college and studying anthropology, Ollie grinned too. It was decided. I'd hide in the oversized empty coat closet off the sitting room behind the Senate president's dais, just feet from the Senate floor.

Before the sun rose, I was in the building. Getting there was easy. Of course when I found it and tried the door, the closet was unlocked. But it wasn't empty as it once had been. Who needed a coat closet in a room no one used?

Swinging my backpack from my back and pressing the antiquated push-button light switch on the wall, I found the eight-by-twelve room contained not only a metal rack and rod populated with several hanging garment bags, but a pile of dress shoes, some sort of cardboard display, probably made by Senate pages, and a shelf stocked with bottled water and two plastic tins of nuts and cookies.

If someone opened the door, I could not just be sitting there. I stuffed my backpack behind the bottled water on the shelf and crawled deep into the garment bags, pushing my butt hard against the wall in the deepest, most hidden corner. All I had to do was wait. I had only twenty-three hours to go.

Our level of confidence that I could remain undiscovered was fairly low. It was low enough that we had a backup plan. Caleb, a young, formerly devout Mormon business owner who'd showed up one day to offer us rides from jail, would hide somewhere in the senators-only men's bathroom or in the little room off the women's restroom with its little couch for those needing to lie down.

Time passed. I took off my shoes. Waited.

Worry crowded in.

By maybe 10 a.m., I couldn't sit there any longer. I put my shoes back on, grabbed my bag and left the closet. I wandered out of the Senate and across the Capitol to find the Speaker of the House. I caught Speaker Scott Bedke in the elevator. That was where he was easiest to ambush, easiest to find. He smiled.

Protest was always our last resort, and on this occasion, I felt I'd failed to ask him one last time if he'd hold a hearing on our bill on his side of the building before we again attempted to shut the Senate down.

He's a smart man and had never exactly said no to me. He was pleased that so far the protests had focused on Senate Pro Tem Hill's side of the building, not his.

"It's not happening," he said flatly, dispensing with niceties.

I like honesty. It saves time. The Speaker was not past leading me to believe he'd be helpful to our cause when he needed to. He also wasn't past hauling me to the woodshed for a scolding when earlier efforts to leak our internal messages left him looking like a gay rights sympathizer.

"We're still friends?" he'd joked earlier in the year after clearing a lounge of lobbyists so he could scold me for the story the reporter for the daily paper was about to post on his blog. It was a story about Bedke supposedly holding a hearing on our bill. Someone had sent a screenshot to the reporter, the same one who'd written many stories on Larry Craig and, over the years, had found many unflattering stories to write about me.

I asked Bedke the same question back, "Friends?"

He nodded, "Yes."

"In spite of my pain-in-the-ass-edness?" I asked.

"In spite of your pain-in-the-ass-edness," he said.

I think mostly I was making his life more interesting.

But, that day, I'd left the closet to find him, it was too late in the session for a hearing.

"Next year," everyone kept saying.

Every year, they said, "Next year."

Now it was midmorning and, as I headed back to the closet, the security desks outside the third floor chambers and the gallery checkpoint on the fourth floor were staffed. For obvious reasons, staff had been told not to let me behind security without an escort. They wanted me nowhere near the Senate floor.

Neither the House nor the Senate had begun their morning sessions so I texted the one legislator, Representative Sue Chew, who I suspected would be down for the task of getting me back in place for a protest. Our legislature's most tireless lawmaker and the only Chinese American woman in office, Sue met me on the House side of the building. Outside the fourth-floor gallery, she walked me quickly past Senate security and down the senators-only staircase to the curved hallway that circled the chamber behind Al.

Outside the Senate Democrats' office, I said goodbye with a hug. She had worked an entire decade on social justice–focused service to the people of the state, but she would pay for this act of aiding and abetting.

Turning to the lounge behind the chamber, I vanished into the coat closet, shutting the heavy door.

Waiting in a closet for one or two hours isn't bad. It wasn't long, though, before I had to pee and realized I'd forgotten the heavy-duty ziplock bags I'd planned to put in my backpack. I vowed not to drink any more tea.

From outside, Ty and James texted. I'd been seen going past the Senate offices on the third floor, outside the chamber but not returning. Security was looking for me. From deep among the garment bags, I heard the door open. The light came on and someone sighed a heavy sigh. After a pause, the light went off and the door closed. A coat now hung on the wall opposite the door.

Blood rushed to my head. This was bad. It meant the closet held not only items like formal TV-ready outfits; it meant it was actively in use. The door might open and close at any time before senators finished their morning session, walked to lunch, and returned to sit through their afternoon committees in the basement rooms three flights below.

The presence of cookies and nuts was hardly reassuring either.

In the sitting room outside the closet, someone turned on the little stereo system that broadcast the day's Senate debate from the other side of the room's long inner wall. Words streamed into the empty lounge and I vaguely recognized the muffled roll call, pledge, prayer, then the reading and debating of bills.

At noon, senators went to lunch. Someone turned off the loudspeaker, cutting off its repetitive break-time elevator music. I survived the retrieving of the coat, but after lunch, the floor session resumed. No one went to their usual committees. Instead, they came back to the chamber to debate more bills.

An afternoon session like this was something I should have expected so late in the year, but without the loudspeaker on, I could no longer tell what was happening. I could hear voices, muffled as if underwater. Clearly some senators were outside the closet, sitting in the unused lounge. Given what I knew of the Senate calendar for the day, they'd be debating killing wolves or deciding whether to vote down or pass a bill to ban whistleblowers from publicizing animal abuse on factory farms. The Senate tended to save its most horrendous bills for the end of the session, hoping everyone would just vote yes so they could all go home.

Outside the closet, in the lounge, senators running for higher office were skipping votes, avoiding taking sides on the stickiest issues. Only when someone walked close to the thick closet door would a voice rise and I'd catch a word or a phrase. I was too deep in garment bags to hear more.

An hour passed. Debate went on.

Suddenly the door opened. Light streamed in and Sarah Jane McDonald, the Senate sergeant at arms's voice rose. This was the last voice I wanted to hear. In the previous weeks, she had accused one of our protesters of assault for walking into her arm on his way down a staircase. She was bold enough to have bodily blocked our passage as we tried to gather in the chamber for another protest. Though we had a friendship around the school bullying bill I had tried to pass, I was afraid of Sarah Jane. Around this time I may have had nightmares populated with her voice.

Now she was there, in the closet.

Wedged against the wall behind the plastic-wrapped clothing, my legs began shaking. I worried that my trembling would rattle the metal hangers on the garment rack above me. From the sound of it, Sarah Jane was directing pages. She had a sort of military staging underway. Bright and obedient, two of them stood at the edge of the pile of shoes, within inches of my outstretched legs, taking instructions about moving food into the closet from some place nearby.

Outside the closet through the wide open door, teenage girls began chatting while they set up serving tables and hauled bags of popcorn and cookies. More and more senators gathered as the Senate went "at ease" on break.

Seated on the Victorian furniture in front of the fireplaces just feet away, lawmakers discussed Senator Cameron's salsa, hot and mild, and sheep rancher Senator Siddoway's homemade cheese.

And through all this, the closet light was on. Pages walked in and out and I breathed carefully.

I recognized this party. A party like this happened on the final day of debate, the last day of session for the year. This party meant we were done. They were going home. It meant no bill to add the words would be heard. I put my head down gently, lifting my phone to text James and Ty.

Debate could last into the night or even morning if the House had different ideas about the bills or wasn't ready to go home. I was stuck there though, maybe without a reason, since the gavel might fall and building might empty, leaving us with no doors to block, no proceedings to delay because lawmakers would be packing bags and boxes and heading home.

The voices grew loud. My name came up two times, both unflattering. I could hear former Senator Stegner's voice as he joined the party. At least I was not the only former senator in the room. The party died down. Only Sarah Jane and the pages remained. Out on the floor in the chamber, the debate had resumed. In the sitting room, pages talked over food and drink. The chatter quieted. Hours passed.

Finally, with a heavy click, the closet door closed. If my absurd luck held, they would all soon leave and I'd stretch out, sleep, and wait for morning.

Debate ended. The building grew nearly silent. I got a text from Caleb. He was in the bathroom, a few hundred feet from me on the opposite side of the Senate floor. He said he'd felt creepy about the idea of being in the women's restroom and was in one of the men's stalls. He was dressed in a suit and tie, formal as we all were when we were in the building. Hours earlier, he'd sat down on a toilet and stayed, convincing enough in his suit and dress shoes that a white-shirted guard had apologized when he looked under the door during a security check.

I waited. My phone died. Minutes ticked. Without warning, the closet door opened. I braced. The light came on. Jerry, the assistant sergeant at arms, cleared his throat. I was still deep in garment bags, but they were neither thick nor opaque. They were mostly thin, see-through plastic sheets and they didn't reach all the way to the floor.

Jerry knelt down near my elbow. I could hear his breath. I pressed my knee hard against the cold outer wall to stop my shaking. I tried not to breathe. If he looked, I knew he could see my legs. They were at least partially visible, stretched out behind the pile of shoes. He began rummaging around near my elbow, gathering up pairs of pumps and loafers. I felt a warm hand on my leg. The hand lifted and came down again. I heard Jerry start.

"Who's there?" he yelled, pushing the curtain of garment bags back so that I sat there, a former senator on a pile of shoes, exposed.

There is no script for what to say in a situation like this.

"Hey!" I said as if I was expecting him and had been waiting.

Jerry froze. He was clearly doing math in his head. Why was I there? I think he knew. I think he was torn, like many staff and lobbyists and even legislators are torn. Civil disobedience is disruptive. Civil disobedience causes discord. It involves the breaking of rules and laws. It cannot be condoned. But lawmakers, staff, and lobbyists do have friends who are gay—children, nieces, brothers—so they see bits of the pain. They see the exodus to the coasts, see the vague obituaries for healthy teens. And they're torn.

I don't know what Jerry thought. He pushed the garment bags back across to cover my body, stood up, punched off the light, and closed the door.

I wondered if he'd leave me there and tell no one, but the answer came soon enough. Senate Democratic minority leader Michelle Stennett opened the door and came in with one of her staff.

She was grinning. "Whatcha doin'?" she asked. Michelle was a runner, strong, calm, and quick to smile.

A closet. That was precious.

"The usual," I think I said.

"Leadership knows you're here. You staying or going?"

"I'll think about it," I said.

It was after 3 p.m. Even in the midst of having been caught hiding in a Senate closet, I was intent on pulling out my tin of magnets. For some reason, I still thought I could jam the lock on the stairway door. I still thought there was a way we could come up the stairs and stand in the Senate in the morning. I still thought there'd be a session to disrupt, a protest to be made the next day.

My optimism is boundless.

The Democrats left the closet, shutting the door behind them. With my phone battery dead, I couldn't text Caleb or anyone to tell them I'd been found.

I climbed out of the garment bags and stood up, digging in my backpack for my charger cable and my tin of lock-fixing flotsam.

This was the moment Brent Hill walked in. The Senate president pro tem stood in the closet door, his face and body like the metal hull of a war ship.

"What are you doing digging in your bag?"

"Looking for my phone charger?" I said. It was less of an answer than a question.

Knowing I needed to comply and leave, I walked out into the bright shining glare of the Capitol rotunda. Tourists climbed the winding marble stairs. Lobbyists reclined on historic furniture. Caleb, too, abandoned his attempt to stay the night in the Senate bathroom.

Across the building I found Ollie, Ty, and our protesters. Twenty or so stood in the gallery overlooking the House floor, hand over mouth. Below, Representative Sue Chew stood at her microphone. For the first time, a member of the legislature was speaking into the cameras during session about the arrests and the bill to add the words. Body compact and braced, she leaned in to the room and her words spun out, crushed by anticipation of the gavel, which the Speaker seemed ready to lift and let fall. She called out her colleagues' failure to hold a hearing. She asked them to hear the bill.

Instead, the House went home. There would be no hearing. No bill.

That night, thirty of us stood in the doorway of the Senate. We went for drama, brought props, medical models, a cliché heart and spine.

What we'd each given up, what I'd asked a hundred people to do in accepting criminal records, had come to nothing. My stay in the closet would be painted as a stunt, a spying mission, an infiltration of the Senate. It would make national news.

I wept. We wept. People who were able sang songs written for us, written for our movement.

Before midnight, state police arrived to arrest us. We left in handcuffs, driven across town in black-and-white state troopers' cars, processed, photographed, left in jail till the sun rose.

21
TESTIFY

2014–2015

Boise, Idaho

Out in the air, the trees were bare but budding. On my car windshield lay pansy seeds in a packet and pear and tangerine candies in plastic baggies, twist-tied to my wipers in the rain. Carol. Only Carol knew my favorites.

It was Valentine's Day. Carol texted, sending photos from the past of us in costume. Our civil union.

I wanted to be done roaming, sleeping in pastures, sleeping with strangers, but I'd tried and failed to go back. I'd stay at the house, try and fail to embrace routine. I'd leave and Carol would hate me, then beg me to come home again. And I'd go, sleep again on Carol's floor for a night or two. Then I'd leave, terrified of making promises, worrying I wasn't done being free and unfaithful, worrying I would cause pain, again and again.

People scolded me, told me I should have reasoned with the legislature before blocking doors. Some said our "stunts" cost the community our chance of a hearing. The House and Senate, people said, were mad enough they'd never consider the bill.

Still, in January 2015, when the legislature convened again, we prepared for more protests and arrests, meeting in secret, knowing the discomfort of attention was our only tool, the only way to pry open their grip on the law. It was time for the House also to feel the pressure, to face blocked doors, sit-ins. Speaker Bedke, too, needed to be offered the choice of taking up our issue or making arrests.

Instead, before our protests began, Bedke scheduled a public hearing on the bill to add the words.

The optimistic celebrated. The pessimistic braced.

From all over the state, people traveled. For three days, the Capitol filled with those coming to testify. When we got a moment alone, the Speaker wanted to hear that the protests would stop, that, in exchange for a hearing, the arrests of 2014 wouldn't be repeated.

I wasn't going to make decisions for us. I would do no negotiating without Ollie, Mistie, Emilie, James, Ty, Joe, and others. I think the Speaker saw that in my eyes. He, too, was loyal to some force outside the building. This wouldn't be about friendship. What was about to happen, I suspected, was beyond us both.

The Lincoln Auditorium filled. An overflow committee room broadcast the hearing live on a big TV screen. Chairman Thomas Loertscher, an LDS Republican from Eastern Idaho, stacked the testimony. He called on people, alternating pro then con, pro then con. This clustered the few who'd come to testify against the bill early in the two-day hearing. By the time the chairman ran out of opponents, much of the media was gone. Queers were left to give a day and half of testimony at the podium without much coverage.

Hundreds testified. LDS representatives Andrus and Bateman were so moved by the stories that they cried. Even the chairman softened. At the roll call, Andrus voted no nonetheless, as did Representative Bateman. All the committee's Democrats voted yes. Every Republican voted no.

Outside the committee room, as I walked with him up the stairway, from the underground to the sidewalk, Ken Andrus, sheep rancher and friend, had tears in his eyes. He told me he wanted to vote yes, but the church told him he could not.

On March 3, more than twenty of us walked through the front doors, right into the Senate, right into the House, into the chambers, right past the doorkeepers. For the first time, we stood in Speaker Bedke's chamber, Ty in his suit, Rabbi Fink, tiny Judy, James, and Ollie—stiff, hands over mouths in the well below the dais. We occupied the space just before the gavel was set to call each house to order.

We went to jail three times that year. Our mugshots flashed across the internet. Scores of us prepared for sentencing.

And the damage went on—in little towns, in schools, and factories; people went into the world bare of law. In the state's few cities, we were protected. Everywhere else, to Senator Hill and the powerful, our pain seemed to be acceptable. It seemed they must have told themselves that our loss was our own. We should choose not to be gay, choose to live small, constricted lives, pretending.

Instead, we sent out love from the Capitol in photographs and arrest records, in sore feet, and wrists rubbed raw. Collectively we tried to help isolated queers bear it all. What is left when one's tried everything peaceful and still the harm goes on?

The day after our hearing in the Idaho Capitol, the Utah legislature began advancing a so-called nondiscrimination law they claimed protected queers. Riddled with exemptions, the legislation they created for LGBTQ people was a hollow version of Utah's law protecting people on the basis of race, religion, sex, and national origin.

These new protections in Utah's non-discrimination statutes applied only to workplaces with seven or more employees. Idaho's Human Rights Act protects rural people better by covering smaller businesses where only five people work. What some called "The Utah Compromise" also quietly denied queers the right of private action, so a person couldn't sue for damages, even if a firing, eviction, or refusal of service was investigated, mediated, and found to be calculated or malicious.

In his office, Senator Davis offered me that same Utah Compromise, saying he could pass it into law.

"No," I said.

Activists in our community had agreed that to pass a special section of lesser nondiscrimination code—a special lesser law just for gay and transgender people—would be to assign ourselves second-class citizenship, to pin on the big pink triangle and comply. It would be like we agreed there was some special problem with being gay, bisexual, or gender nonconforming. It would be like we agreed we were less than, more repugnant, more problematic, less worthy of the right to work, support our families, and exist.

Months passed. When it came time again for Idaho courts to sentence us, we paid more fines and court costs and were sentenced to ten hours of community service for each arrest. Those with only one arrest were set free. Even conservative judges scolded prosecutors for trying to use our arrests as an excuse to bar us from the Capitol, strip us of our right to redress. From the bench, some praised our use of nonviolent civil disobedience, our peaceful behavior with the legislature and the police.

Ty, James, Ollie, Joe Kibbe, Judy, and I spent more months deep in public service. I'd been assigned to the nature center where I raked leaves, weeded native plant displays, shoveled snow, left my motorhome in the goat pasture and logged hours I had to report to jailers until my sentence was done.

22
THE FOURTH DIMENSION

2015, MAY

Napa, California

Above my head in the hospital room, machines beep. Dad's beard is lost behind the clear plastic bulk of an oxygen mask. His wife, Faith, roams the back of the room as if circling a car wreck she cannot look at. Her voice lilts, transcends disaster. Dad has gone from a coma to a shaky thumbs up. The stroke has not caused the typical motor cortex trauma. Both sides of Dad's face are animated. The damage is in the thinking part of his brain. This, I'm certain, is the one place he would wish had been spared.

Cree navigates hospitals with ease; staff demure to her. She is pointed and able to cut through the niceties and rules. But Dad is blind, or near blind. In the hospital bed it's apparent he travels in three-minute intervals across decades of time. He flits from our ranch, to Aspen, to Ketchum, to California, landing on occasion in the belief that he exists in some postapocalyptic chaos of contagion where we are recovering from some plague. I hold his hand, stare into his blue eyes, try to anchor him. "This is here, Papa. This is now."

I tried dating to find human kindness, to be seen for any part of myself that may still have been beautiful, but this failed me. I was a fifty-one-year-old, pancake-flat person with scars where a woman's breasts and nipples once had been.

I was intimate and vulnerable with people who cared only that I had some of the right holes arranged in roughly the right places. They could fill in the rest.

I mistook men who wanted sex for men who gave a shit. My oblivion and gullibility is infinite.

Desire is nothing like love. It is not connected to respect. It does not require kindness. At all.

And Carol kept texting.

One morning I lay in a man's bed, a place I'd slept for months of winter mornings, and I listened to the radio come on, watched the light careen in from the trees, and I rose out of my own body, or maybe I sank back into it.

This man I'd met on a dating site had noticed I'd stopped shaving, waxing, and bleaching. After all the primping, powder, and preparation to appear in person half as young, feminine, and vibrant as the veneer of my profile picture, it was now really me there in the bed, not the physical mythical naked husk of myself.

Desire had shrunk in me to a fine point of bile in my chest. I could not be the person who would stand in to fill whatever hole in himself he hoped to fill. He certainly could not fill the whirling center of me. He had no interest in that frantic and sorry place.

I found a scrap of myself then, the breastless person with gray curls, always too forward, too loud, too certain. As my sister, Cree, once said of me, I am the one tripping on rocks and sidewalks because my mind is focused too far above the ground.

I visited Dad. His wife moved him to Washington and a modest house near the ocean with a garden and nut trees. He was still nearly blind, and had no short-term memory to keep him oriented. He still believed he cooked for us, fed us his gifts. In his mind, he could write, travel. He went to work in a kitchen each day. But the present tense where he stood still slipped from decade to decade. He had not regained a sense of where on the vast plain of the earth or the dimension of time and space he stood.

Then I could have told him, "Papa, the fourth dimension is time."

But dimensions are thought experiments, not places any physical things inhabit. Dad lived in some other unfolding of the cosmos, a universe where time doesn't flow in a line; it loops backward, then forward, slippery, illusive as gender or water.

Mom at eighty has fallen twice, done damage to her memory just as the whisky has. I move her to Boise after she loses her partner, Sharon, to cancer. Mom grieves, drinks. We set a cup of Sharon's ashes to rest under the apricot tree at Mom's place in the desert. Slowly she regains her wicked humor. I shop for her, clean her house, make sure she remembers to feed her cat and dog. When she isn't sleeping or eating, she reads.

She drinks less when she is happy. So I'd take her on adventures, back to Challis, on boats, to hot springs, the ocean, or the art museum.

In downtown Boise, Mom and I step into the crosswalk near the Capitol headed for lunch. From skateboards, three teenage boys leer at us. Mom stomps her cane on the ground as their wheels roar. They swerve, then pass. She lets go of my arm and turns.

I glimpse her middle finger. "Mom, did you flip them off?"

She grins.

This is the woman I found one night, thirty-five years earlier, standing naked on her cafe roof with her shotgun in her hands. Sometime earlier, she'd hurled her ex-lover's furniture off a nearby cliff into the Salmon River below.

Mom lifts her handmade cane forward on the sidewalk. She's sweeter, tamer now. She drinks to excess mostly when her dreams haunt her. She's still afraid at night when the dog barks or headlights scan the walls. I've hidden her guns. In nightmares, I fear she'll shoot someone.

When we are with her, Mom tells Cree and me to tuck in the fat of our bellies, to pluck whiskers, not to touch our faces. She comments on Carol's weight too, thinking she can help us, not thinking we all know we're no longer young. She mothers—as if offering up correction, adventure, and sweet good nights were all the proof we'd ever need that she loves us. It is for me. I see no point in judging her for the mother she was or was not. She is more than that.

We are all more than that.

That is the thing with forgiveness, that gift we set out for others.

With time, we have to save a little for ourselves.

Night after night, I sat in my motor home, the old disco ball from the women's dances hanging, throwing specks of light onto worn wood paneling, my phone wired to play music through a set of speakers. In my head, I pushed to make all the love songs about Carol.

I didn't want to grow old with anyone else. But I didn't trust myself. I worked those nights to scrub three years of pointless desire from music and words. Few people even knew that I didn't date women after I left Carol. Binaries are simple, less messy, comfortable. Most assumed I was gay, the pure and wholesome kind of gay. And I let them.

I went on adventures with Meg and with my friend from the closet, Caleb. Young people who'd been arrested beside me made a place for me. They let me rest in a world without weight and pressure. We cooked dinner in a kitchen, played pool. With time, we laughed.

In the evening, I'd picture Carol at the big table in a new living room, in a new house. I knew what plate Carol would use, which spoon or fork or knife. I knew that when dinner was done, the cold would press at the pane of the kitchen window while Carol might stand at the sink, washing that fork and plate.

I could guess when Carol was out walking our dog on a ridge in the foothills, jogging trails back down through the cold, each morning getting up from a half-empty bed to take conference calls, meet a friend for beers, go on a date with a woman now and then.

A fourth year passed. I didn't go home. Instead, I bought a brambled city lot set in elm trees. I moved an eight-by-sixteen-foot wooden shed there and forty friends came, Carol came and helped me lift the tiny building onto its foundation so I could turn it into a house.

For years, I punished myself for leaving Carol—and for not going back.

My fingers find the wall switch in the dark. Lights land me in a deep yellow room with high ceilings, heated cement floors, a bathroom with a shower, a flush toilet, and sink.

I breathe. My house is artful and spectacular in its tininess. It's my material masterpiece, a museum of time and found objects, a miracle of carpentry, budget, and carefully navigated city building code. No one, it seems, builds a 288-square-foot house on a foundation. Outside, under the sticky elms, my motor home is at last for sale.

I clean house more than I once did. I host parties where I drink more, too. I find washing dishes with hot water soothing, a luxury I never used to appreciate.

Solid for the first time in four years, I've drawn lines in myself, reminders of the cost of vanity and of all the meaningless sex I inhaled like a feast. And I don't miss that. The need to be desired by men, by strangers, feels like a state I've escaped, a hormone-laced physical place I grew lost in, a place inside my body maybe, a place that formed when I grew too thin to have a soul, too worn down to hear it call.

It happens sometimes that we run to fill a void in ourselves, to escape age, to avoid change or the headlights of loss, death, or irrelevance. We go somewhere else, thinking the answer is there. What we find might keep us busy, but we still have to wake in the morning. We still have to look at ourselves in the mirror and decide if there'll be anything to show for this bit of reality we're about to live, something that makes our efforts tangible in the world outside.

Yes, sex can be beautiful in its gritty intimacy. Even with strangers.

It can be transcendent as a connection to self or another life. It cannot be life itself.

There's more. For me there'll always be more. I am one who lives with that need to wake and do something to help stem the flow of loss in the world. I need to shove something, some fragment of my unimaginable surplus, into the breach.

In my house, I stand with the light falling through the trees, streaming through the windows onto the concrete and colored walls, and the reality of the present, of this postage stamp of time is certain, "I am a teacher, an activist. I am loved and hated. Now I will grow old."

23
ASPEN TREES

2016–2025

Boise, Idaho

Forgiveness is delicate. It's like the eye inside a storm. Always out there are the memories, a gale of glass shards and torn bushes flying just inches from the calm.

Outside, in Boise, winter has begun to gather again. My tiny house lies small and warm, its foundation dug so its kitchen floor sits four feet below ground. Hot water courses through its concrete veins. On the stove, I mix basil, garlic, ginger, and lemongrass into coconut milk, mashing my herbs with a mortar and pestle like Dad taught when I cooked in his kitchens. He'd bark orders in perfect, staccato Thai.

A meal was always love to Dad. Cooking was one of many ways he fed us as we grew. He'd look out from behind his blue eyes and smile.

I cook for love, out of habit, and in honor of him. Tonight I am cooking for Carol.

Sometimes we build or cook a thing knowing we intend it for someone other than ourselves. It is a thing we must share. I built my house for one, but I gave it wild color and angular beauty that I hoped someone else might love.

Carol has brought champagne. We open a bottle and toast, play music, grin, and dance. I look into those eyes, ones that see well the maze within the tornado that is me.

I see in Carol that light which brings everything into focus with a beautiful calm. Trust between us took time, but I know Carol is my pilot fish, the one in the water beside me, whispering the path forward into to my ear.

Even the self inside myself—the place where the air is still—is easier for me to reach when we are in each other's lives. With Carol, I am free to move, free to exist in my complexity. There is no requirement that I tether myself to some part of gender. I am free to roam.

I think, if my work can be done with someone who makes the task feel less endless—someone whose brain and humor makes the journey worthwhile, whose life I can slip into and feel safe and capable in a way nothing else allows—then that is what I choose.

I reach out one hand. I pull Carol in. We dance in the kitchen between the concrete countertops. I lean in for a kiss when the song is done.

Carol is my pilot fish. I am our tornado.

Some people love us for the whole us—chaos or no chaos. Perhaps with Hunter and Juan, or with Mom and Dad, it was that way. Some love the chaos inside a person, the adventure of it, the wildness—at least a little more than they dread it.

Cranes call from the valley below and light slants through huge ponderosa pines. In bed, back to me, Carol wakes, shaking, crying. I reach out, whispering, "What's wrong?"

Through long breaths, tears trail cheeks sideways. "I dreamed you left me." Then those blue eyes close and I float in a tub of water, the ramp fallen down.

"Oh," I whisper. "No. No. I won't. I won't." But I deserve this. Nothing I could say can convince Carol not to worry. Nothing in the world could help me prove now that these things are impossible. So I reach out, curl around Carol tight.

Later, we stand outside.

"Sometimes I'll be angry," is what I hear.

"You should be," I say shifting in my big shoes.

"Sometimes I hated you."

"I know." I smile. "I got those texts, my sweet."

"I meant it."

"I know," I say, kissing Carol, taking each lip between mine in turn, dipping the tip of my tongue in to taste that mouth.

Forgiveness is an allowance, some form of belief that a circumstance was exceptional, that it won't be repeated, that there are still redeeming qualities in the forgiven person, an intention we love.

In taking me back, Carol now carries my betrayal like a spider in a box. And I carry a new certainty, one deep enough to let me make promises again.

I have dressed up, climbed the wide front steps of the Capitol again, circling four flights of marble stairs.

The gray-blue dome with its painted stars curls over me.

I feel panic.

I breathe.

Passing the security desk, I head for the gallery perched above the Senate floor. Following the curved walkway, I sit looking down at the men and women in their suit jackets and ties. Senator Cherie Buckner-Webb looks up, smiles, rises to stand before her microphone, a lone Black woman in that White, White place. With love, she makes the required nod to my presence in the velvet seats above. On both sides of the aisle, senators clap or wave politely. Some gesture is expected from them when a former senator visits. Still, I'm surprised when they don't sit stiff in their seats or turn away.

Pro Tem Hill is gone. Though his church became a road block, its influence, on occasion, pulls our state back from in the precipice of now. Words from archconservative Senator Winder, the new pro tem, echo up out of memory, a whispered, "Keep it up. It's working!" This man and I passed each other, years before in a hallway, mid-protest. I imagine he meant the arrests, the blocked doors. Lobbyists and powerful people on the inside told me this. "Keep it up," they said. This helped my exit plan grow vague, caused us to keep throwing ourselves at the Senate. And I wonder, Should we have ever stopped? Did the loss of tension, the absence of pressure, allow extremism to grow?

I scan the room below, the faces. I feel shrunken and small. I know there'll be no reward in this place, no return to grace after what I've done.

I lean back in my seat. My dreams have been full of Armageddon. I picture how, both in politics and personally, I've come to roam two worlds: one in which I am occasionally heroic—and another in which I've broken the rules of politics, gender, and sexuality, and live in disgrace.

I don't want to cry here, so I look across the open air to the balcony on the far side. How could so much love for the world, so much good intent, amount to so little?

Then I see across from me an ambling body in a dark suit. It moves toward me in the gallery from the far end of the curving hall that leads from the security desk to the high rows of theater chairs. It's a figure I know well. I watch it grow nearer, headed for where I sit.

Senator Davis. He notices me alone in the bank of empty seats and smiles.

No longer a senator, he's been appointed by President Trump as Idaho's US attorney. He prosecutes hate crimes, the death penalty, and is charged with enforcing unpopular federal law. He's visiting the chamber, just as I am, back where we both once rose to microphones, did battle with words, ethics, and the constitution, with the good of our people in mind.

Senator Davis. I struggled for more than eight years to rise to his standard for Senate service and to push drafts of legislative language past his gatekeeping desk. But he served many masters. Only one of them was his conscience.

He and Senate Republicans never had to vote yes or no on adding the four words. They were never asked to choose between justice and loyalty to party or church.

Soon, in the Bostock case, the Supreme Court will agree that the Civil Rights Act of 1964 should protect LGBTQ Americans from discrimination in employment and housing. Bias against people because of their gender identity, their gender expression, or the gender of the person they love is, they said, bias on the basis of sex. Though the protection we in red states get from these rulings does not give us a right to eat at lunch counters or require businesses to sell us goods and services, the direction of change is a basis for hope, a glimpse of it.

The chamber echoes. Senator Davis reaches the spot where I sit.

He meets my eyes. He is still smiling. I worry how I should greet him, unsure what is fitting after all the years.

His smile is one of those once reserved for pages and maybe puppies. Always in public he's tried to cover it with a scowl. I stand and reach out to shake his hand. Instead, he leans in, hugs me tight, there on the balcony where all the Senate can see.

The yellow walls of the tiny house I built glow. Carol and I live there together. Deep in moving boxes, I sort papers at our dinner table, stacking photographs, bill drafts, and newspaper clippings printed with my name. The wood ceiling curves over me and high up in the walls, windows funnel the sky.

Slowly, our little house empties.

It is 2022 and Idaho has been sketched into the center of the great American Redoubt, a White Nationalist place of retreat for when society breaks down. Already a hangman's gallows has towered outside the US Capitol. Again, as in 2020, our capitol city is besieged by lines of pickup trucks hauling armed men and women flying blue-lives-matter flags, Confederate flags, and Trump banners.

Idaho's population swells with White flight. Families from blue states arrive via ConservativeMove.com. The state's extreme politics draw in the faithful, the fanatical, and those who seem to love only the second amendment of the Constitution, not the first or the rest. Farmlands fill with subdivisions. Quiet trails and lake basins are worn raw by wheels, boots, and gear. The wealthy maneuver to put up gates and carve mansions into forests and public land.

In the north of our state, now local militias parade the streets and sidewalks with automatic weapons. Proud Boys march. From across the US, Patriot Front members gather with clubs and shields, plotting to storm the Coeur d'Alene Pride parade. Hate crimes rise as sitting legislators call trans women and drag performers "groomers" and "predators." Men online threaten execution and violence, whispering at local Black organizers, synagogues, Islamic centers, Latinos, queers, and refugees. Anger reigns.

Still, Carol and I are not fleeing Idaho, only going deeper in. We know it takes very few people to make entire communities live in fear. We refuse to let terror paralyze us.

My seven years of caring for Mom ends with her eyes fixed on mine. Carol and I hold her hands. As the fire in her fades, she squeezes tight. At her cafe on the Salmon River, Cree and I spread her ashes with Sharon's under the apricot and the lone aspen sapling now grown so that the young trees in its clone almost circle the old building, casting shade.

Now I'm going home to that place. Carol and I have bought that empty restaurant in the desert. We are the third generation of queers to live there in the arms of mountains, at the edge of the wild.

We play pickle ball with Trump loyalists and conservatives, volunteer at the ski hill and thrift store. We burn wood for heat, plant squash and beans, pull weeds. Our neighbors work hard, often at more than one job. They live in simple homes or campers, scattered in the desert and farmland. Still, for too many, rent exceeds what they earn. Hundreds who clear trail, clean outhouses, fight fire, and manage weeds have lost their jobs. Government is stepping away. Until collectively we set it right, it will be up to us to care for the land and for our neighbors.

I wake on a summer night, window open to the click of bats and the odd "eeettt" of owl-like nighthawks hunting insects in the dark. All around us, in the dry where the land seems brown, native rice grass grows, primrose blooms, tiny blue penstemons hang from the cliff edge. The nighthawks have flown to our canyon from South America for the hatch of the salmon flies, huge soft insects that climb by the millions from the river and take to the sky. Curled in bed next to Carol, I stare out and imagine the stars blotted out by their transparent wings, a soup of sky cut by the warm skin of bats, the banded, knife-sharp flight of nighthawks, launching from their nests on the ground between cactus and sage.

What will protect the otter and the salmon fly? What will protect the vulnerable or us from each other if not the Constitution, if not a government with a conscience that serves others and the whole before itself?

For half my life, I struggled with the conscience of Idaho. I waited for the federal government to draw lines that defined me and those like me as human, as deserving of basic freedoms, as endowed with certain inalienable rights. But the bluebirds and the nighthawks grow scarce, and from the desert, I watch the shameless rise, seeking power for its own sake. Such power built on fear surges out of neglected states like ours where it has festered unchecked, unanswered for two decades. It dances in religious clothes, sets fire to the Constitution, which I hoped would save us.

It's convenient to say that our choices make us suffer. We are too wealthy a nation for so many to struggle. The American dream cannot just be about those who climb. It is about how to balance freedoms and legislate away the obstacles so *every* American is allowed to prosper.

But Idaho has become a hard place to raise children. If queers once were absent from law, now we are a focal point. Our stories are censored, our bodies are regulated, and our identities are stripped from records. Queer friends leave the state, hoping for somewhere safer. But, in coastal cities, sweeping deportations rise. The growing army of ICE walks the streets in masks, and its list of targets widens. For those who dissent, all this White Christian conformity promises violence.

But Carol and I would rather die than hide or run away.

I am a pacifist. Yet at the feed and grain store, the two of us stand in jeans and flannel shirts to study an aisle packed with boxes of ammunition. I have always been a pacifist. Yet the bag of heavy boxes Carol and I carry home is a thread that ties me to a culture I was raised in. It is an echo of Idaho's long tradition of people arming themselves in fear of the federal government. I will stay and defend people I care for, defend people I do not yet know, people who stand here in the face of this now and say, "No."

I wander outside, into the desert to see what new weeds have grown. The job is endless, a fool's errand, I'm told. I tell myself to focus just here, just at my feet, to pull there, that plant and that one, to free the native grasses and the flowering vetches, in just this spot. Carol waits, watching from the yard while I vanish into the evening, brush bucket by my side, hands calloused, promising I will be done soon, promising for hours that I am almost done.

The next morning, the two of us wake and step outside to sit with the cactus on the river as it rises in spring flood. We are still here. Aspen leaves clatter from the trees behind us. Native needle grasses turn green and the land blooms.

ACKNOWLEDGMENTS

This book is dedicated to those in red states like Idaho where, outside major cities, federal nondiscrimination law is not enforced and it remains legal for restaurants, gas stations, bakeries, and hardware stores to refuse to serve hardworking human beings simply because they're gay, bi, or gender nonconforming.

To all whose bravery pushes our world toward justice and to the queers in hard places, I send my love and sorrow for your need to persist and be strong in spite of the growing threat of violence. May we change minds by reaching out in grocery store lines and over fences, by setting an example, or simply by walking this universe of gender and love in our own beautiful ways.

Throughout my life, I walked beside and in the arms of friends, activists, volunteers, arrestees, coconspirators, and countless others. You all made the work I did possible.

Most of all, to the love of my life, Carol Growhoski, for all the years of patience, brilliance, wry humor, and love, thank you. Thank you for dancing and for pulling weeds with me. To my dad, Bruce LeFavour, for loving, inspiring, and believing in me. I miss you. To my mom, Pat LeFavour, may you always be wild and, in spirit, ever free.

Thank you to Carol Growhoski, Sally Neil, reporter Anna Means, Babette Munting, Jan Holmgren, Linda Crozier, Terry Crozier, Mary Rebecca Grant, Nancy Stouffer, Sheri Johnson Hughes, Ollie Shannon, Caleb Hansen, Meg Roberts, Hosanna Jean Cardeño, Jennifer Purvine, Mary and Wally Smith, Ava McKenzie, Rebecca Stone; writers Jessica Holmes, J. Ruben Appelman, Mark Seiler, James Tidmarsh Blazor, Brandon Follett, John McCarthy, Misty Schymtzik, Mike Caughey, Raina Phillips; as well as Rob Weisbach, David McCormick, and all those who helped me through the process of writing this book and all the attempts I made at telling this story before it. Thank you also to my agent, Leslie Meredith, at Dystel, Goderich and Bourret; my editor, Joanna Green; and the amazing Beacon Press. May these pages inspire.

For the queer activists and community organizers who birthed a movement and those who still keep it burning with love: especially Mistie DelliCarpini-Tolman, Emilie Jackson-Edney, James Tidmarsh Blazor, Hannah Brass Greer, Finn Greer, Amy Herzfeld-Copple, Don Curtis Jr., Judy Cross, Lindsay Madsen, Karen McMillan, Cody Hafer, Mary Rebecca Grant, Ashley Matthews, Representative Sue Chew, Nikki Leonard, Lori Watsen, Javier Smith, MaryEvelyn (Evie) Smith, Ollie Shannon, Ty Carson-Eisenman, Joseph Kibbe, Ashley Loosli-Thomson, Bonnie Violet Quintana, Preston Pace, Jenna Damron, Rebecca De Leon, Brandon Connolly, Ruby Mendez-Mota, Becky DelliCarpini-Tolman, Nikson Matthews, Reilly O'Connor, and all who still do the work in this hard place.

For Corbin Harney whose work brought to a close an era of nuclear weapons testing and to those everywhere who brave discomfort to peacefully call attention to tragedy and need for change.

For allies who gave of themselves again and again: Pam Baldwin, Bill Roden; Idaho Human Rights Commission directors Marilyn Shuler, Leslie Goddard, and Pam Parks; Rabbi Dan Fink, Lee Flinn, Janet Lawler, Linda Crozier, Janet Lawler, Jenn Blair, Gretchen Bates, Babette Munting, Sara LaWall, Cindy Gross, Lisa Perry, Gene Chandler, Stacy Ericson, Jonathan Carkin, Fred Roe, Leta Harris Neustaedter, Roger Sherman, Leo Morales, Jeremy Woodson, Ken and Michelle Bass, Michael and Angie Devitt, Ruth Garrison, Schuyler Enochs, Carole and Ron Blakely, Susan and Don Curtis, Sydney and Clark Fiddler, Bill and Leslie Drake, Sarah Huntley, Chris Huntley, and many others.

For the Republicans who sponsored or, at some point when it was hard, voted or worked to protect us from oppression, discrimination, and harm: former Governor Phil Batt, former Senate Majority Leader Bill Roden, Ed Lodge, Senator Sheila Sorensen, Senator Tim Corder, Senator Joe Stegner, Senator Chuck Coiner, Representative Tom Trail, Senator Gary Schroeder, Senator John Andreason, Senator John Goedde, Senator Shawn Keough, Representative Carlos Bilbao, Representative Janet

Miller, Senator Dick Compton, Senator Tom Gannon, Senator Linda Wright Hartgen, Representative Matthew Bundy, Senator Geoff Schroeder, former Senate Majority Leader Bart Davis, former Speaker of the House Bruce Newcomb, Lieutenant Governor Scott Bedke, former Senate President Pro Tem Chuck Winder, and Idaho Governor and once-upon-a-time ally and Senator Brad Little.

For the many who mentored, taught, inspired, and spurred me on: Cree LeFavour, Dwight Garner, Penn LeFavour, Hattie Garner LeFavour, Joseph Growhoski, Sidney LeFavour, Angela and Jeremy Foster, John and Catherine Smith, Billy Noonan, Hunter S. Thompson, Juan Thompson, Sondi Wright, Betty Benton, Katy Smith, Joseph Anderson, Ted Anderson, Sophia Jon Winegarner, Polly Read King, Don King, Sharon Chamberlain, Carolyn "C" Rose, Patricia Gregson Millington, Faith Echtermeyer, Bob and Sylvia Markley, Meg Roberts and Mark Torf, Wally Smith; teachers Mary Clagett Smith, Mike Straughan, Ellen Fisher, John Rember, Peter Phillips, Bill Smallwood, Lanny Montgomery, George Lakoff, Thom Gunn, Linda Kaboolian, Marty Linsky, David King, Jennifer Lerner, Ted McConnell; Thane Lever, Michael Tobin, Eric Schocket, Andrea Pritchett, Julie Morfee, Kelly Wells, Carolyn Bevington, Elena Farmer, Jon Knapp, Martha Stevens, Pat Clark, Beatrice Brailsford, Kerry Cooke, Jean Boyles, Deanah Messenger, Craig Gehrke, Bob Digrazia, Diane Sands, Mary Rohlfing, Jen Ray, Brian Bergquist, John Hummel, Scott Stewart, Doug Flanders, Alan Virta, MaryEvelyn (Evie) Smith, Rich Keefe, Bert Allen, Nicole Prehoda, Stephanie Franks, Joan Dodd, Dean Worbois, Susie Randall, Jim Smith, Steve Martin, Nikki Leonard, Misty Schymtzik, Sharon Matties, Jill Gill, Pam Baldwin, Andrew Putz, Andy Hedden-Nicely, Bob Huntley, Carole King, Rebecca Scott, Vicki Stagi, Yolanda Matos, Chani Lyles, Rochelle Smith, Zella Bardsley, J. Dallas Gudgell, Eric K. Ward, Moira Bowman, Scot Nakagawa, Tarso Luis Ramos, Sharon Gary-Smith, JoAnn Hardesty, James Du Toit, Robin Brand, Ollie Shannon, Liz Merril, Yul Kim, Zach Mallavia, Maria Andrade, Nancy Tiger Spittle, Wendy Fox, Jessica Holmes, Sally Neil, Lori Wright, Lori Watsen, Sue Latta, Andrea Altmayer, Rachel Winer, Daelan Crystal McDaniel, Hosanna Jean Cardeño, Camilla Barnes-Kelly, Jeanne Huff, Bob Neal, Marcus Hunter, Chrystal Sowell, Ryan Fay, Brandon Follett, Marie Boyle, Josie Erskin, Janie Burns, Tara Wolfson, Nathaniel Hoffman,

Gloria Munoz, Roger Sherman, Cathy Steuart Sherman, Brent Marchbanks, Kelly Buckland, Jim Baugh, Joanie Fauci, Ed Cannady, Char Roth, Tom Pomeroy, Rickie Brady, Rialin Flores, Ryan Hill, Xochitl Sierra Hernandez, Luke Mandel Anorak-Neill, Betty Richardson, Shawn Novak, Caleb Hansen; Margaret Marti, Joy Palmer, Calvin Udall, Malia Collins, Develynn Hall, Mike Sakelaris, and my students and colleagues at Harriman State Park, The Cabin, College of Western Idaho, and the Shoshone-Bannock Tribes' Fort Hall Recreation; to former Sandpoint City Council Member John Reuter, Boise Planning and Zoning Commissioner Ester Ceja, Boise City Council Member Ann Hausrath, Boise Mayor Lauren McClean, Representative Shirley Ringo, Representative Sue Chew, Senator and former Boise City Council Member Maryanne Jordan, Representative Lenore Hardy Barrett, Senator Gail Bray, Representative Elmer Martinez, former House Minority Leader Wendy Jaquet, former Speaker of the House Bruce Newcomb, former Senate Minority Leader Clint Stennett, former Senate Minority Leader Michelle Stennett, Senate Minority Caucus Chair James Ruchti, and especially former Senate Assistant Minority Leader Cherie Buckner-Webb, former Senate Majority Leader Bill Roden, and former Senate Minority Leader Edgar J. Malepeai.

To all the trainers, organizers, and chorus for Add the Four Words: Judy Cross, Madelynn Lee Taylor, Ty Carson, Oliver Shannon, James Tidmarsh Blazor, Diane Tipton, Karen Kelley, Emilie Jackson-Edney, Mike Butts, Sharon Gregory, Meredith Butts, Joseph Kibbe, Babette Munting, Sylvia Ramirez, Matthew Montoya, Ashley Loosli-Thomson, Caleb Hansen, Fred Roe, James Blakely, Kieth Blazor, Mike Caughey, Sue Bolen, Angel Petregallo, Gretchen Bates, Ben Wilson, Jennie Rylee, Diane Terhune, David Thompson-Elliot, Dallas Gudgell, Senator Steve Scanlin, Spencer Duncan, Jonathan Nicholes, Tim Walsh, Mike Bishop, Dalton Warr, Donelle Lee, Rodney Busbee, Jessica Irwin, Paddy Smith, and many more. Thanks to the hundreds who trained for arrest and to the countless generous people who paid our bail, court costs, and legal fees. Thanks to tireless lead attorney Dan Skinner, and to Jeff Brownson, Rich Rayhill, and the many phenomenal lawyers who gave their time to defend and counsel us.

To the *Add the Words* documentary filmmakers Cammie Pavesic, Michael D. Gough, and Eugene Boyle who followed the work and the more than 190 arrests through the heat of it. What you made is beautiful and powerful.

To Julie Zicha and Carmen Stanger with such sorrow for the loss of your children. To you and all the other parents who faced such loss, may we soon make it truly better for the generations to come.

For those from Add the Four Words arrested in the Idaho Capitol in 2014 and 2015: Barbara Anne Abersold, Krishelle Jeanette Amlin, Shelley Axtell, Richard Chaddon Axtell, Gretchen Bates, Nancy Diane Berto, James Michael Blakely, Kieth Vincent Blazor, James Robert Tidmarsh Blazor, Susan L. Bolen, Jeannette Bowman, Gene Edwin Bray, Casie Briese, Jim Rodney Busbee, Michael Butts, Meredith Jordan Butts, Denae Carson, Tyler R. Carson, Carmine Emilio Caruso, Michael Caughey, Stefan Alexander Cavin, Joseph Ambrose Christophersen, Frances Collette, Shelly Denise Costa, Judy Ellen Cross, Alexandra Storm Daniels, Ellen Louise DeAngelis, Salem Christian Djembe, Daniel Everhart, Rabbi Daniel Fink, Susan K. Gelletly, Daniel James Gonzalez, Reverend Deborah M. Graham, Sharon Gregory, Cynthia Ann Gross, John Grubbs, Carly Hanna, Caleb Foster Hansen, Donna Harwood, Kerstyn Leann Hastings, Boise City Council Anne Stites Hausrath, Alan Richard Hausrath, Nicole Betty Haworth, Rich Holm, Colin C. Howard, Gabriel Ibarra, Emilie Jackson-Edney, Neysa Jensen, Jerry Jerrems, Deja Jones, Senator James Richard Just, Jo-Ann Kachigian, Rachel Kaufman, Reverend Edwin Keith Keener, Karen S. Kelley, Joseph Larell Kibbe, Kristine Ann Kirsch, Rebecca Lampman, Jessica Nicole Lema, Nicole Leonard, Ashley C. Loosli-Thomson, Sheena Marie Loosli-Thomson, Rosie Luna, Debbie Ann Mallis, Kaitlin P. Mandigo, Cay Marquart, Ron Marquart, Arla Catherine McEvoy, Terry B. McKay, Patricia Lee McKernan, Evangel Kealy McVicker, David Milton Monsees, Matthew Montoya, Stephen Francis Murphy, Justin Robert Ness, Molly Anne O'Shea, Dianne Grace Piggott, Pamela Jyll Piper-Ruth, Patricia Brightwing Raino, Hilary Kay Rayhill, Jacqueline Rhuman, Patricia Richardson, Kelly Lynae Robinson, Elliott Kristopher Rowen, Jennie Gay Rylee, former Boise City Council Member Maria E. (Lisa) Sanchez, Jenna Avery Preheim Schlegel, Pastor Marcus Schlegel, Oliver Shannon, Terri Lee Simmons, MaryEvelyn (Evie) Smith, Paddy Smith, Martha Lou Spiva, Alonzo Statham, Karissa Sutton, Madelynn Lee Taylor, Mary Lou Taylor, Lisa Marie Tenney, Kyle

Lindsey Tikala, Diane Tipton, Kerstyn Tracy, Benjamin Brian Tupaz, Donna Marie Vasquez, Jade Walker, John Sidney Wargo, Reverend Janine M. Watkins, Cody Rodney Weight, Benjamin Dale Wilson, Janelle Davis Wintersteen, Gayle Michelle Woods, Mitchell Garrett Wortman, and Frances Eileen Wray.

With love and gratitude . . . cole